TIME-SAVING SOLUTIONS FOR YOUR BOARD

ECFA TOOLS AND TEMPLATES

FOR EFFECTIVE BOARD GOVERNANCE

DAN BUSBY AND JOHN PEARSON

For free download of templates associated with each Tool, please visit
ECFA.org/ToolsandTemplatesDownloads

ISBN: 978-1-949365-18-4

CONTENTS

TOOLS AND TEMPLATES

Part 5: Policies and Board Responsibilities

Part 6: Ideas for Better Board Governance

RESOURCES AND WORKSHEETS

INTRODUCTION: Why Are Tools & Templates Important?

Leverage the right tool or template to enrich board effectiveness and create a climate of trust and candor.

Don't Dump on Directors the Night Before!

Trust Can Be Broken at Any Point

Why are tools and templates so important? "A virtuous cycle of respect, trust, and candor can be broken at any point."[1]

According to Jeffrey Sonnenfeld, building an effective board involves at least five critical elements:

- ☑ Creating a climate of trust and candor
- ☑ Fostering a culture of open dissent
- ☑ Utilizing a fluid portfolio of roles
- ☑ Ensuring individual accountability
- ☑ Evaluating the board's performance

He adds, "A virtuous cycle of respect, trust, and candor can be broken at any point. One of the most common breaks occurs when the CEO doesn't trust the board enough to share information.

"What kind of CEO waits until the night before the board meeting to dump on the directors a phone-book size report that includes, buried in a thicket of sub clauses and footnotes, the news that earnings are off for the second consecutive quarter? Surely not a CEO who trusts his or her board."[2]

With the right tools and templates, board chairs and CEOs will build and enhance trust.

Peter Drucker on Tool Competence:

"Although I don't know a single for-profit business that is as well managed as a few of the nonprofits, the great majority of the nonprofits can be graded a 'C' at best. Not for lack of effort; most of them work very hard. But for lack of focus, and for lack of tool competence."[3]

---

[1] Jeffrey A. Sonnenfeld, "What Makes Great Boards Great," Posted September 2002. Harvard Business Review: *https://hbr.org/2002/09/what-makes-great-boards-great.*

[2] Ibid.

[3] Peter F. Drucker, Frances Hesselbein, and Joan Snyder Kuhl, *Peter Drucker's Five Most Important Questions: Enduring Wisdom for Today's Leaders* (Hoboken, NJ: John Wiley & Sons, 2015), 2.

Tools and Templates Will Enhance Boardroom Trust . . .

. . . if you build your trust with these two principles in mind:

❑ PRINCIPLE NO. 1: The Faith Based Foundation

This resource, *ECFA Tools and Templates for Effective Board Governance*, is built on a foundation of Christ-centered governance. These tools have been tested hundreds of times in Christ-centered ministries. As David McKenna wisely notes in *Call of the Chair*, **"A major difference between Christ-centered ministries and for-profit or nonprofit organizations is in the question, 'Who gets the credit?'"**[4]

Certainly nonprofit boards of all types will find value in these tools and templates, but those who serve in Christ-centered organizations will understand the language, our lexicon—and our motivation.

❑ PRINCIPLE NO. 2: Leverage for Impact!

If you knew that by leveraging a specific tool or template it would exponentially enhance your communication, your outcomes, your results, and your governance joy—you'd do it right? Then heed this simple, but powerful premise from *TRUST: The Firm Foundation for Kingdom Fruitfulness*:

"Christ-centered ministries with Trusted Governance, Trusted Resource-raising, and Trusted Resource Management experience elevated Kingdom outcomes."[5]

When leaders and board members leverage the right tools and templates—at the right time and for the right reasons—they will build trust. And trust will pave the way for God-honoring results.

Example: CEOs and senior pastors have told us that by using the "5/15 Monthly Report to the Board" template, they have enhanced communication—and trust—with their board members. One CEO even called the template a "home run."[6]

We encourage you to read *Lessons From the Nonprofit Boardroom* (Second Edition, 2018) as a companion resource to this book. You'll find additional color commentary on several tools and templates including the "Board Policies Manual," "Ten Minutes for Governance," and the "5/15 Monthly Report to the Board."

Finally, we're grateful for all of our colleagues, coaches, and mentors over the years who have introduced us to numerous tools and templates that we've revised, customized, and maximized for boardrooms across North America and worldwide.

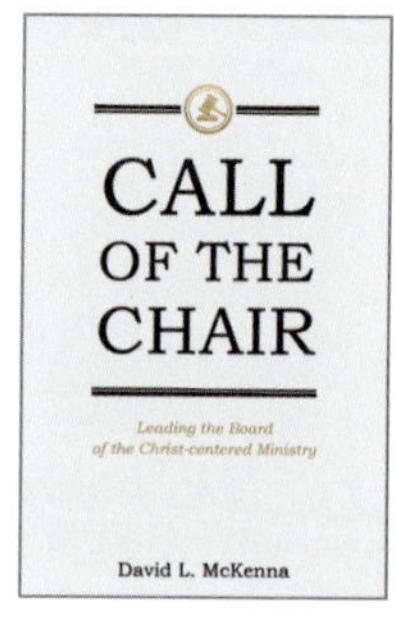

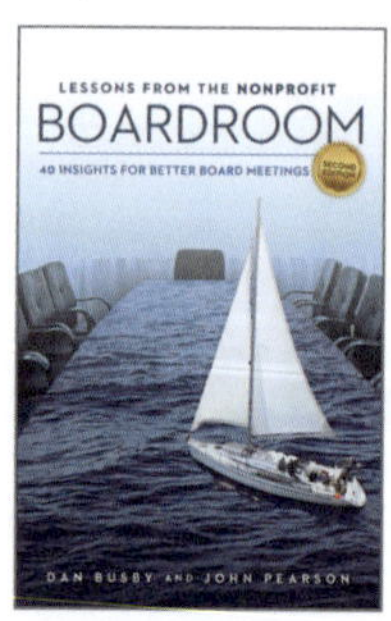

[4] David L. McKenna, *Call of the Chair: Leading the Board of the Christ-Centered Ministry* (Winchester, VA: ECFAPress, 2017), 93.

[5] Dan Busby, *TRUST: The Firm Foundation for Kingdom Fruitfulness* (Winchester, VA: ECFAPress, 2015), 2.

[6] Dan Busby and John Pearson, *Lessons From the Nonprofit Boardroom: 40 Insights for Better Board Meetings*, 2d ed. (Winchester, VA: ECFAPress, 2018), 29.

Many of these tools and templates were created by John for the ECFA Governance Forums in earlier years and adapted from webinars he led for ECFA and Christian Leadership Alliance (formerly Christian Management Association). Then, as lead facilitator for five years for the M.J. Murdock Charitable Trust's Board Leadership and Development Program, John packaged several tools into a printed resource for cohort participants. In 2017, at the request of the Thriving Boards program of Christian Camp and Conference Association, the tools were first published in this workbook format. And note this—it's unlikely that John can talk governance for more than five minutes without mentioning one of these tools!

Along the way, Dan has added his boardroom savvy and experience to these tools based on—imagine this!—more than 110 man-years on nonprofit boards. As president of ECFA and having served in leadership positions with ECFA for over 20 years, Dan's email inbox is constantly bulging with governance questions from top leaders and board members. So this book is long overdue and we believe it will be so helpful to so many.

"At least once every five years, every form should be put on trial for its life."[7]

Peter Drucker

When we introduce these tools, you'll note that sometimes we'll add personal notes ("…one of my top-10 life experiences…"). You can guess whether it's Dan or John who is over-sharing, but mostly, we trust you will enjoy learning more about why we're such big fans of tools and templates.

Be assured! These resources have been tested in hundreds of boardrooms and we are commending them to you and your board—with great hope—that they will enhance God-honoring governance in your boardroom. We pray that your board members will be better equipped for their sacred calling as stewards of God's work.

Dan Busby
Winchester, VA

John Pearson
San Clemente, CA

P.S. Reminder! If you, or your organization, purchased this book (or received it as part of a board training/enrichment experience), you are authorized to download the templates. (See the templates webpage on page ii of this book.)

Attn: Church Boards

Watch for this "church symbol" throughout these pages. You'll find special instructions and resources especially for church governance issues and opportunities.

[7] Peter F. Drucker, *The Practice of Management* (New York: HarperBusiness, 2006), 135.

Definitions

Top Leader

The paid employee who reports directly to the board of directors. This person's title might be:

- Chief Executive Officer or President
- Senior Pastor or Lead Pastor
- Executive Director

Governance

Here are several of our favorite definitions of governance:

- ❑ "Within Christ-centered organizations, governance is the stewardship of powers to accomplish the mission in service of the Church's calling."[8]
- ❑ "Governance is a collective effort, through smooth and suitable processes, to take actions that advance a shared purpose consistent with the institution's [organization's] mission."[9]
- ❑ "Governance is an activity, an action word; it is what boards do. The essence of the verb to govern is being a steward and trustee of an organization's resources and capacities. Governance is a team sport. Boards exercise collective influence; their members have no individual power. Boards exist only when they meet, that is, between 'raps of the gavel.'"[10]
- ❑ "The purpose of governance is to ensure, usually on behalf of others, that an organization achieves what it should achieve while avoiding those behaviors that should be avoided."[11]

Aspirational Core Competency of Christ-Centered Boards

"We believe that board members must sense God's call to serve on the board of directors. We invest time in cultivating, recruiting, orienting and engaging board members in their strategic role as stewards of our organization. The first step in organizational sustainability is to inspire board members to be highly committed and generous partners in ministry."[12]

Boards Are Highly Passionate About Their Christ-centered Mission.

ECFA Research Says...

clearly see the board's work as **Christ-centered**

strive to conduct their work with **Christ-centered character**

pray regularly for the ministry and the CEO

---

[8] David Tiede, President Emeritus, Luther Seminary (This definition was confirmed by Rebekah Basinger, governance consultant, who heard Dr. Tiede share this statement numerous times in workshops and personal conversations.)

[9] Richard P. Chait, Thomas P. Holland, and Barbara E. Taylor, *Improving the Performance of Governing Boards*, 1st ed. (Lanham, MD: Rowman & Littlefield Publishers, 1996), 1.

[10] Dennis D. Pointer and James E. Orlikoff, *The High-Performance Board: Principles of Nonprofit Organization Governance* (San Francisco: Jossey-Bass, 2002), 2.

[11] John Carver, *Boards That Make a Difference: A New Design for Leadership in Nonprofit and Public Organizations*, 3d ed. (San Francisco: Jossey-Bass, 2006), xxvii-xxviii.

[12] John Pearson, *Mastering the Management Buckets: 20 Critical Competencies for Leading Your Business or NonProfit* (Ventura, CA: Regal Books, 2008), 191.

TOOL #1: The Pathway to the Board

Give this internal document to your Governance Committee to guide them along the six steps…from suggestion to election.

"Your board candidate does not need to be wealthy—just generous. Generally that means that during this person's term of service on the board, he or she will make your ministry their first, second or third highest annual giving priority. No exceptions. Remember, Jesus said, 'For where your treasure is, there your heart will be also.'

"Where this core value is practiced, board members attest to the remarkable culture change that happens on the board. Passionate, highly committed board members—who follow their money with their heart—become incredible zealots for your mission. Wow!"[1]

Cultivation→Recruitment→Orientation→Engagement

6 Steps on the Pathway to Board Service

> Ask an administratively-gifted person on your Governance Committee (or perhaps the executive assistant to your CEO) to track names and next steps in your "Prospect Pipeline" using this internal document, "The Pathway to the Board."

Reminder! "Date" board prospects before proposing "marriage" (board service). Bring board prospects inside the circle of involvement.

Thoughtful adults don't propose marriage on the first date. Effective boards don't propose board service to prospects they don't know well. Think of this as a 36-month dating experience. But don't mention marriage (board service) up front.

As you pray through the process, slowly bring the prospect inside the circles of involvement. Today, he or she may be unfamiliar with your ministry, so add them to your mailing list and invite them to an event. Test their interest with a volunteer role. Just like in dating, continue to evaluate over many months if your prospect demonstrates growing interest, and ultimately passion, for your important mission.

YES OR NO? If "Cliff" turns out to be a lousy volunteer, drop him as a board prospect! You've avoided untold problems by not marrying an ineffective or uncommitted board member. But—if Susan volunteers with energy and effectiveness, plus recruits friends and families beyond expectation, you've likely found a great board prospect! Keep dating![2]

[1] John Pearson, *Mastering the Management Buckets: 20 Critical Competencies for Leading Your Business or Nonprofit* (Ventura, CA: Regal, 2008), 194–95.

[2] Adapted from Pearson, *Mastering the Management Buckets*, 193.

The Pathway to the Board

Go Slow...and Keep Reminding the Board About the Process for Recruiting New Board Members

Track these six steps for each name in your "Prospect Pipeline."

Ask an administratively-gifted person on your Governance Committee (or perhaps the executive assistant to your CEO) to track names and next steps in your "Prospect Pipeline" using this internal document, "The Pathway to the Board."

- ❑ **Step 1: SUGGEST.** A board member submits a "Board Nominee Suggestion Form" for a possible prospect—and the Governance Committee creates a "Pathway to the Board" file.
- ❑ **STEP 2: REVIEW.** The Governance Committee prays, discerns, and reviews the candidate's biographical information and qualifications against board-approved criteria. (Example: See the "6 D's Criteria.")
- ❑ **STEP 3: INQUIRE.** The Governance Committee assigns the next step on "building the relationship" to a specific board or committee member (perhaps in tandem with the CEO) and, possibly, the individual is invited to participate in a ministry event and/or accept a volunteer role.
- ❑ **STEP 4: APPLY.** The individual, after adequate time for dating, has a formal discussion about board service and—if it goes well—may be invited to complete an application for board service. The conversation should be crystal clear: the individual would still be subject to numerous next steps, including board approval and formal election.
- ❑ **STEP 5: ORIENTATION.** Should the candidate be recommended to the board by the Governance Committee—and receive board approval—begin the orientation steps immediately.
- ❑ **STEP 6: ENGAGE.** Create the expectation that every board member is highly committed to the sacred calling of God-honoring governance. Provide feedback and affirmation regularly!

RESOURCE:

Once a year, view the "Recruiting Board Members" short video at a meeting of the Governance Committee.[3]

[3] *ECFA Governance Toolbox Series No. 1: Recruiting Board Members – Cultivation, Recruitment, Orientation, Engagement* (Winchester, VA: ECFAPress, 2012). Visit *www.ECFA.org/Toolbox* and download the *Board Member Read-and-Engage Viewing Guide* and the *Facilitator Guide.*

Think 18 to 36 Months When "Dating" a Board Prospect

You'll know when it's time to propose marriage (board service). The prospect will have already demonstrated a high level of commitment, all the time moving towards the center of the involvement circle. This person will meet all of the previously established board criteria. Plus, the Lord will confirm it to you and your Governance Committee—as you devote time to prayer and discernment.[4]

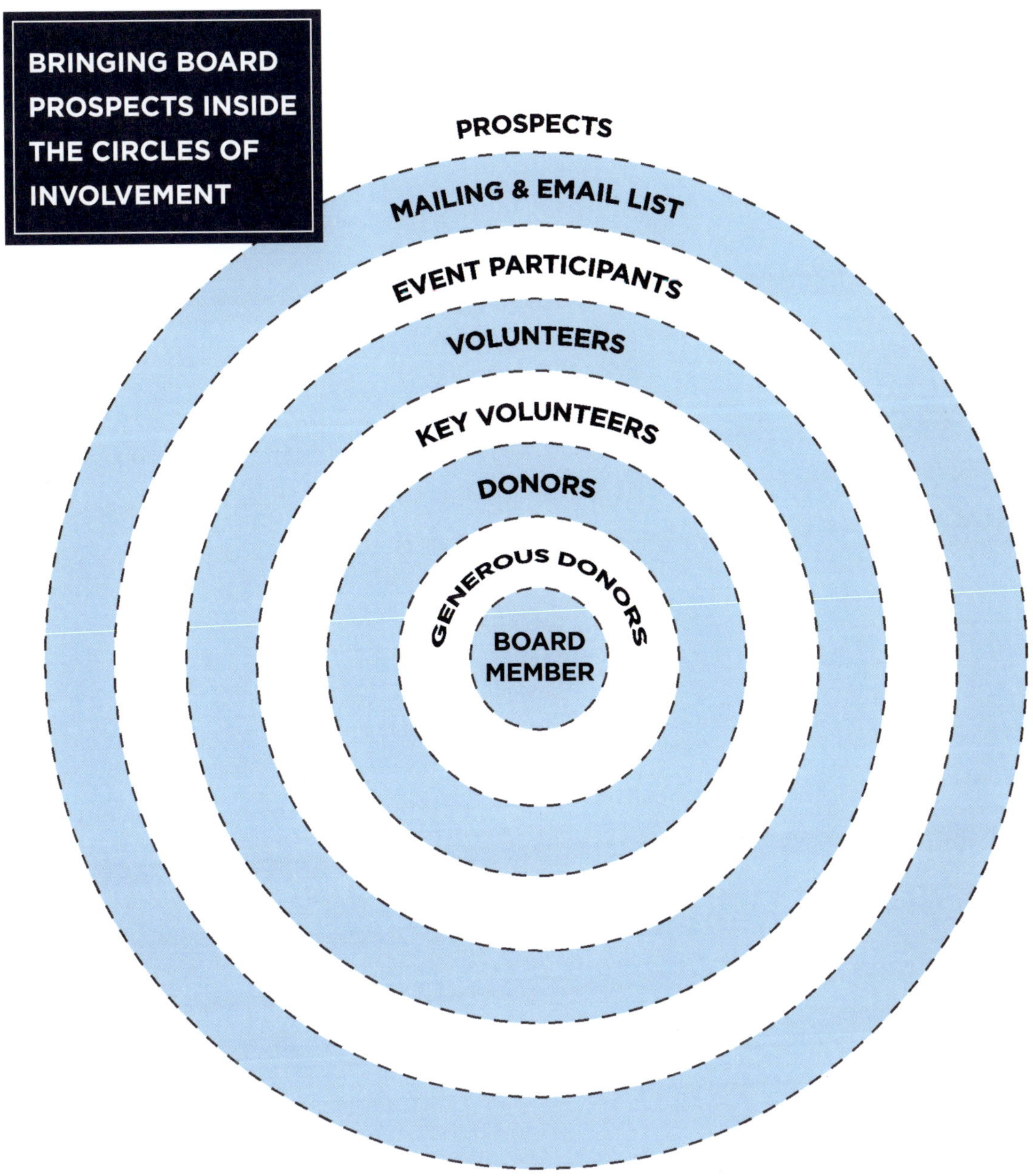

Mastering the Management Buckets. Used by permission.

[4] Adapted from "The Board Bucket" chapter in Pearson, *Mastering the Management Buckets*, 194–95.

THE PATHWAY TO THE BOARD

The 18- to 36-Month Steps for Bringing Highly Qualified Candidates Onto the Board

XYZ INTERNATIONAL

Version 1.0 – This form was approved by the board on (date): ___________.

(one name per form)

6 STEPS	
❑ 1. Suggest	❑ 4. Apply (Nomination & Election)
❑ 2. Review	❑ 5. Orientation
❑ 3. Inquire	❑ 6. Engage

CULTIVATION→RECRUITMENT→ORIENTATION→ENGAGEMENT	
❑ **STEP 1: Suggest** CONFIDENTIAL	**Submitted to Governance Committee** Attn: Committee Chair
Board Prospect Name and Contact Information:	
Submitted by:	
Date:	
"Board Nominee Suggestion Form" received:	❑ Yes ❑ No (do not proceed without form)

❑ **STEP 2: Review** CONFIDENTIAL	**Reviewed by Governance Committee** within 30 days
Review Biographical Information and/or Resumé	
Review Qualification as a Board Member (including Statement of Faith)	
Review Preliminary Qualification Per Written Board Member Nominee Criteria	
Prayer and Spiritual Discernment Process	
Action & Date: ❑ Decline or Postpone ❑ Move to Step 3: Inquire	

❑ **STEP 3: Inquire** **CONFIDENTIAL**	**Confidential "Dating Process" Begins**
"Build the Relationship" process assigned to (board member and/or CEO):	
Document past involvement with our ministry (if any):	
Possible invitation for current involvement and/or volunteer role in our ministry: ❑ Task Force ❑ Advisory Council ❑ Informal Input/Focus Group/etc. ❑ Attend Annual Event ❑ ________________	
Other:	
Action & Date: ❑ Decline or Postpone ❑ Move to Step 4: Apply ❑ Inform the Board	

CULTIVATION→**RECRUITMENT**→ORIENTATION→ENGAGEMENT	
❑ **STEP 4: Apply** (including nomination & election— if recommended)	**Formal Recruitment Begins**
Formal Meeting: "Would you consider, sometime, in the future (this year or next year), perhaps/maybe serving as a board member, should the Governance Committee recommend you and the board elect you?" • Here's why we think God is leading us to you (your background, experience, etc.)... • Here's how this might give you joy, fulfillment and rich relationships as you leverage your strengths, spiritual gifts and social style...	
Review Board Nominee Orientation Materials With Applicant, including: ❑ Board Member Position Description ❑ Board Member Annual Affirmation Statement ❑ Board Policies Manual (BPM) ❑ Annual Calendar of Board Meetings & Annual Board Retreat ❑ Briefing on "The 3 Board Hats: Governance, Volunteer, Participant"[5]	
Get-Acquainted Meal: Applicant and Spouse (if married) with 2-3 Board Members (including CEO)	
Invitation to Submit Application: Governance Committee authorizes next step and Board Chair (and/or CEO) invites individual to submit Application (and resume): ❑ Invitation extended ❑ Board informed	
Application & Resume Submitted: Application submitted and permission given to proceed on reference checks, etc.	
Reference Checks: to affirm applicant meets "Board Member Criteria" standards: ❑ Pastor and/or Church/Small Group Leader ❑ Spouse ❑ Employer and/or Fellow Employees ❑ Background Checks (must be legal and authorized!) ❑ Social Media Check ❑ Colleague or Outside Board Member Where Applicant Serves or Has Served ("Is he/she knowledgeable in governance and a Christ-centered team player?)	

[5] *ECFA Governance Toolbox Series No. 2: Balancing Board Roles: Understanding the 3 Board Hats: Governance, Volunteer, Participant* (Winchester, VA: ECFAPress, 2013). Visit *www.ECFA.org/Toolbox* and download the *Board Member Read-and-Engage Viewing Guide and the Facilitator Guide.*

CULTIVATION→**RECRUITMENT**→ORIENTATION→ENGAGEMENT	
❑ **STEP 4: Apply** (including nomination & election— if recommended)	**Formal Recruitment Begins**
Prayer and Spiritual Discernment: Engage the Board in praying and discerning God's direction regarding this candidate.	
Governance Committee Recommendation: Due diligence by Governance Committee and recommendation to the Board	
Board Approval/Election: Governance Committee recommendation is approved by the Board of Directors: ❑ Candidate notified ❑ Candidate is/will be elected on ____________ and term begins on ____________.	

CULTIVATION→RECRUITMENT→**ORIENTATION**→ENGAGEMENT	
❑ **STEP 5: Orientation**	**Formal Orientation Begins**
Customized Orientation: With assigned "board buddy" and CEO, create the customized six-month orientation process, to likely include: ❑ Attendance at board member professional development workshop or conference ❑ Online course(s)/orientation (if available) ❑ Detailed Review of Board Nominee Orientation Binder ❑ Walk-through/briefing of ministry departments and introductions to staff, etc. ❑ Password for online board portal and documents ❑ ____________________ ❑ ____________________	
Professional Development/Reading: Read ____ of the following books/articles within the next six months. For additional reading options, visit *ECFA's Governance of Christ-Centered Organizations* blog:[6] ❑ *StrengthsFinder 2.0* by Tom Rath (take the CliftonStrengths assessment—and share your Top-5 strengths with the board) ❑ *The Imperfect Board Member* by Jim Brown ❑ *Owning Up: 14 Questions Every Board Member Needs to Ask* by Ram Charan ❑ "What Makes Great Boards Great" by Jeffrey A. Sonnenfeld, (*Harvard Business Review*) ❑ *Called to Serve: Creating and Nurturing the Effective Volunteer Board* by Max De Pree ❑ *Lessons From the Nonprofit Boardroom*, Second Edition, by Dan Busby and John Pearson ❑ *More Lessons From the Nonprofit Boardroom* by Dan Busby and John Pearson ❑ *Lessons From the Church Boardroom* by Dan Busby and John Pearson ❑ *The Council*, by Gary G. Hoag, Wesley K Willmer, and Gregory J. Henson	
Orientation Evaluation: Within six months of the first board meeting, submit an evaluation and suggestions for improving the orientation process for future new board members.	

[6] John Pearson, "Best Board Books: Index to 18 Good Governance Stimulators," *Governance of Christ-Centered Organizations* (blog), March 12, 2019. *http://ecfagovernance.blogspot.com/2019/03/best-board-books-index-to-18-good.html.*

CULTIVATION→RECRUITMENT→ORIENTATION→**ENGAGEMENT**	
❑ **STEP 6 Engage**	**Engagement Begins**
Inspiring Engagement: Based on engagement expectations for all board members, continue to engage at the highest level—stewarding the responsibilities of a Christ-centered board member. Customize your plan to include: ❑ ____________________ ❑ ____________________ ❑ ____________________	
Annually: ❑ Sign the Board Member Annual Affirmation (to include the board's generous giving expectations) ❑ Sign the Annual Conflicts of Interest Statement ❑ Attend the Annual Board Retreat (with spouse) ❑ Complete the Annual Board Self-Assessment Survey	
Quarterly: ❑ Attend board meetings: • Read and review all board meeting materials in advance of the meeting • Complete "homework" assignments on time ❑ Attend committee meetings ❑ Expect to hear from God about the critical issues of our governance work—through our formal and informal times of prayer and spiritual discernment ❑ Maintain standards of board member governance literacy as documented in the Board Policies Manual (BPM) ❑ ____________________	
Daily/Weekly/Monthly: ❑ Pray regularly for our Board, staff and CEO ❑ Respond promptly to emails and phone calls regarding board work ❑ ____________________	

As a Volunteer	
Conduct all volunteer work through appropriate employee channels (per our board policy) versus "going around" normal channels to senior management or our CEO.	

The 6 D's Criteria:

Attn: Governance Committee: Review the Suggestion Forms for two or three applicants—and compare them to each other. *What is God saying to you about them?*

Rate Applicants on a Scale of 1 to 10 (10 is high):

Board Nominees Must Meet our 6 D's Criteria [7]	**Applicant #1**	**Applicant #2**	**Applicant #3**
1. **Discerning Decision-Maker:** Prior experience in making wise policy, financial, strategy and personnel decisions. (*Is this person competent in both hiring and firing situations?*)			
2. **Demonstrated Passion:** Gives high priority to and cares deeply about our cause. (Limits board service to one or two boards at a time.)			
3. **Documented Team Player:** Competent in group process skills, effective listener; leverages own spiritual gifts and those of others (Rom. 12, Eph. 4, 1 Cor. 12). Knows and leverages his or her strengths.			
4. **Diligent and Faithful Participant:** Documented history of fulfilling our volunteer assignments (if applicable) on schedule and under budget. Keeps promises and keeps confidences. Inspires others.			
5. **Doer: Walks the Talk!** Reference checks affirm a God-honoring lifestyle and character. Humble, prayerful, high integrity in all relationships. Affirms our statement of faith.			
6. **Donor:** Because Jesus said in Matthew 6:21, "Where your treasure is, there your heart will be also," this board prospect is *already* a generous giver to our ministry. (Note: Many organizations define "generous" as prioritizing your organization in the Top-3 of a person's annual giving. Board members at all income levels can be generous.)			

Other criteria could include:

- ❑ Highly knowledgeable and/or competent in ________________ and ________________.
- ❑ Highly knowledgeable and/or influential in this niche/network/profession/etc.____________.
- ❑ ____

[7] *ECFA Governance Toolbox Series No. 1: Recruiting Board Members.* Visit *www.ECFA.org/Toolbox* and download the *Board Member Read-and-Engage Viewing Guide* and the *Facilitator Guide.*

TOOL #2: Board Nominee Suggestion Form

Give this suggestion form to board members to help them discern who to recommend for board service.

"For where your treasure is, there your heart will be also" (Matt. 6:21, NIV).

"Recruit intentionally, with generosity in mind, and you'll breathe new life into your ministry. As you 'date' board prospects, spiritually challenge them to become generous givers to your ministry. Explain why you need a team of highly committed givers who demonstrate through their giving where their hearts are."[1]

Recommend People for Your Prospect Pipeline That Meet the "6 D's Criteria"

Pray Before Prospecting

Today . . . begin your Top-50 Prospects Prayer List. Effective CEOs, senior pastors, board chairs, and development officers know that it takes up to 36 months to bring exceptional board prospects into the board circle.

Jim Brown, author of *The Imperfect Board Member*, writes,

> The problem is, most board cultures are developed by default, not by design.[2]

Change that! The Lord wants you to have an extraordinary board. Imagine the potential when you energize exceptional board members who give spiritual oversight and excellent governance to your God-given mission.

Why settle for second best? Why recruit untested, uncommitted good prospects when—with prayer and hard work—the Lord could bless you with a sterling team of board members?[3]

---

[1] John Pearson, *Mastering the Management Buckets: 20 Critical Competencies for Leading Your Business or Nonprofit* (Ventura, CA: Regal, 2008), 191, 194.

[2] Jim Brown, *The Imperfect Board Member: Discovering the Seven Disciplines of Governance Excellence (San Francisco:* Jossey-Bass, 2006), 102.

[3] Pearson, *Mastering the Management Buckets*, 192.

Board Nominee Suggestion Form

Date Board Prospects Before Proposing!

8 steps for inspiring your board to recommend exceptional prospects for board service

Inspire your board members to pray and discern who—in their networks—might be possible prospects for board service. Follow these steps:

- ❑ **1. Affirm Criteria.** Establish criteria for board service (see the "6 D's" on page 19).
- ❑ **2. Adopt the Affirmation Statement.** Adopt the "Board Member Annual Affirmation Statement" (Tool #21), and customize it for your specific board member roles and responsibilities related to the three board hats: Governance, Volunteer, Participant.
- ❑ **3. Assign Responsiblities.** Assign board recruitment responsibilities to the Governance Committee (or perhaps your Nominating Committee, or your Executive Committee). Review your bylaws and your Board Policies Manual to confirm who has primary responsibility for recruiting new board members.
- ❑ **4. View the Video.** Encourage your Governance Committee to view and discuss the video and materials in the *ECFA Governance Toolbox Series No. 1: Recruiting Board Members – Cultivation, Recruitment, Orientation, Engagement.*[4]
- ❑ **5. Review Recruitment Steps.** Review the seven steps in board recruitment ("dating a board prospect") from "The Board Bucket" chapter in *Mastering the Management Buckets.*[5]
- ❑ **6. Suggest Names.** Inspire your board members to pray, discern, and then recommend individuals who meet the criteria for board service. Give all board members a Word document of this tool, "Board Nominee Suggestion Form."
- ❑ **7. Keep Confidential.** Remind board members that board recruitment is a process (similar to dating!) and not to discuss board service (marriage!) with any prospects until the Governance Committee has reviewed the suggestion forms and approved any next steps.
- ❑ **8. Update the Prospect Pipeline at Every Board Meeting** Include on every board meeting's agenda a brief report from the Governance Committee, with "The Prospect Pipeline" report—indicating where prospects and nominees are in the discerning, dating, and discussion phases. (See Tool #1, "The Pathway to the Board.")

[4] *ECFA Governance Toolbox Series No. 1: Recruiting Board Members – Cultivation, Recruitment, Orientation, Engagement* (Winchester, VA: ECFAPress, 2012). Visit *www.ECFA.org/Toolbox* and download the *Board Member Read-and-Engage Viewing Guide* and the *Facilitator Guide.*

[5] Pearson, *Mastering the Management Buckets*, 191–99.

BOARD NOMINEE SUGGESTION FORM
XYZ International

(one name per form; request Word document from: _______________)

Version 1.0 – This suggestion form was approved by the board on (date): ____________.

MY NAME	
Date Submitted	

ATTN: Governance Committee

I am suggesting that the Governance Committee consider the following person for service on:

❏ Check one:
[ ] ____________________________ (example: Advisory Council, etc.)
[ ] Board of Directors (*3-year term, or unexpired term*)

To the best of my knowledge, this person meets the criteria as described in the following documents:

☑ Pathway to the Board

☑ Board Member Annual Affirmation Statement

☑ "The 6 D's" (see page 19) – Adapted from the *ECFA Governance Toolbox Series No. 1: Recruiting Board Members*

Name	
Active with XYZ? If yes, for approximately how many years?	
Spouse Name	
Home Address	
Home Phone	
Mobile Phone	
Email Address	
Employer (& City)	
Resume Highlights	• Use bullet points here •
Education Highlights	• Use bullet points here •
Describe this person's walk with God	
Church Involvement (church name and city)	
Describe the strengths, gifts and expertise that this person would bring to the position	
Service to other boards (past and present)	

Describe this person's understanding and philosophy of governance	
Availability to faithfully attend: • Quarterly Board Meetings • Committee Meetings • Annual Meeting • Other "Participant Hat" Events	
Could this person (and spouse) participate in the Annual Board Retreat **every year**?	
Could this participant meet these additional requirements? • ____________________ • ____________________	
Other Comments	

Governance Committee **Next Steps ➜**	☑ A member of the Governance Committee will contact you for additional information, usually within 30 days. ☑ Then…the Governance Committee will prioritize the person's name on the master list of suggested names ("The Prospect Pipeline"). ☑ When that name is prioritized near the top, then a member of the Governance Committee will call you about next steps (such as who will make the direct contact and when).

IMPORTANT!

Please do NOT contact the suggested person directly about service on our board, until such time as the Governance Committee may ask for your involvement. But you are encouraged—as with all members—to inspire this person to become more involved in our organization and to become a "raving fan" of our organization by inspiring others to become engaged in the ministry.

Engagement Next Steps Might Include:

☑ "Liking" our organization on Facebook—and posting "satisfied customer" comments

☑ Encouraging family members to participate in organizational events

☑ Encouraging his/her local church to participate in organizational events (and giving)

☑ Encouraging other strategic influencers to participate in organizational events

☑ Attending major organizational events

☑ Serving on a Focus Group, Task Force or other volunteer role

The 6 D's Criteria:

Board Nominees Must Meet our 6 D's Criteria [7]	Describe Your Observation of This Person Relative to Each of the 6 D's
1. **Discerning Decision-Maker:** Prior experience in making wise policy, financial, strategy and personnel decisions. (*Is this person competent in both hiring and firing situations?*)	
2. **Demonstrated Passion:** Gives high priority to and cares deeply about our cause. (Limits board service to one or two boards at a time.)	
3. **Documented Team Player:** Competent in group process skills, effective listener; leverages own spiritual gifts and those of others (Rom. 12, Eph. 4, 1 Cor. 12). Knows and leverages his or her strengths.	
4. **Diligent and Faithful Participant:** Documented history of fulfilling our volunteer assignments (if applicable) on schedule and under budget. Keeps promises and keeps confidences. Inspires others.	
5. **Doer: Walks the Talk!** Reference checks affirm a God-honoring lifestyle and character. Humble, prayerful, high integrity in all relationships. Affirms our statement of faith.	
6. **Donor:** Because Jesus said in Matthew 6:21, "Where your treasure is, there your heart will be also," this board prospect is already a generous giver to our ministry. (Note: Many organizations define "generous" as prioritizing your organization in the Top-3 of a person's annual giving. Board members at all income levels can be generous.)	
7. ***Other:**	

**Example:* this person is a "raving fan" of our organization and has a significant circle of influence (large church or churches, denomination, parachurches, business community, associations/networks, etc.) that he or she will strategically leverage to bring others into our organization's circle.	

[7] *ECFA Governance Toolbox Series No. 1: Recruiting Board Members.* Visit *www.ECFA.org/toolbox* and download the *Board Member Read-and-Engage Viewing Guide* and the *Facilitator Guide.*

TOOL #3: Board Nominee Orientation: Table of Contents

Inspire qualified board prospects to consider board service by giving them a comprehensive overview of your governance documents.

"Recruit board members for their passion, not their position. Don't swallow the board myth that says you need a CPA, an attorney, a pastor and a fundraiser on your board. People in those positions might make great volunteers, but less-than-loyal, uncommitted board members are the last thing your organization needs."[1]

Recruit for Passion—Not Position!

The Board Bucket Core Competency

We believe that board members must sense God's call to serve on the board of directors. We invest time in cultivating, recruiting, orienting and engaging board members in their strategic role as stewards of our organization. The first step in organizational sustainability is to inspire board members to be highly committed and generous partners in ministry.

The 7 Steps in the Board Prospect Pipeline

1. **Recruit** for passion, not position.
2. **Pray** before prospecting.
3. **Date** before proposing.
4. **Inspire** your prospect to give generously.
5. **Propose** marriage.
6. **Continue** dating!
7. **Leave** a legacy.[2]

Effective Boards Report a High Level of Ministry Passion

ECFA Research Says...

5. Increase Board Member Passion

"Our board members are passionate about our organization's primary mission/vision and invest time, talent, and treasure in personally enhancing our mission."

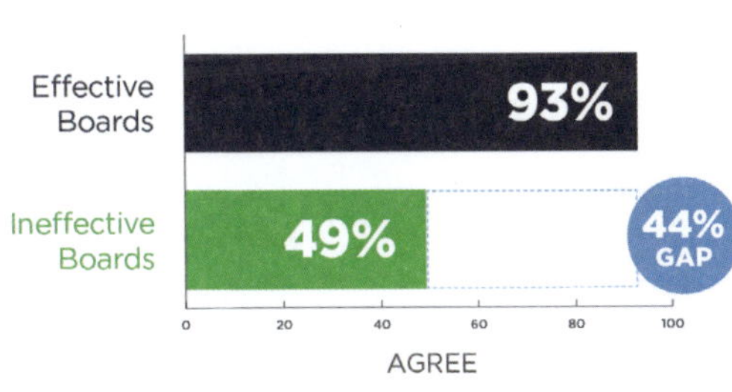

[1] John Pearson, *Mastering the Management Buckets: 20 Critical Competencies for Leading Your Business or Nonprofit* (Ventura, CA: Regal Books, 2008), 192.

[2] Ibid., 191. Read Chapter 14, "The Board Bucket," pages 191-200, for the narrative of the seven steps in board member recruitment.

Board Nominee Orientation Materials

Table of Contents

Picture this! You've been "dating" a board prospect who is on the board-approved "Prospect Pipeline List."

The Nominating Committee has affirmed that this person…

- ☑ …is already a generous giver to your organization.
- ☑ …has served with distinction as a faithful volunteer.
- ☑ …has stellar character from your due diligence reference-checking with the person's pastor and others (Check on: character, competency, chemistry, keeps confidences, and much more.)
- ☑ …has prior board governance positive experience and understands the "3 Board Hats: Governance, Volunteer, and Participant" and the policy governance continuum.
- ☑ …and all the other boxes are checked with "Outstanding!"

So with approval from the Nominating Committee (following your "Pathway to the Board" protocol), it's now time for your first meeting with the prospect to discuss the possibility that he or she might have passion for serving on your board…someday. (*Don't pop the question yet!*)

Use this **"Board Nominee Orientation Materials: Table of Contents"** as an outline for communicating a comprehensive and very transparent look at your governance documents.

Guarantee! This will be the first time that this board prospect has ever received such a comprehensive overview. Your prospect will be impressed! And, you will pick up signs and signals as to whether the prospect is the *right* person to invite on the board at *this* time.

REMINDER! Customize your one-on-one presentation, based on your prospect's social style. (One size doesn't fit all.)[3]

The 4 Social Styles	This Person Values:
Analytical	Facts and information
Driving	Bullet points and executive summaries
Amiable	Relationships and stories
Expressives	4-color documents and the Big Vision for the future

How to Deal With Annoying People: What to Do When You Can't Avoid Them

by Bob Phillips and Kimberly Alyn

Inspire your board to read this humorous and faith-based book on the four social styles. The chapter on "Dispelling Ten Stereotypical Gender Myths" is worth the price of the book. If you've bought into the myth that women are relationship-oriented and men are task-oriented, you've misread God's unique design in people—male and female. It's a must-read chapter.[4]

[3] Pearson, *Mastering the Management Buckets*, 192. For more on the four social styles, read Chapter 7: "The People Bucket." Learn more about social styles at *www.tracomcorp.com/social-style-training/*.

[4] Bob Phillips and Kimberly Alyn, *How to Deal With Annoying People: What to Do When You Can't Avoid Them* (Eugene, OR: Harvest House, 2011), 145–56.

Board of Directors – Board Nominee Orientation Materials

Table of Contents – [Organization Name Here]

Section	**Introductory Materials**
1	Introduction from the Chair of the Board of Directors
2	General Brochures, Publications, (eNewsletter, Website outline, etc.)
3	Historical Snapshot, Honors, Awards, Notable News Clippings
	Board of Directors
4	Current Board Members (Mini-Bios), Committees, and Volunteer Structure
5	Board Member Annual Affirmation Statement, Calendar of Future Board Meetings, Board Member Application Form, and Biographical Sketch Form
6	Nomination and Election Procedures
7	Bylaws, Articles of Incorporation, etc.
8	Board Policies Manual (BPM)
9	Conflict of Interest Disclosure Letter
10	Former Board Members & Board Chairs
11	Board Meeting Agenda/Pages (of most recent meeting) – *sample*
12	Board Issues/Challenges for Next 3 Years (including: "Any skeletons in boardroom closet?")
	Finance, Budget, IRS, ECFA Reports
13	Annual Budget
14	Current Financial Reports
15	Audited Financial Statements
16	ECFA Membership, Profile and Public Statistics
17	IRS Form 990 (*Return of Org. Exempt from Income Tax*)
	Strategic Plan and Metrics
18	Rolling 3-Year Strategic Plan & Strategic Plan Placemat (one-page summary: 11" x 17")
19	Annual Customer Satisfaction Surveys
20	CEOs Annual S.M.A.R.T. Goals & Board/CEO Accountability Process (Monthly Dashboard)
21	Leading Indicators/Key Performance Indicators (KPIs), Statistics (charts and graphs)
22	Our Answers to Peter Drucker's "Five Questions Every Nonprofit Organization Must Answer"
23	"Radar Issues" (1-page) – "Our Assumptions About the Next 3 Years"
	Team Members
24	Organizational Chart & Mini-Position Descriptions: Staff Contact Info
25	Team Member Mini-Bios; CEO Bio, CEO's Top-5 Strengths (StrengthsFinder.com)
26	Confidential Compensation Schedule
	Development
27	Donor Development Program - Snapshot
28	Direct Mail, Campaign/Project, Brochure Samples
29	Development Program Annual and 3-Year Goals (and the fundraising role of board members)
	Programs and Services
30	"Menu" of Programs, Products, and Services for "Primary Customers" and "Supporting Customers" (and annual program evaluation process)
31	Other

Board Member Recruitment Resources:

ECFA Governance Toolbox Series No. 1: Recruiting Board Members
Leveraging the 4 Phases of Board Recruitment: Cultivation, Recruitment, Orientation and Engagement

www.ECFA.org/Toolbox

Lessons From the Nonprofit Boardroom:
40 Insights for Better Board Meetings, Second Edition (2018)

by Dan Busby and John Pearson

- ❑ Lesson 13. If You Need a Volunteer, Recruit a Volunteer
- ❑ Lesson 14. If You Need a Board Member, Recruit a Board Member
- ❑ Lesson 16. Date Board Prospects Before You Propose Marriage
- ❑ Lesson 34. Envision Your Best Board Member Orientation Ever

Read blogs on these topics (and all 40 lessons) at:
http://nonprofitboardroom.blogspot.com/

Board Member Orientation:
The Concise and Complete Guide to Nonprofit Board Service

by Michael E. Batts

Hooey Alerts! Most handbooks on board governance are dry and boring. Batts remedies that sin by sprinkling "Hooey Alerts!" throughout the book. He defines hooey as "false or misleading information, malarkey, or bunk."[5]

[5] Michael E. Batts, *Board Member Orientation: The Concise and Complete Guide to Nonprofit Board Service* (Orlando: Accountability Press, 2011), i. Read the review of *Board Member Orientation* at: *http://urgentink.typepad.com/my_weblog/2012/07/board-member-orientation.html*

Board Member Recruitment Resources:

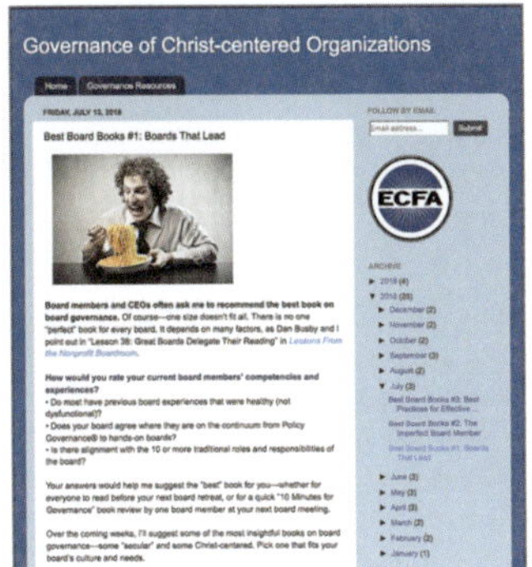

Read ECFA's blog for more governance insights:

http://ECFAgovernance.blogspot.com

Governance of Christ-Centered Organizations Blog

by John Pearson

Check out the series on "Best Board Books" beginning with Book #1: *Boards That Lead: When to Take Charge, When to Partner, and When to Stay Out of the Way*, by Ram Charan, Dennis Carey and Michael Useem.

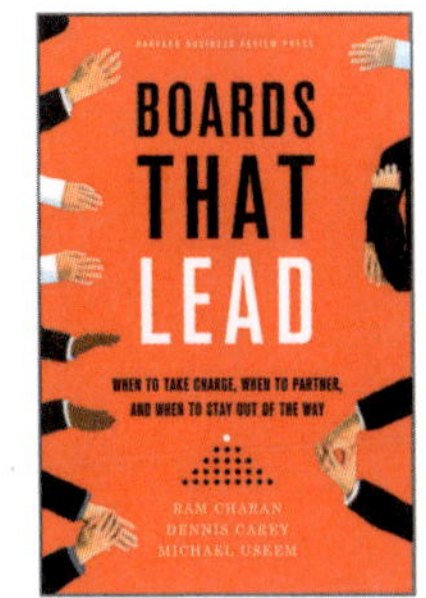

Visit:
http://ECFAgovernance.blogspot.com/2018/07/best-board-books-1-boards-that-lead.html

Mastering the Management Buckets Workbook
Management Tools, Templates and Tips From John Pearson

by John Pearson

The Board Bucket:

> **"I've searched all the parks in all the cities and found no statues of committees."**[6]
>
> G.K. Chesterton

Development 101
Building a Comprehensive Development Program on Biblical Values

by John R. Frank and R. Scott Rodin

Ask a board member to read and report on Part 3, "The Role of the Board in Development." The authors note: "Understanding the role of the board in the development process may be one of the greatest sources of frustration for CEOs, development staff, and board members."[7]

[6] John Pearson, *Mastering the Management Buckets Workbook: Management Tools, Templates and Tips From John Pearson* (San Clemente, CA: A Pearpod Resource, 2018), 131.

[7] John R. Frank and R. Scott Rodin, *Development 101: Building a Comprehensive Development Program on Biblical Values* (Colbert, WA: Kingdom Life, 2015), 27.

When meeting with a board prospect, it's important to discuss whether or not your board has practices or policies regarding annual giving requirements. And, it is good to outline expectations for board members to encourage *others* to give financially to your organization.

Board Member Stewardship Roles
ECFA's 2019 Comprehensive Nonprofit Governance Survey

What do boards indicate as the places where they're weakest? ECFA's national survey of ECFA-accredited ministries asked people to rate their board on best practices. The numbers range from low to high, from undesirable to very desirable. These self-scores are from everyone combined—CEO, board chair and board member.[8]

Where Boards Are the Weakest

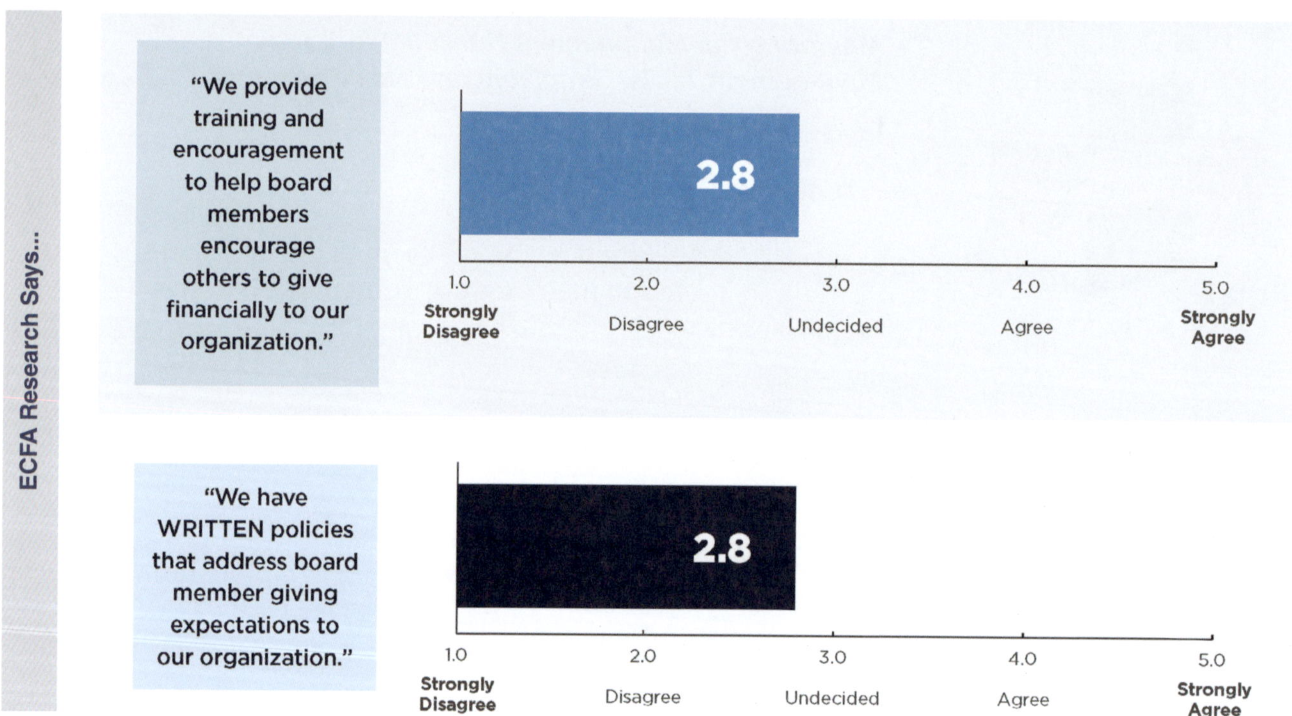

[8] *Unleashing Your Board's Potential: Comprehensive Report from ECFA's Nonprofit Governance Survey* (Winchester, VA: ECFAPress, 2019).

Effective Boards Have a Lot Going for Them

But what happens when survey participants are compared to those who rated their boards as effective with those who don't think their board is effective?

ECFA Research Says...

Develop Additional Giving

"We provide training and encouragement to help board members encourage others to give"

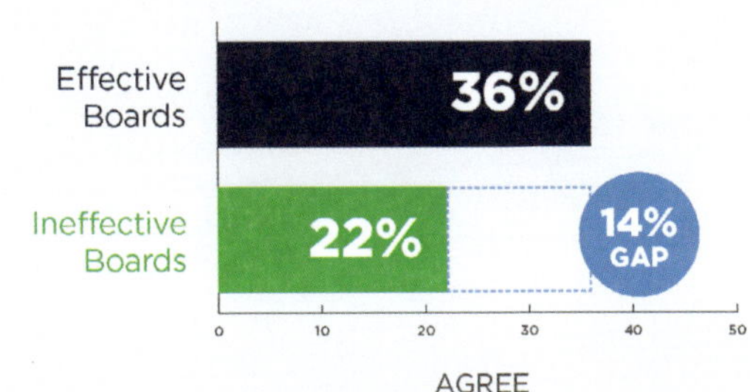

Different Views on Stewardship Expectations

ECFA asked about **expectations for financial giving** from board members. The questions with the biggest contrast between CEO, board chair, and board members are depicted below. On both, the CEO has a higher expectation than others do.

ECFA Research Says...

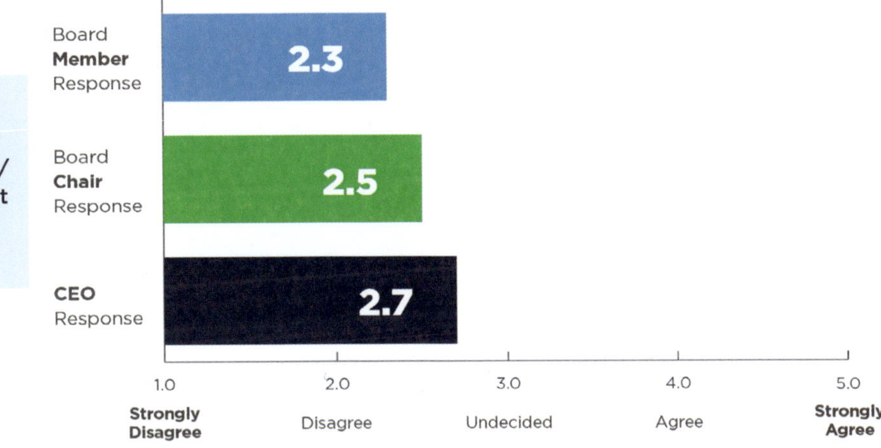

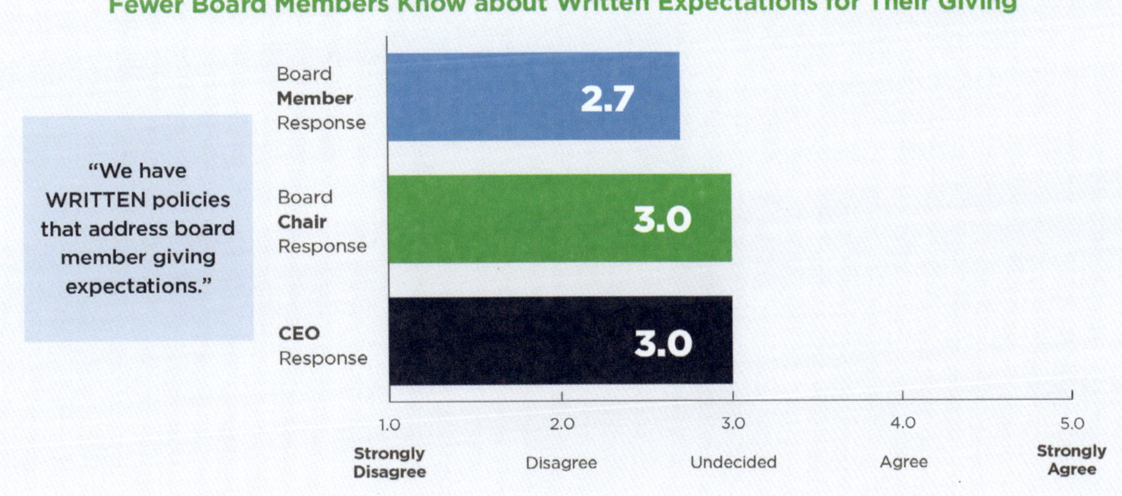

Big Difference Between Effective and Ineffective Boards

ECFA Research Says...

Set Clear Expectations

"Our board understands its roles and responsibilities."

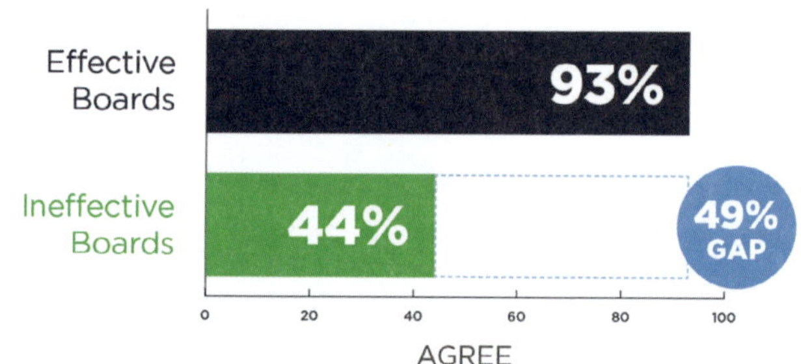

Not Enough Board Members Feel They Have the Right Board Composition for the Future

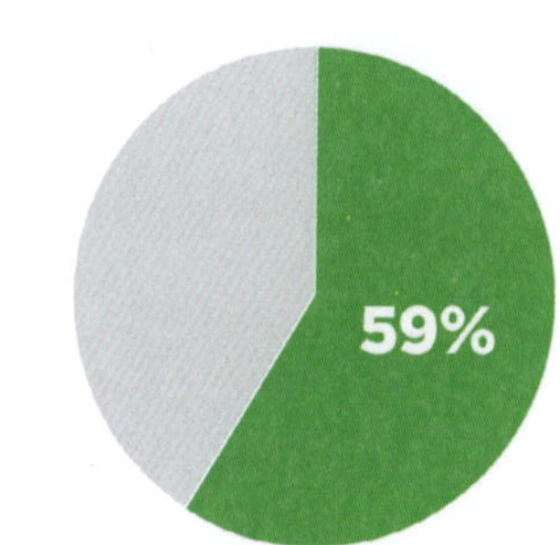

59% answer affirmatively to "Is our board composition right for the challenges ahead?"

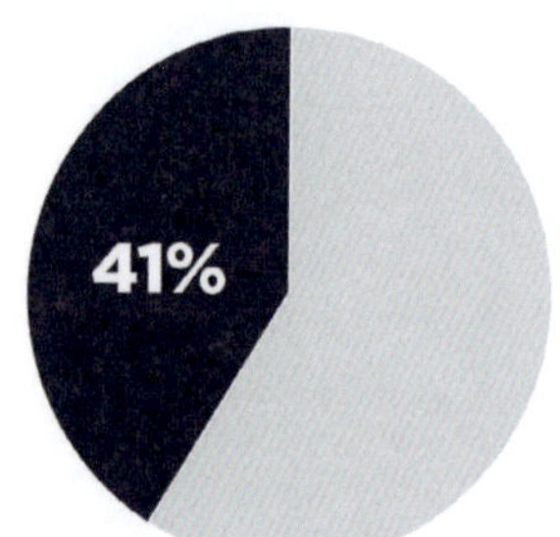

41% say they need "some," "much," or "major" help to remove ineffective board members.

Note: "ECFA Research Says . . ." inserts appear throughout this book. All findings come from *Unleashing Your Board's Potential: Comprehensive Report from ECFA's Nonprofit Governance Survey* by Warren Bird. It is available for free download at *ECFA.org/Surveys* and is described further on page 38 of this book.

TOOL #4: Five-Finger Feedback

Use this tool to enrich engagement and immediate feedback..

Fast Feedback Tool

Here's a Fast Feedback Tool that will immediately improve your board and committee meetings.

At the conclusion of a board's Nominating Committee meeting we facilitated, the newly elected committee chair asked for feedback.

"At every board or committee meeting I chair," he told us, "I always ask each participant to rate the effectiveness of our meeting. So on a scale of one to five (five is high), I'll ask each of you to give me your rating. How did we do?"

The committee members each shared their rating—holding up the appropriate number of fingers—and also shared the rationale for the rating. Next, the Nominating Committee chair gave his rating—a five—which was an encouragement to everyone.

At our next meeting, I know two things will happen:

1) We'll be asked to rate the meeting.
2) Throughout the meeting, we'll be thoughtfully contributing (listening more than talking) to help the ratings stay high!

It's a brilliant idea—and it took less than three minutes.

Romans 12:3 reminds us: "Do not think of yourself more highly than you ought, but rather think of yourself with sober judgment…" This Fast Feedback Tool will remind everyone to do just that.

QUESTION: What if…you're the chair and the Fast Feedback Tool exercise reveals low scores? What would you say?[1]

[1] John Pearson, "Fast Feedback Tool," *Governance of Christ-centered Organizations* (blog), February 20, 2013. ECFA: *http://ECFAgovernance.blogspot.com/2013/02/fast-feedback-tool.html.*

Bonus Feedback Tool

The board members at Christian Community Credit Union use this feedback tool frequently:

BOARD MEETING EVALUATION – 5 Minutes at End of Meeting
Submit to: Jane Doe

Date: April 26, 2019

Name: ______________________________

✓ **How Effective Was:**	**5** Extremely Effective	**4** Very Effective	**3** Moderately Effective	**2** Slightly Effective	**1** Not at all Effective
My Preparation?	○	○	○	○	○
My engagement in this meeting?	○	○	○	○	○
The board's overall engagement in this meeting?	○	○	○	○	○

Highlight:

Lowlight:

I leveraged my strengths, social style, spiritual gifts, and/or passion when I:

Next month's meeting would be more effective if:

TOOL #5: The Board's Annual Self-Assessment Survey

Select the board self-assessment survey option that best fits your board's culture and your board's aspirations for continual improvement.

"Writing in the Dark Is Hard!"

Self-Assessment Is Not an Optional Task

"Board self-evaluation is an inseparable part of governing, not an extraneous or optional task. To see how integral evaluation is to the task, try writing in the dark. If you cannot see where your pen marks, you will not write well and may not even write legibly. Yet writing is a familiar skill with which you have a lifetime of experience. It is so automatic that you scarcely give the arm, and hand, finger muscle movements a conscious thought. But writing in the dark is hard. How much more must we need feedback for a complex social task such as governance?"[1]

Peter Drucker on Self-Assessment:

"**Self-assessment** is the first action requirement of leadership: the constant resharpening, constant refocusing, never really being satisfied."[2]

"**Self-assessment** can and should convert good intentions and knowledge into effective action—not next year but tomorrow morning."[3]

Attn: Church Boards

While the following board self-assessment options are designed for nonprofit boards, they can easily be customized for church boards.

[1] John Carver, *CarverGuide 8: Board Self-Assessment* (San Francisco: Jossey-Bass, 1997), 16. This is one of several short booklets from *The CarverGuide Series on Effective Board Governance.*

[2] Peter F. Drucker, Frances Hesselbein, and Joan Snyder Kuhl, *Peter Drucker's Five Most Important Questions: Enduring Wisdom for Today's Leaders* (Hoboken, NJ: John Wiley & Sons, 2015), 5.

[3] Ibid., 6

The Board's Annual Self-Assessment Survey

Options and Opportunities

Select your option from these three sections:

Section	Process
❑ Section 1	Do-It-Yourself
❑ Section 2	Facilitated by a Consultant or Board Coach
❑ Section 3	Template: "Best Governance Practices" Survey (use with SurveyMonkey)

INTRODUCTION: Why Assess?

Why assess?

Assessment is one of the most effective ways to move your board to the next level of performance. And that is a worthy goal for all boards.

Why conduct a board self-assessment?

Are you wondering whether you should change your board's size or governance model? Restructure your committees? Put term limits in place? Do you want to step up your board's engagement? Explore how to improve board members' stewardship roles? Or determine how to keep your board from tilting towards micromanagement?

A board self-assessment is an effective way to get input from all of your board members on how the full board is performing against generally accepted best practice standards and use that information to create positive change! It leads to a shared understanding of the board's responsibilities related to compliance, accountability, financial oversight, and ultimately, setting direction for the organization. And it provides the framework for setting priorities that will maintain your strengths and will address areas in need of improvement.

Is Enough Self-Assessment and Outside Assessment Happening?

ECFA Research Says...

In the last two years, have you had an **outside person** help your board look in the mirror to do self-assessment for how it could improve?

31% said yes

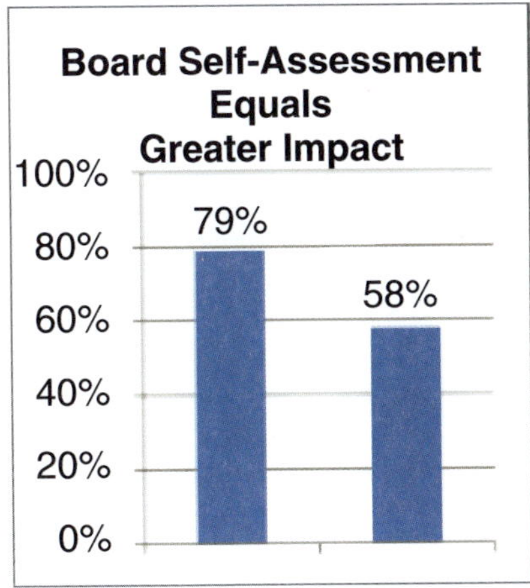

Leading With Intent:

Research From BoardSource

According to BoardSource's research with nonprofit CEOs:

> **"...boards that have conducted a self-assessment have greater impact on the organization's performance than those that have not (79% vs. 58%)."**[4]

From the *Leading With Intent* Research:

While there are many ways boards can be intentional about reflecting on board performance, a formal board self-assessment ensures that board members are engaging in a process of group- and self-reflection.

Boards that assess themselves regularly perform better on core responsibilities.

Boards that assess their own performance get higher grades across all areas of board performance, as rated by chief executives. The largest positive variances are in the following categories:

- ✓ Evaluating the chief executive
- ✓ Adopting and following a strategic plan
- ✓ Monitoring organizational performance and impact against strategic plan goals
- ✓ Understanding board roles and responsibilities

The majority of boards are prioritizing performance assessment, with 58 percent reporting their board has conducted a formal self-assessment at some point; up from 23 percent of boards in 1994. Only 40 percent of all boards have done an assessment in the past two years, however, which is BoardSource's recommended practice.[5]

ECFA Research Says...

Ineffective Boards Reveal a Greater Need for Outside Intervention
Board Members Who Agree They Need "Much Help" or "Major Help" with...

	Effective Boards	**Ineffective** Boards	Difference
Assessing ministry results and kingdom outcomes	8%	37%	29%

[4] BoardSource, *Leading with Intent: 2015 National Index of Nonprofit Board Practices, https://leadingwithintent.org/previous-reports/.*

[5] BoardSource, *Leading with Intent: 2017 National Index of Nonprofit Board Practices, https://boardsource.org/research-critical-issues/nonprofit-sector-research.*

SECTION 1:

Do-It-Yourself

7 OPTIONS

❑ **OPTION #1. NonprofitBoardScore™**

ECFA has developed an online tool called NonprofitBoardScore™ to help your board evaluate its performance. It is very easy to use, absolutely free, and only takes a few minutes to complete.

NonprofitBoardScore™ gives you instant feedback, lets you take the evaluation over and over (you may want to take it every six months or annually), and allows you to save and print the results to share with your board, including a matrix reflecting the results specific to your ministry.

NonprofitBoardScore™ Sample Matrix

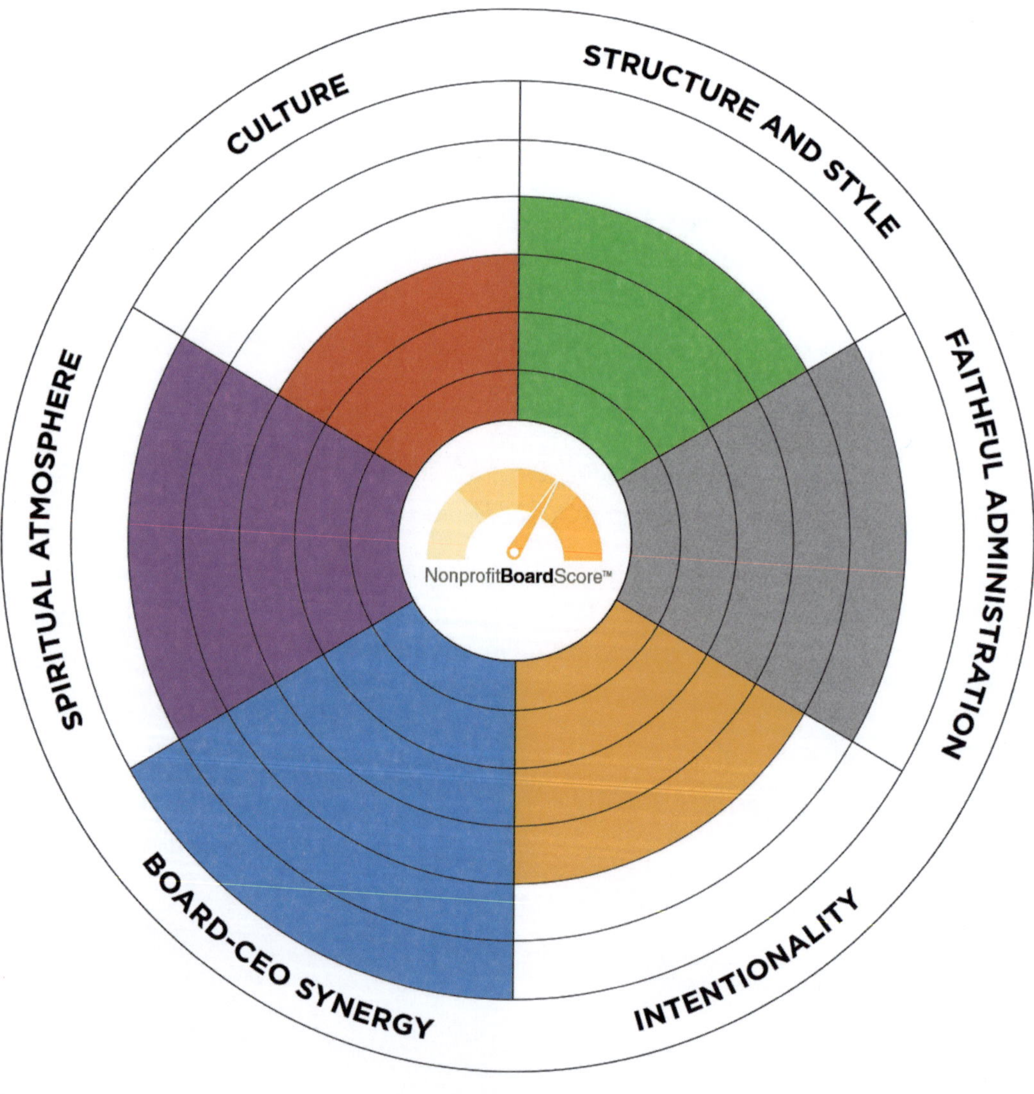

www.ECFA.org/Score

Governance Elements	Sample Topics Included
1 Spiritual Atmosphere	Scripture reading, prayer, discernment, silence, Christ-centered character, spiritual gifts inventory, humble service, and loving community of grace and truth
2 Board-CEO Synergy	Regular fellowship, attention to physical health and soul care, board assessment, and annual review of CEO's performance and compensation/benefits
3 Intentionality	Clear agendas, Board Policies Manual, Prime Responsibility Chart, 80/20 focus on strategy, risk prioritization, and protection of all God's children from abuse
4 Faithful Administration	Avoid conflicts of interest, implement controls to prevent fraud and properly handle designated gifts, budget responsibly, and report with appropriate transparency
5 Structure and Style	Committed chair, board size, majority of independent board members, roles and responsibilities, meeting frequency, and annual commitment form
6 Culture	Spirit-led, mission-minded, self-disciplined, proactive, respectful, keen listeners, lifelong learners, integrity, accountability, confidentiality, and full of grace and truth

How to use. Ideally *every board member* including the CEO, should take the survey so the board can compare and discuss the results. Alternatively, the board chair (or the vice chair, if the CEO is the chair) should take the survey for the board.

Attn: Church Boards

ChurchBoardScore™ is also available at *www.ECFA.Church/Score.*

❑ OPTION #2. BoardSource Assessments

Visit *www.BoardSource.org* to review several options for board self-evaluations and board self-assessments.

Assessments Lead to Good Governance
WHAT ASSESSMENT TOOLS DOES BOARDSOURCE OFFER?
https://boardsource.org/board-support/assessing-performance/

From BoardSource:

> BoardSource offers a variety of assessment tools for both boards and chief executives. In fact, we feel so strongly about assessment as a driver of nonprofit effectiveness that we offer either complimentary or discounted assessment tools as a benefit of our organizational membership program. If you are considering one of BoardSource's assessment tools, you may want to consider becoming an organizational member.

Board Performance Assessment Tools

- **Board Self-Assessment (BSA)** survey gathers feedback from individual board members and measures the collective performance of the board.
- **Peer-to-Peer Assessment (P2P)** survey asks board members to evaluate their individual performance and that of their peers to learn how the performance and culture of the full board is affected by the style and engagement of its individual members.

Visit...
https://boardsource.org/board-support/assessing-performance/board-self-assessment/

...and click on "SAMPLE SURVEY" at the bottom of the page—for several pages of the BoardSource survey.

ECFA Note to Christ-centered Organizations and Churches:

While BoardSource serves both secular and faith-based boards, the materials do not reference what we believe are the unique distinctives of Christ-centered boards. Should you create your own "do-it-yourself" tools/process, we encourage you to add those distinctives for Christ-centered boards such as: spiritual discernment practices, prayer, understanding strategic planning and mission outcomes from a theological perspective, Matthew 18 principles of conflict management, and much more.

RESOURCES:

Read these two helpful resources for ministry boards: *The Choice: The Christ-Centered Pursuit of Kingdom Outcomes*[6] and *The Council: A Biblical Perspective on Board Governance.*[7]

[6] Gary G. Hoag, R. Scott Rodin, and Wesley K. Willmer, *The Choice: The Christ-Centered Pursuit of Kingdom Outcomes* (Winchester, VA: ECFAPress, 2014).
[7] Gary G. Hoag, Wesley K. Willmer, and Gregory J. Henson, *The Council: A Biblical Perspective on Board Governance* (Winchester, VA: ECFAPress, 2018).

❑ OPTION #3. Book/Assessment: Ten Basic Responsibilities of Nonprofit Boards

Ten Basic Responsibilities of Nonprofit Boards (Third Edition), by Richard T. Ingram (106 pages, BoardSource, 2015), includes an 18-question self-assessment survey example.

The first title of six in BoardSource's "Governance Series" delivers the generally agreed-upon list of the 10 roles and responsibilities of nonprofit board members. (Boards of faith-based organizations will likely add one or two more.)

The book includes an excellent 18-point self-assessment for board members, with probing questions like:

- ☑ Are there ways in which your talents and interests can be more fully realized at or between board or committee meetings?
- ☑ As a director, are you reasonably clear about what is expected of you?
- ☑ Which aspect of your service on the board has been the least satisfying and enjoyable?[8]

Read John Pearson's review of *Ten Basic Responsibilities of Nonprofit Boards*, along with three other governance books here: *http://urgentink.typepad.com/my_weblog/2014/11/serving-as-a-board-member-4-books.html*

- ☑ *Ten Basic Responsibilities of Nonprofit Boards*, 3rd ed., by Richard T. Ingram (106 pages, BoardSource, 2015)
- ☑ *Serving as a Board Member: Practical Guidance for Directors of Christian Ministries*, by John Pellowe (188 pages, Canadian Council of Christian Charities, 2012)
- ☑ *Best Practices for Effective Boards*, by E. LeBron Fairbanks, Dwight M. Gunter II, and James R. Couchenour (191 pages, Beacon Hill Press of Kansas City, 2012)
- ☑ *Board Essentials: 12 Best Practices of Nonprofit Boards*, by David L. Coleman (109 pages, Andrew/Wallace Books, an imprint of BoardTrek Nonprofit Consulting, 2014)

[8] Richard T. Ingram, *Ten Basic Responsibilities of Nonprofit Boards*, 3d ed. (Washington, DC: BoardSource, 2015), 98–99.

❑ OPTION #4. Book/Assessment: *Owning Up*

Another helpful approach is to take Ram Charan's book, *Owning Up: The 14 Questions Every Board Member Needs to Ask* and assign the five most significant chapters (out of the 14 questions) to five different board members and work through those. (See the "Read and Reflect" worksheet to be used with the book in Tool #13.)

Board Member Self-Assessment

Note: Several questions from *Owning Up* (Question 5: "Does Our Board Really Own the Company's Strategy?") were adapted for use in *Unleashing Your Board's Potential: Comprehensive Report from ECFA's Nonprofit Governance Survey* (see Option #5).

What do boards indicate as the places where they're weakest? ECFA's national survey of accredited ministries asked people to rate their board about best practices. The numbers range from low to high, from undesirable to very desirable. These self-scores are from everyone combined—CEO, board chair and board member. The following question had the lowest best-practice score:

ECFA Research Says...

The Board Struggles with Staying at 30,000 Feet

"How often does the board discuss tactical versus strategic topics?"

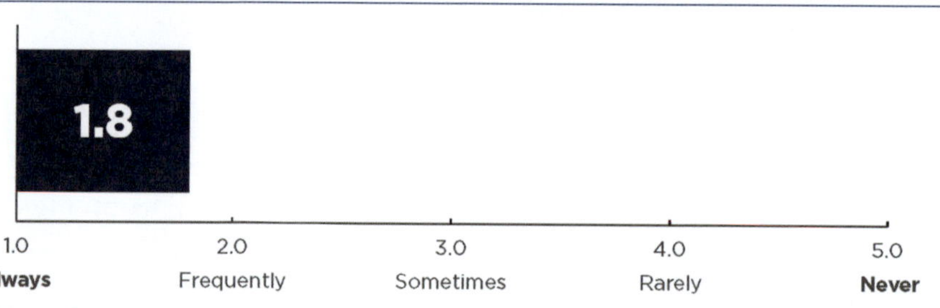

Effective Boards Have a Lot Going for Them

But what happens when we compare survey participants who rated their boards as effective against those who don't think their board is effective?

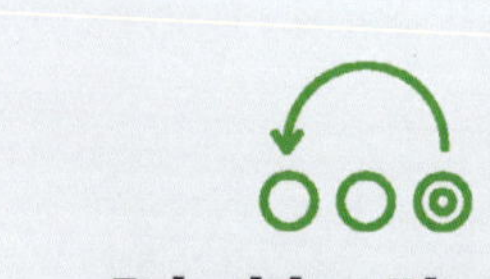

Prioritize Planning and Strategizing

"Our board ensures that the ministry has an active strategic planning process in place."

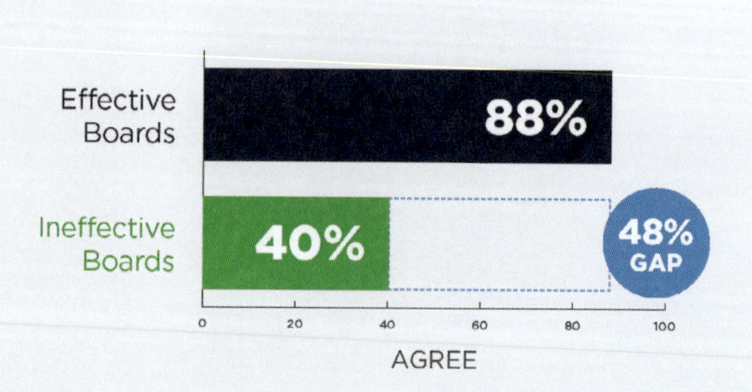

❑ OPTION #5. Self-Assessment: *ECFA Survey*

Unleashing Your Board's Potential: Comprehensive Report from ECFA's Nonprofit Governance Survey[9] included 20 questions that are included on the following page as the "Board Member Self-Assessment." The one-pager includes the average scores for those questions from more than 1,700 board members.

Download a PDF of the survey findings here:
www.ECFA.org/Content/Surveys

See the next page for the ECFA "Board Member Self-Assessment" survey with 20 questions. →→→

This self-assessment will help you evaluate those areas in which your board can improve as it governs your ministry with integrity and effectiveness. For more governance resources, visit *ECFA.org/surveys* or email *survey@ECFA.org*.

> ***"Boards need to understand basic strategy, but it's not their job to create it."***[10]
>
> Ram Charan

[9] *Unleashing Your Board's Potential: Comprehensive Report from ECFA's Nonprofit Governance Survey* (Winchester, VA: ECFAPress, 2019).

[10] Ram Charan, quoted in "Leadership Tip of the Day" email from the (now named) Frances Hesselbein Leadership Forum, Sept. 26, 2013, *www.HesselbeinForum.org*.

Board Member Self-Assessment

Unleashing Your Board's Potential: Comprehensive Report from ECFA's Nonprofit Governance Survey

(photocopy for your next meeting)

Use these 20 questions to compare your board with the Average ECFA Scores. For each question, place a checkmark ☑ in the box that best represents your level of agreement with the statement on the left.

How Does Your Organization Compare?	Strongly Disagree (1)	Disagree (2)	Undecided (3)	Agree (4)	Strongly Agree (5)	*Average ECFA Scores
1. Our board carves out time to creatively address the current and future needs of our "customers."						3.6
2. Our board clearly sees its work as Christ-centered.						4.7
3. Our board has been very effective over the last 12-18 months.						3.9
4. Our board understands its roles and responsibilities.						4.0
5. Our board ensures that the ministry has an active strategic planning process in place.						4.0
6. Our board annually affirms and "owns" the ministry strategy.						4.0
7. We know the spiritual gifts (Rom. 12, 1 Cor. 12) of every board member.						3.0
8. Our board members have high passion for the ministry.						4.5
9. We expect every board member to be an annual giver.						4.2
10. We provide training and encouragement to help board members encourage others to give.						2.8
11. Most people on the board help the CEO in appropriate ways by offering strategic input (as opposed to tactical input).						3.9
12. Outside of board meetings, most people avoid offering opinions that differ from agreed-upon board decisions.						3.9
13. Our board devotes creative energy and board meeting time to assess risks and opportunities—and thus is well informed about the outside forces impacting the organization.						3.8
14. Our board has policies—and the spiritual integrity required—to ask an underperforming board member to resign.						3.3
15. Our board is very focused on measuring mission impact.						3.8
16. Our board conducts an annual performance review of the CEO.						3.8
17. Our board approves the CEO's annual measurable goals that align with the strategy.						3.9
18. The working relationship between our CEO and Board Chair is excellent.						4.5
19. Our board chair (or a designated board member) regularly encourages our CEO to address "soul care" topics in his or her own life.						3.8
20. Board members pray regularly for the ministry and the CEO.						4.6

Add up checkmarks in each column	___x 1 ⬇	___x 2 ⬇	___x 3 ⬇	___x 4 ⬇	___x 5 ⬇	**Overall Score** ⬇
Column Total X Column Value (See next page for scoring legend.)						= ______ See next page

*Average ECFA Score based on responses from 1,754 board members of ECFA-accredited organizations.

How to Interpret This Self-Assessment	Strongly Disagree (1)	Disagree (2)	Undecided (3)	Agree (4)	Strongly Agree (5)	*Average ECFA Scores
A. Compare your "strongly disagree" and "strongly agree" choices with the choices of others on your board. Discuss with your board. Add up checkmarks in each column						
B. Compare your choices with the ECFA averages. Circle three where your score is closest to the ECFA averages. Draw squares around those where your score is farthest from the ECFA averages. Discuss with your board.*						
C. Add up your total score and compare it to the interpretations below. Now discuss with your board.	How many 1's? ___	How many 2's? ___	How many 3's? ___	How many 4's? ___	How many 5's? ___	
	Multiply by 1 —	Multiply by 2 —	Multiply by 3 —	Multiply by 4 —	Multiply by 5 —	
	Create a total score by adding the five numbers in the row above: If your total score is: 91-100, your board is well above average 81-90, your board is above average 75-80, your board is average 65-74, your board is below average 0-64, your board is well below average (The ECFA survey average is 78.)					

*For more details on the comparison numbers, see *Unleashing Your Board's Potential: Comprehensive Report from ECFA's Nonprofit Governance Survey* by Warren Bird, available for free download at *ECFA.org/surveys.*

❑ OPTION #6. Book/Assessment: *Boards That Lead*

Boards That Lead: When to Take Charge, When to Partner, and When to Stay Out of the Way, by Ram Charan, Dennis Carey and Michael Useem, is an excellent resource and could also be an important book for the board to read prior to a board retreat or a strategic planning day.

Just when you thought you were knowledgeable in governance, along comes a 219-page poke-in-the-ribs, plus an incredible 40-page section with 18 checklists for board members, a bonus chapter on "Trends in Director Monitoring and Leading," a director evaluation worksheet, and six golden pages on "Division of Responsibilities Between the Board Leader and the CEO."

If you're leading a board, on a board, or considering board service, you'll want to read Chapter 3, "Recruit Directors Who Build Value." The co-authors, including Ram Charan, author of *Owning Up: The 14 Questions Every Board Member Needs to Ask*, are big on questions. This chapter asks eight mission-critical questions of prospective board members, including: "Will the candidate be ready to stand tall and engage constructively when vital issues are on the line, the stakes and stress are high, and leadership of the company becomes even more essential?"

"Root Out Dysfunction" is Chapter 4's theme. "In our experience, as many as half of Fortune 500 companies have one or two dysfunctional directors." The authors identify three types:

- "Some see themselves as the smartest person in the room.
- Others seek recognition.
- Others are frustrated would-be CEOs."

They add, "Whatever their personal motives, they tend to micromanage or take boardroom discussions down dark alleys. We have seen a director interrupt the first five minutes of a CEO's boardroom presentation and sour the mood of both board and management for the remainder of the day. The result is to impair, even negate, a board's capacity to lead the firm. As in any group, a dysfunctional member can sabotage the entire team."

The authors recommend six personal qualities to look for in a board leader (often the board chair in nonprofit circles): 1) Executive experience, 2) Respect and confidence, 3) Collaboration and restraint, 4) Personal bonding, 5) Personal comfort, and 6) Resilience. (*Frame these qualities, perhaps, into your annual board self-assessment survey.*)

Board service is not for the weak-hearted! Board leaders (or board chairs) "can anticipate at least one major crisis during their tenures." Under the "personal comfort" commentary, they share this wisdom: "Yet another factor defining the board leader is a sense of comfort in one's own skin and place in life, with nothing yet to prove or still to achieve, most often the product of a long and successful career as a corporate leader in one's own right—no coveting of the chief executive's office, no longing for operational control."

❑ OPTION #7. Self-Assessment: *Alliance for Board Effectiveness*

80-Question Self-Assessment
http://boardeffectiveness.org

The Alliance for Board Effectiveness provides a free do-it-yourself 80-question self-assessment on their website, based on the governance tool "80 Principles/Practices of Effective Boards" from the Good Governance Toolbox of The Andringa Group.

Sample Self-Assessment Questions

Below are Questions 74 to 80 from the five-page "Board Self-Assessment" of Alliance for Board Effectiveness (used by permission). To download all 80 questions, visit *http://boardeffectiveness.org.*

Other Characteristics of Good Governance	We need to make significant changes	We need to make minor adjustments in this area	We need to discuss this for possible changes	We are doing well, no changes needed	We are excelling in this area
74. We invest in professional development for board members, staff, and volunteers.	1	2	3	4	5
75. Our board protocols are documented, including our commitment to confidentiality.	1	2	3	4	5
76. We ensure that technology is maximized for efficiency in governance and programs.	1	2	3	4	5
77. We ensure that contracts and agreements with others include alternative dispute resolution.	1	2	3	4	5
78. We make sure to thank and honor board members and staff when they depart.	1	2	3	4	5
79. We regularly review Articles and Bylaws to reflect changing culture, laws, and regulations.	1	2	3	4	5
80. Our board knows why, when, and how it would close or merge with another organization.	1	2	3	4	5

SECTION 2:

Board Self-Assessment Facilitated by a Board Coach/Consultant

2 OPTIONS — A or B

❑ **OPTION A. Coach/consultant customizes the ECFA Self-Assessment Survey specifically for your board**

In this option, your coach or consultant could customize *Unleashing Your Board's Potential: Comprehensive Report from ECFA's Nonprofit Governance Survey* for your use (free download at *ECFA.org/Surveys*). Drop the questions into a survey software program, such as *www.SurveyMonkey.com.* You could then benchmark your responses against the responses of ECFA-accredited organizations. Your coach or consultant could include some value-added elements, such as phone coaching.

Details:

- Approximately 30-35 questions with 7 to 10 optional questions.
- Approximately 12 to 15 minutes required to complete the assessment, depending on how many optional questions a board member answers.
- Anonymous—but all open-ended responses/comments will be included in the results.

Process:

- From beginning to end, the process generally can be accomplished in 30 to 60 days, depending on urgency and board meeting schedules.

No.	Steps
1	Board Chair and CEO (or senior pastor) review customized survey (Draft #1) and suggest edits (by email or phone). Depending on the consultant, this could include up to three drafts; and could include additional questions that are not part of the ECFA survey.
2	When survey is finalized, the Board Chair or CEO (or senior pastor) sends an email to all board members with a brief memo (written by your consultant) with a link to the online survey. • Survey deadline (usually 14 days, with a reminder sent 2 days before the deadline)
3	Survey Results delivered via 3 options (see next page)

"When is the last time you as a board member acknowledged that another board member was right and you were wrong?"[11]

Peter Greer and David Weekley

[11] Peter Greer and David Weekley, *The Board and the CEO: Seven Practices to Protect Your Organization's Most Important Relationship* (Scotts Valley, CA: CreateSpace, 2017), 72.

Delivery of Survey Results by Consultant/Coach:

Options	Description of Services (including survey design)	Coach's Time
Option 1: Results Only	Survey Results emailed in PDF format • Your Executive Committee or Governance Committee discerns how best to analyze and review the information; and how best to share it with the board.	About 4 hours
Option 2: Briefing via *Go to Meeting*	Survey Results emailed in PDF format to Executive Committee or Governance Committee with one-hour "Go to Meeting" session: • PowerPoint presentation of Survey Results • Q&A • Recommended Next Steps	About 6 hours
Option 3: Presentation at Committee or Board Meeting	On-site Briefing of Survey Results with full Board and/or Executive Committee or Governance Committee to include: • Survey Results (photocopied for each participant) • PowerPoint presentation • Q&A • Recommended Next Steps	1 day

"Social sector leaders are not less decisive than business leaders as a general rule; they only appear that way to those who fail to grasp the complex governance and diffuse power structures common to social sectors."[12]

Jim Collins

[12] Jim Collins quoted in the "Leadership Tip of the Day" email from the (now named) Frances Hesselbein Leadership Forum, August 3, 2010, *www.HesselbeinForum.org.*

❑ **OPTION B. Coach/consultant creates an original self-assessment survey—unique to your current needs**

In this option, your coach or consultant would start from scratch and create a customized survey tool—based on numerous factors unique to your board, including:

- Your current governance model
- Experience of current board members
- Tenure and experience of the CEO/Senior Pastor and/or senior team
- What season or cycle you're in (example: google Charles Handy and the Sigmoid Curve)

  Or…read how Jim Collins identifies five stages of decline in his book, *How the Mighty Fall: And Why Some Companies Never Give In.* The five stages:

  ✓ Stage 1: Hubris Born of Success

  ✓ Stage 2: Undisciplined Pursuit of More

  ✓ Stage 3: Denial of Risk and Peril

  ✓ Stage 4: Grasping for Salvation

  ✓ Stage 5: Capitulation to Irrelevance or Death[13]

- Previous governance enrichment help from other consultants and/or board training
- Other factors (Are you in chaos? Growing? Declining? Healthy? God-honoring? Board dissension? Staff departures? Community concerns? Inability to agree on a governance model, perhaps due to the recruitment of new board members, with different views and past board experiences and/or dysfunctions?)

Options	Description of Services (including survey design)	Coach's Time
Option 1: Bronze	Design customized survey based on: • Phone interviews with up to 5 board members (including the CEO/Senior Pastor and board chair) • On-site presentation of results and next steps	1.5 days
Option 2: Silver	Design customized survey based on: • Phone interviews with all board members (including the CEO/Senior Pastor) • On-site presentation of results and next steps • Phone coaching over the next 6 months (about 4 hours)	2 days
Option 3: Gold	Your suggestions!	___ days

[13] Jim Collins, *How the Mighty Fall: And Why Some Companies Never Give In* (New York: HarperCollins, 2009), vii.

Bonus Resources on Board Self-Assessment

Carver Guide 8
Board Self-Assessment
CarverGuide Series on Effective Board Governance
by John Carver 1997, 18 pages

Even if your board does not function as a true Policy Governance® Model board, John Carver's work in this area is worth noting. Perhaps inspire a board member to read *Boards That Make a Difference: A New Design for Leadership in Nonprofit Organizations* by John Carver. Carver's book is over 400 pages, but his booklet series might be more realistic for you.

In the 18-page booklet, *Board Self-Assessment*, Carver summarizes his definition of the process. Check the paragraph that resonates most with your board's needs.[14]

- ❑ The primary purpose of evaluation is not to reward or punish but to achieve continual improvement in performance. A board can engage in healthy and useful self-evaluation if it lays aside the judging connotation. I want boards to see self-evaluation as similar to what goes on between eyes, brain, and muscles when you practice a skill. Typically, you make little comparisons, little adjustments—a nip here, a tuck there, hold your mouth a little differently—in a never-ending sequence.

- ❑ Self-evaluation is most meaningful when related to established expectations. Evaluation requires a standard of comparison, an expectation. Unless a board is clear about what constitutes responsible governance, its attempt at evaluation will merely meander. Evaluation, therefore, done as a freestanding action, can never make up for not having put into place carefully considered expectations, against which the board then does its evaluation.

- ❑ Board self-evaluation is an inseparable part of governing, not an extraneous or optional task. To see how integral evaluation is to the task, try writing in the dark. If you cannot see where your pen marks, you will not write well and may not even write legibly. Yet writing is a familiar skill with which you have a lifetime of experience. It is so automatic that you scarcely give the arm, and hand, finger muscle movements a conscious thought. But writing in the dark is hard. How much more must we need feedback for a complex social task such as governance?

- ❑ Self-evaluation is a continual rather than sporadic activity. If you want to improve performance, evaluation must be continual. **Consequently, I have little use for the annual board self-evaluation.**

Board self-evaluation is the responsibility of the board—not the staff. Because self-evaluation is integral to the job to be done, and because governance is surely the board's job, the board has little choice but to accept the responsibility of evaluating how well it is doing its job. Like other parts of the board's job, people outside the board may be engaged to help the board evaluate itself, but it is critical that the board begin with the sense that it alone is responsible in a very direct and personal way.

[14] John Carver, *CarverGuide 8: Board Self-Assessment* (San Francisco: Jossey-Bass, 1997), 16.

More Bonus Resources on Board Self-Assessment

ECFA Knowledge Center – Nonprofit
www.ECFA.org/KnowledgeCenter

ECFA Knowledge Center – Church
www.ECFA.church/KnowledgeCenter

ECFA Blog:
Governance of Christ-Centered Organizations
http://ECFAgovernance.blogspot.com

John Pearson's Board Bucket webpage:
http://managementbuckets.com/board-bucket

SECTION 3:
"Best Governance Practices" Survey

Customize this survey for your board!

Drop these survey questions into the SurveyMonkey software (or your preferred survey software). *www.SurveyMonkey.com*

Background

The following "Best Governance Practices" survey questions were developed in 2016 with the help and feedback of over 20 governance consultants, many who served as board coaches in one of the board enrichment programs funded in part by M.J. Murdock Charitable Trust.

John Pearson asked consultants to rank order several laundry lists of "best governance practices." The responses were summarized by John and provided to Kay Edwards, President & CEO of Outsight Network (*www.outsightnetwork.com*).

The attached survey was then completed by the CEOs and board members in the 2016 CCCA Thriving Boards Program, an initiative of Christian Camp and Conference Association (*www.CCCA.org*), and funded in part by Murdock Trust. For more information, visit: *www.ccca.org/ccca/Thriving_Boards.asp* and *www.BoardLeadership.org*.

Survey Contents

- ❑ 1. & 2. Introductory Questions
- ❑ 3. Mission, Vision, and Values
- ❑ 4. Executive Leadership
- ❑ 5. Governance
- ❑ 6. Board Member Recruitment and Engagement
- ❑ 7. Board Member Character and Relationships
- ❑ 8. Strategic Planning and Strategy
- ❑ 9. Sustainability, Financial and Fiduciary Oversight
- ❑ 10. Tools and Templates: Board Best Practices
    - Part 1: The Board's Role With the CEO
    - Part 2: The Board's Governance Role

Attn: Church Boards

While the following board self-assessment survey is designed for nonprofit boards, ask a board member or staff member to customize it for the unique needs of your church board.

Customize this survey for your board!

Drop these survey questions into the SurveyMonkey software (or your preferred survey software). www.SurveyMonkey.com

Introduction to the BEST GOVERNANCE PRACTICES Survey

Cover memo and introduction on first page of survey:

SURVEY DEADLINE: __________(date)

Attn: All Board Members

As part of our board's annual self-assessment process, we're asking all board members to complete this important survey. Your survey responses will be anonymous, and your participation is extremely important to the process. We will be using your responses to improve our governance, so thanks for investing your time on this.

Survey results will be shared with the full board at our next meeting.

IMPORTANT! Survey references to "CEO" (chief executive officer) refer, of course, to ____________, *the one staff person who reports directly to our board.*

Thank you for your board service as we continue on our journey to become a more healthy and more effective governing board!

Name

Board Chair

Organization

Introductory Questions

✦ 1. How many years have you served on the board?

- ❑ Less than 1 year
- ❑ 1 – 3 years
- ❑ 4 – 6 years
- ❑ 7 – 9 years
- ❑ 10 – 12 years
- ❑ 13 or more years

✦ 2. Counting our board, how many other boards (including your local church board) are you currently serving on?

- ❑ 1 board
- ❑ 2 boards
- ❑ 3 boards
- ❑ 4 boards
- ❑ 5 boards
- ❑ More than 5 boards

✦ 3. Mission, Vision, and Values

One of the board's fundamental responsibilities is to establish the mission, vision, and values of the organization. The board should review the mission at least every three years. Each member of the board should understand and support the mission, vision, and values.

For each statement, please indicate how much you agree, on a scale of 1 to 7, with 7 being "Describes Completely" and 1 being, "Does Not Describe At All."

Mission, Vision, and Values	1 Does Not Describe At All	2	3	4	5	6	7 Describes Completely
Our board members have high passion for our mission, vision, and values.							
Our board ensures that our programs align with our mission, vision and values.							

✦ 4. Executive Leadership

One of the most significant decisions a board makes is the selection of a chief executive. An effective board will provide a clear job description that outlines the duties of the chief executive, and will undertake a carefully planned search process to fill the position. The board will support its chief executive by providing him or her with frequent and constructive feedback, and by conducting an annual evaluation to help the chief executive strengthen his or her performance.

For each statement, please indicate how much you agree, on a scale of 1 to 7, with 7 being "Describes Completely" and 1 being, "Does Not Describe At All."

Executive Leadership	**1 Does Not Describe At All**	**2**	**3**	**4**	**5**	**6**	**7 Describes Completely**
Our board agrees that their most important responsibility is having the right CEO in place.							
Our board approves our CEO's annual measurable goals.							
Our board monitors our CEO's annual measurable goals at least quarterly.							
Our board conducts an annual performance review of our CEO.							
Our board has a written plan for an emergency CEO transition—and it is reviewed annually.							
Our board ensures that we have an on-going continuous process of succession planning.							
Our board agrees that compensation/benefits for our CEO are at the right level.							

✦ 5. Governance

Effective boards ensure effective governance by putting organizational policy documents in place and periodically reviewing and updating those documents.

For each statement, please indicate how much you agree, on a scale of 1 to 7, with 7 being "Describes Completely" and 1 being, "Does Not Describe At All."

Governance	1 Does Not Describe At All	2	3	4	5	6	7 Describes Completely
Our board member roles and responsibilities are in writing.							
Our board members understand their roles and responsibilities.							
Our board members are knowledgeable about the numerous governance models, including the "policy governance" model.							
Our board agrees that our current governance model is appropriate for us.							
Our board has a dynamic written document (such as a "Board Policies Manual") to ensure that both long-standing and the latest board policies are easily accessible by the board, CEO, and senior team.							
Our board meetings are well-planned, well-led, and achieve our desired results.							
Our committee meetings are well-planned, well-led, and achieve our desired results.							

✦ 6. Board Member Recruitment and Engagement

An effective board needs a plan to identify and recruit qualified people to serve on the board. It is the responsibility of the board to effectively orient new members to their responsibilities and to the activities of the organization.

For each statement, please indicate how much you agree, on a scale of 1 to 7, with 7 being "Describes Completely" and 1 being, "Does Not Describe At All."

Board Member Recruitment and Engagement	1 Does Not Describe At All	2	3	4	5	6	7 Describes Completely
Our board (not our CEO) owns the responsibility to recruit and build a competent board.							
Our board has a formal orientation process for new board members.							
Our board members understand the unique "roles/hats" that board members wear (in and out of board meetings), such as the Governance Hat, the Volunteer Hat, and the (Event) Participant Hat—and there is agreement on the protocol for each unique role.							
Our board members sign an annual "re-commitment/reminder" document such as a "Board Member Annual Affirmation Statement."							
Our board has written policies addressing charitable giving expectations for board members.							
Our board's self-evaluation process improves the functioning and output of the board.							
Our board has policies in place—and the spiritual integrity required—to ask an under-performing board member to resign.							
Our board is prepared to do its job well when a crisis erupts.							

✦ 7. Board Member Character and Relationships

Board members must act with integrity and be exemplary role models of the organization's values and character, carrying out their duties in a Christ-like manner. An effective board will display healthy relationships with each other, and between the board and staff.

For each statement, please indicate how much you agree, on a scale of 1 to 7, with 7 being "Describes Completely" and 1 being, "Does Not Describe At All."

Board Member Character and Relationships	1 Does Not Describe At All	2	3	4	5	6	7 Describes Completely
Our board members conduct our work and relationships with Christ-centered character.							
Our board practices spiritual discernment in our decision-making.							
Our board ensures that there is a healthy and effective relationship between our board chair and our CEO.							
Our board members annually read and sign our "conflicts of interest" policy that addresses legal and ethical integrity.							
Our board "speaks with one voice, or not at all."							

✦ 8. Strategic Planning and Strategy

The board is responsible for establishing the organization's direction and goals. The board engages in a formal strategic planning process, and monitors changes in the environment that may present new challenges or opportunities that call for new direction.

For each statement, please indicate how much you agree, on a scale of 1 to 7, with 7 being "Describes Completely" and 1 being, "Does Not Describe At All."

Strategic Planning and Strategy	1 Does Not Describe At All	2	3	4	5	6	7 Describes Completely
Our board ensures that there is an effective and on-going planning process in place.							
Our board "owns" the organization's strategy to achieve our mission.							
Our board regularly addresses the risks that could send our ministry over the cliff.							
Our board reviews program reports that address measurements and ministry outcomes.							

✦ 9. Sustainability, Financial and Fiduciary Oversight

The board is responsible for stewarding the organization's resources and assets. This includes ensuring that income is managed wisely, financial guidelines are established and adhered to, and the organization is properly reporting sources and uses of funds. It also includes making sure the organization is complying with local, state, and federal requirements.

For each statement, please indicate how much you agree, on a scale of 1 to 7, with 7 being "Describes Completely" and 1 being, "Does Not Describe At All."

Sustainability, Financial and Fiduciary Oversight	**1 Does Not Describe At All**	**2**	**3**	**4**	**5**	**6**	**7 Describes Completely**
Our board ensures that there are adequate financial resources to achieve the mission.							
Our board is competent in protecting organizational assets and providing proper financial oversight to ensure our sustainability.							
Our board monitors the organization's compliance with all applicable local, state, and federal laws and regulations that govern our operations.							
Our board has the information, including financial information, it needs to govern well.							

✦ 10. Tools and Templates: Board Best Practices

PART 1: The Board's Role with the CEO

So they don't have to "re-invent the wheel," many boards look for tools and templates that other nonprofit boards have found helpful—and then each board customizes the templates to their unique situation. (One size doesn't fit all.)

Below is a list of frequently used tools and templates that embody one or more of the most common board best practices.

Check YES or NO if your board is currently using the following tools and/or templates (or a variation of the template).

Tools and Templates: Board Best Practices	Yes	No	Not Sure	N/A
CEO's "5/15" Monthly Board Report. A standardized monthly report from the CEO, updating the board with agreed-upon topics and metrics—and takes just 5 minutes to read and normally just 15 minutes for the CEO to write.				
CEO's Annual S.M.A.R.T. Goals. A board-approved list of 3 to 5 annual goals for the CEO that meet the "S.M.A.R.T." test: Specific, Measurable, Achievable, Realistic, Time-related.				
CEO's Monthly Dashboard Report on CEO's Annual S.M.A.R.T. Goals. A one-page dashboard reporting the year-to-date progress on the CEO's 3 to 5 annual "S.M.A.R.T." goals (often color-coded in green, yellow and red).				
CEO's Position Description. The document that describes the roles and responsibilities of the CEO.				
Board's Annual Evaluation of the CEO. The agreed-upon process and written (or online) survey instrument completed by all board members for the board's annual assessment of the CEO.				

✦ 10. Tools and Templates: Board Best Practices

PART 2: The Board's Governance Role

So they don't have to "re-invent the wheel," many boards look for tools and templates that other nonprofit boards have found helpful—and then each board customizes the templates to their unique situation. (One size doesn't fit all.)

Below is a list of frequently used tools and templates that embody one or more of the most common board best practices.

Check YES or NO if your board is currently using the following tools and/or templates (or a variation of the template).

Tools and Templates: Board Best Practices	Yes	No	Not Sure	N/A
Board Policies Manual. A 15- to 20-page document that gathers all board policies into one document; and revised occasionally—based on the ever-changing environment (financial, leadership, strategy, etc.).				
Prime Responsibility Chart. A one-page document clarifying roles between the board, committees, board chair, board treasurer, CEO, CFO, etc.				
Board Meeting Agenda & Recommendations Template. A board-approved template for each board meeting's agenda, recommendations, reports, minutes, etc.—and mailed or emailed to board members at least X days prior to every board meeting (per policy).				
Board Position Description & Board Member Annual Affirmation Statement. A board-approved document that includes the board member position description, signed annually by every board member.				
Board Chair Position Description. The written position description for the board chair that details roles and responsibilities, plus protocol for enriching the important relationship between the board chair and the CEO.				
Board Nominee Orientation Resource. The annually-updated resource that the Nominating Committee uses to inspire and inform both board prospects and board nominees.				
Board's Annual Self- Assessment Survey. The written (or online) annual survey completed by every board member, assessing his or her own performance on the board, and the performance of the full board.				
The Board's 3 Powerful S's: Strengths, Spiritual Gifts and Social Styles (and/or Other Assessments). The assessments that many boards use to help members better understand themselves, each other, and their CEOs.				

Check YES or NO if your board is currently using the following tools and/or templates (or a variation of the template).

Tools and Templates: Board Best Practices	Yes	No	Not Sure	N/A
Key Performance Indicators (KPIs): A monthly or quarterly report that identifies agreed-upon metrics or measurements, outcomes, and impact for programs, products, and services.				
Dashboard Reports. The monthly or quarterly dashboard reports that help "nonprofit leaders focus their attention on what matters most in their organizations, and in doing so, gain greater insight and ascribe greater meaning to other available data."[15]				

Attn: Church Boards

While this board self-assessment survey is designed for nonprofit boards, ask a board member or staff member to customize it for the unique needs of your church board.

[15] Lawrence M. Butler, *The Nonprofit Dashboard: A Tool for Tracking Progress* (Washington, D.C.: BoardSource, 2007), vii.

TOOL #6: The Board's Annual Financial Management Audit

Use this TRUE OR FALSE audit annually as a first step in assessing your ministry's financial health and integrity.

"In the worst case scenario, clarity of ministry finances is a key to avoiding a financial shipwreck. In the best case, clarity prevents a ministry from becoming an embarrassment to Christ."[1]

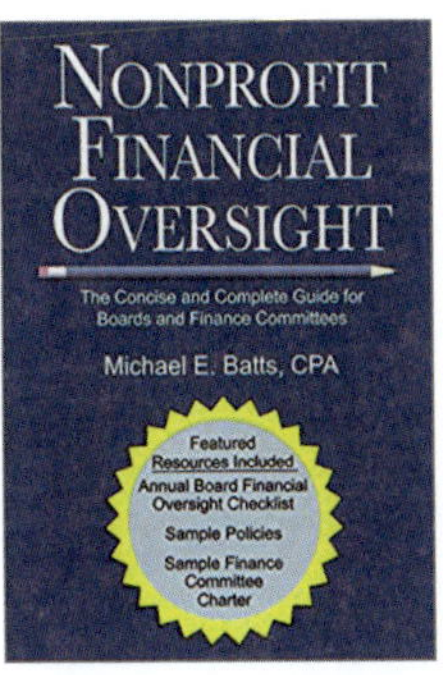

"The vast majority of nonprofit organizations have a strong desire to do the right things for the right reasons, while working to improve the lives of people."[2]

Trusted Ministries Manage Resources with Integrity

The 3 Foundations of Trusted Resource Management

Trusted ministries manage resources with integrity. Christ will only be honored if revenues and expenses are adequately managed, if adequate reserves are developed and maintained, and if obligations are properly fulfilled.

The Foundations of Trusted Resource Management are:

- ❑ 1. **Understanding Finances:** Trusted ministries acknowledge the challenges of understanding nonprofit finances. It is certainly not a one-to-one correlation with the finances of a for-profit organization.
- ❑ 2. **Achieving Appropriate Transparency:** Facing an insatiable desire for transparency, trusted ministries must find the balance between being appropriately transparent while recognizing privacy concerns and administrative burdens.
- ❑ 3. **Minimizing Fraud:** Trusted ministries are keenly aware of their susceptibility to fraud. They establish and continually test internal controls to minimize significant fraud.[3]

THE FOUNDATIONS OF TRUSTED RESOURCE MANAGEMENT

UNDERSTANDING FINANCES	ACHIEVING APPROPRIATE TRANSPARENCY	MINIMIZING FRAUD

[1] Dan Busby, *TRUST: The Firm Foundation for Kingdom Fruitfulness* (Winchester, VA: ECFAPress, 2015), 177.

[2] Michael E. Batts, *Nonprofit Financial Oversight: The Concise and Complete Guide for Boards and Finance Committees* (Orlando, FL: Accountability Press, 2017), 5.

[3] Busby, *TRUST*, 175–76. Inspire your board's finance committee to read the three short chapters in Part 4: "Understanding Finances," "Achieving Appropriate Transparency," and "Minimizing Fraud." See pages 175–98.

The Board's Annual Financial Management Audit

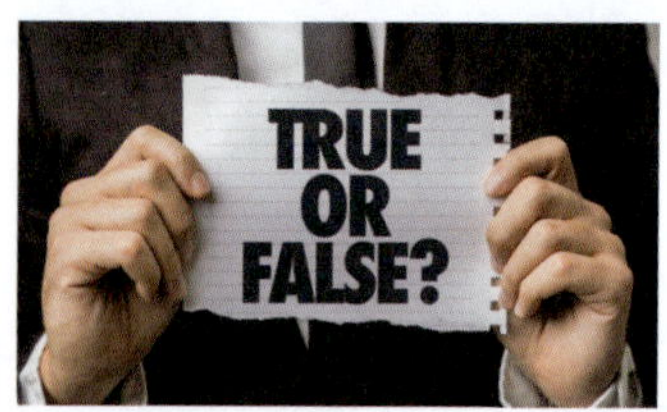

20 Statements the Board Must Address Annually

Your board should expect clarity and honesty from the CEO, the CFO, staff, and the board's finance committee. To provide clarity—so board members understand financial reports and financial trends—the information should be presented with a variety of approaches (for the diverse learning styles of your board members) and can include verbal and written reports, dashboards, and graphs. But there's another important step—an annual checklist.

TRUE OR FALSE? Here are 20 statements that can be adapted for your ministry. Ask your CFO to provide the answers for the question, "How does the board know?" Ultimately, of course, for the board to have faith and trust in the accuracy and veracity of the answers to these statements—the board will be dependent on the honesty and integrity of the CEO and the staff.

Adapt these statements for your ministry—and review the answers at least annually.

See pages 64–65 for a sample completed financial management audit.

The Board's Annual Financial Management Audit	True/ False	How does the board know?
1. Our board receives timely, relevant, and accurate financial information that is readily understood by the board.		
2. Our board has assessed the ministry's financial health within the last year and appropriately addressed any concerns.		
3. We orient new board members on how to interpret the ministry's periodic financial statements and board-approved benchmarks.		
4. Cash reserves compare favorably with the ministry's goal for: a. Operations b. Donor-restricted net assets c. Mortgage covenants d. Capital needs e. Other ministry expansion opportunities		
5. Our significant revenue elements are increasing.		
6. The average size of our contributions is increasing across all gift size ranges.		
7. The number of regular contributors is increasing.		

The Board's Annual Financial Management Audit	True/ False	How does the board know?
8. Our total unrestricted revenue is increasing.		
9. Our ministry is adequately communicating with our financial institutions regarding loan renewals, international fund transfers, line of credit, and bank accounts.		
10. Accounts payable, payroll taxes, and other current liabilities are being paid on time.		
11. Our net assets without donor restrictions, after deducting net property, plant, and equipment less related debt, shows a positive trend.		
12. Our financial statements do not reflect designated net assets in excess of what is available for designation.		
13. We have an appropriate investment policy and it is followed.		
14. Our bank accounts do not exceed FDIC limits.		
15. We have engaged an independent CPA firm to perform an audit, review, or compilation or applied other appropriate accountability measures.		
16. The staff has provided a written response to the board in relation to any management letter comments from the CPA firm.		
17. We have identified the three greatest financial risks of our ministry and the steps we should take to mitigate those risks.		
18. All significant related-party transactions are reported to the board for their review and action.		
19. The staff has informed the board of the total compensation, including fringe benefits taxable and non-taxable, of any member of the top leader's family who is employed by the organization or any of its subsidiaries or affiliates.		
20. Our board complies with ECFA's Policy for Excellence in Compensation-Setting: *https://www.ECFA.org/Contents/Comment6a.*		

Sample completed Board's Annual Financial Management Audit[4]

The Board's Annual Financial Management Audit	True/ False	How does the board know?
1. Our board receives timely, relevant, and accurate financial information that is readily understood by the board.	T	At the last board meeting, the board confirmed this is a true.
2. Our board has assessed the ministry's financial health within the last year and appropriately addressed any concerns.	T	Our board assesses the organization's financial health at each meeting.
3. We orient new board members on how to interpret the ministry's periodic financial statements and board-approved benchmarks.	T	A thorough board orientation is provided for all new board members.
4. Cash reserves compare favorably with the ministry's goal for: a. Operations b. Donor-restricted net assets c. Mortgage covenants d. Capital needs e. Other ministry expansion opportunities	F	The board does not set cash reserve targets so we don't know if we compare favorably to ministry goals. However, we do know that our cash balances have been decreasing over the last five years.
5. Our significant revenue elements are increasing.	F	Our most significant revenue elements have been flat over the last five years.
6. The average size of our contributions is increasing across all gift size ranges.	F	The average size of our contributions has been decreasing over the last three years.
7. The number of regular contributors is increasing.	F	The number of regular contributors has been flat over the last three years.
8. Our total unrestricted revenue is increasing.	F	Our total unrestricted revenue has been flat over the last five year.
9. Our ministry is adequately communicating with our financial institutions regarding loan renewals, international fund transfers, line of credit, and bank accounts.	T	The CFO verified this is true as of September 30.
10. Accounts payable, payroll taxes, and other current liabilities are being paid on time.	T	The CFO verified this is true as of September 30.
11. Our net assets without donor restrictions, after deducting net property, plant, and equipment less related debt, shows a positive trend.	F	Our net assets without donor restrictions have been decreasing over the last five years.

The Board's Annual Financial Management Audit	True/ False	How does the board know?
12. Our financial statements do not reflect designated net assets in excess of what is available for designation.	T	The CFO verified this is true as of September 30.
13. We have an appropriate investment policy and it is followed.	T	The CFO verified this is true as of September 30.
14. Our bank accounts do not exceed FDIC limits.	F	Our bank accounts occasionally exceed FDIC limits by modest amounts.
15. We have engaged an independent CPA firm to perform an audit, review, or compilation or applied other appropriate accountability measures.	T	We have an annual audit by an independent CPA firm.
16. The staff has provided a written response to the board in relation to any management letter comments from the CPA firm.	F	The board receives an annual management letter but staff does not provide a written response to the board in relation to the auditor's recommendations.
17. We have identified the three greatest financial risks of our ministry and the steps we should take to mitigate those risks.	F	The board has not identified the ministry's three greatest financial risks.
18. All significant related-party transactions are reported to the board for their review and action.	T	The board carefully follows its conflicts of interest policy.
19. The staff has informed the board of the total compensation, including fringe benefits taxable and non-taxable, of any member of the top leader's family who is employed by the organization or any of its subsidiaries or affiliates.	F	The board is not informed of compensation paid to members of the top leader's family.
20. Our board complies with ECFA's Policy for Excellence in Compensation-Setting: *https://www.ECFA.org/Contents/Comment6a*.	F	Our board has not referenced ECFA's Policy for Excellence in Compensation-Setting

4 Read more on dashboards in Lesson 5 – "Dashboards Are Not a Secret Sauce for Sound Governance" from *More Lessons From the Nonprofit Boardroom: Effectiveness, Excellence, Elephants!* by Dan Busby and John Pearson (Winchester, VA: ECFAPress, 2019), 28–34.

TOOL #7: The Board's Annual Legal Audit

Use this TRUE OR FALSE annual audit as a first step in assessing your ministry's compliance with applicable local, state, and federal laws and regulations.

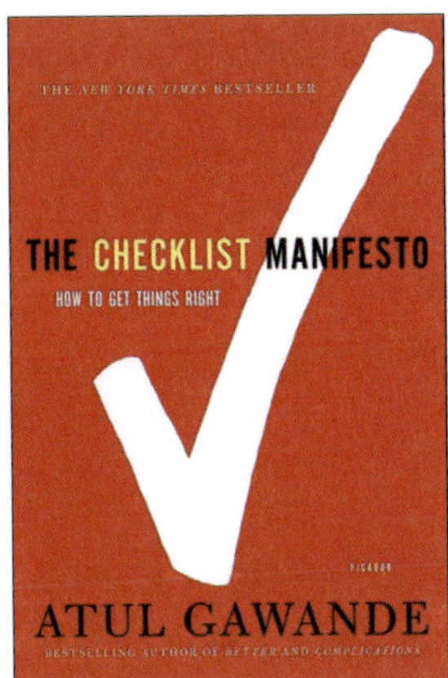

Atul Gawande, the author of *The Checklist Manifesto*, interviewed the managing partner of a California investment firm who is a checklist zealot. He cited the "cocaine brain" that researchers often experience when investigating company financial reports. Without a thorough checklist (honed over years of experience), a greed mode kicks in for investors and wipes out thoughtful discernment.

Another firm uses a "Day Three Checklist" (what to ask on the third day of analysis).

"Forty-nine times out of fifty, he said, there's nothing to be found. 'But then there is.'"[1]

What Could Possibly Go Wrong?

Where's the Checklist?

Imagine this scenario. It's Saturday 7:30 a.m. in the boardroom. You have hot coffee with your favorite creamer. Your "board buddy" (a person assigned to all new board members) has guided you through two informative orientation sessions. You've reviewed the ministry's rolling three-year strategic planning process—and learned how it was birthed by prayer and spiritual discernment. You've read the Board Policies Manual, and you've signed the Board Member Annual Affirmation Statement, the Confidentiality Policy, and the Conflicts of Interest Policy.

It gets better! This Christ-centered board is forward-looking, yet humble, and board member micromanaging is gently prohibited. The board has welcomed you and the new class of board members with warmth and affirmation. You're ready to deploy your spiritual gifts, your top-five strengths from the CliftonStrengths® assessment, and the board chair knows your social style—you're an "analytical" (one of four styles).

What could possibly go wrong?

The board chair begins. "Thank you, everyone, for attending this early morning special meeting of the board. We have just one agenda item: a bookkeeper in our accounting department has been accused of diverting payroll taxes to his own checking account. We have no funds to cover the delinquent taxes and penalties."

Yikes! This is new territory for you. The room goes quiet. "Lord, help us…" you plead silently to the heavens. Then your beating heart calms as you realize…surely, there must be a best practice checklist for this kind of crisis. Surely there is a policy and a step-by-step procedure. Airline pilots have emergency checklists. Surgeons have checklists.

Hmmm. Maybe a checklist would have prevented this?[2]

[1] Atul Gawande, *The Checklist Manifesto: How to Get Things Right* (New York: Metropolitan, 2009), 166–67.

[2] Adapted from Dan Busby and John Pearson, *Lessons From the Church Boardroom: 40 Insights for Exceptional Governance*, 2d ed. (Winchester, VA: ECFAPress, 2019), 17–18.

The Board's Annual Legal Audit

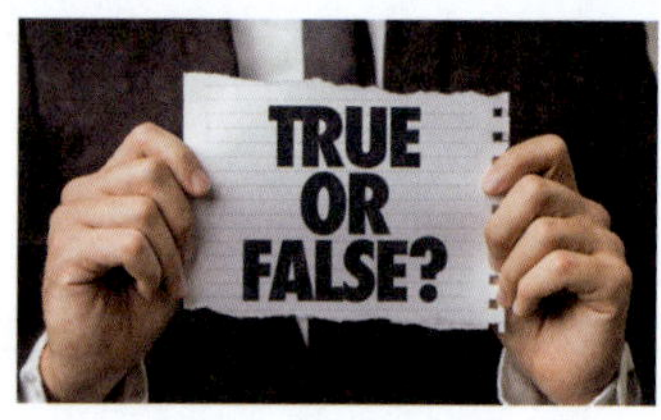

17 Statements the Board Must Address Annually

Your board should expect clarity and honesty from the CEO, the COO, the CFO, staff, and all of the board's committees. To provide clarity—so board members understand basic legal issues and legal trends—the information should be presented with a variety of approaches (for the diverse learning styles of your board members) and can include verbal and written reports, dashboards, and graphs. But there's another important step—an annual checklist.

TRUE OR FALSE? Here are 17 statements that can be adapted for your ministry. Ask your CFO and COO to provide the answers for the question, "How does the board know?" Ultimately, of course, for the board to have faith and trust in the accuracy and veracity of the answers to these statements—the board will be dependent on the honesty and integrity of the CEO and the staff.

Adapt these statements for your ministry—and review the answers at least annually.

See pages 70–71 for a sample completed legal audit.

The Board's Annual Legal Audit	True/ False	How does the board know?
1. The board has reviewed organizational practices within the past year to ensure compliance with its corporate documents (Articles, Bylaws, etc.) and applicable state and federal law.		
2. Appropriately experienced legal counsel has reviewed the articles of incorporation, bylaws, and board policies in the last three years.		
3. Our annual filings with each applicable state are current to maintain our corporate status.		
4. Our annual filings with each applicable state are current for charitable registration purposes.		
5. We are in compliance with our loan covenants, if applicable.		
6. All payroll tax filings are current with federal, state, and local governments. If so, what is the basis for that determination?		

The Board's Annual Legal Audit	True/ False	How does the board know?
7. All informational filings with the federal government (Forms 1098, 1099, 5578, and others, as applicable) are current.		
8. The annual filings of Form 990 and 990-T, if applicable, are current.		
9. The ministry is in compliance with all significant contractual agreements.		
10. All filings for the ministry's copyrights and trademarks are current.		
11. The ministry's insurance coverages are adequate and all insurance policies are in force.		
12. The ministry uses written memos of understanding or contracts to specify the roles and responsibilities of the parties to any partnership, joint venture, or other collaboration, signed by all parties to the agreements.		
13. All ministry funds are being expended consistent with the organization's mission and for tax-exempt purposes (for ministry purposes, not private benefit).		
14. The board has approved the establishment of each type of restricted fund.		
15. Giver-restricted funds are being disbursed in a timely manner.		
16. Giver-restricted funds are always used for the intended purpose.		
17. We have not borrowed any of the restricted asset balances to fund operational expenses in the last year.		

Sample completed Board's Annual Legal Audit[3]

The Board's Annual Legal Audit	True/ False	How does the board know?
1. The board has reviewed organizational practices within the past year to ensure compliance with its corporate documents (Articles, Bylaws, etc.) and applicable state and federal law.	F	We are three years past due on completing this review.
2. Appropriately experienced legal counsel has reviewed the articles of incorporation, bylaws, and board policies in the last three years.	T	Tax counsel completed the most recent review in October of this year. Recommendations were presented to the Governance Committee. The committee will report on these recommendations at the next board meeting.
3. Our annual filings with each applicable state are current to maintain our corporate status.	T	The CFO has verified that all state filings are up-to-date for the current year.
4. Our annual filings with each applicable state are current for charitable registration purposes.	T	The VP of Development has verified that all state charitable solicitations have been filed for the current year.
5. We are in compliance with our loan covenants, if applicable.	F	On September 30, the ministry was $100,000 below the cash reserves threshold required by the mortgage loan covenants.
6. All payroll tax filings are current with federal, state, and local governments. If so, what is the basis for that determination?	T	The CFO verified that all tax filings and related payments are current as of September 30.
7. All informational filings with the federal government (Forms 1098, 1099, 5578, and others, as applicable) are current.	T	The CFO verified that all informational filings are current as of September 30.
8. The annual filings of Form 990 and 990-T, if applicable, are current.	T	The Forms 990 and 990-T were filed on May 15.
9. The ministry is in compliance with all significant contractual agreements.	F	External legal counsel has not reviewed all the ministry's significant contractual agreements.

The Board's Annual Legal Audit	True/ False	How does the board know?
10. All filings for the ministry's copyrights and trademarks are current.	T	External legal counsel has reviewed the status of all copyrights and trademarks and has verified that all filings are current as of August 31.
11. The ministry's insurance coverages are adequate and all insurance policies are in force.	T	The CFO verified this is true as of September 30.
12. The ministry uses written memos of understanding or contracts to specify the roles and responsibilities of the parties to any partnership, joint venture, or other collaboration, signed by all parties to the agreements.	T	The CFO verified this is true as of September 30.
13. All ministry funds are being expended consistent with the organization's mission and for tax-exempt purposes (for ministry purposes, not private benefit).	T	The CFO verified this is true as of September 30.
14. The board has approved the establishment of each type of restricted fund.	F	The board has not been approving the establishment of all types of restricted funds.
15. Giver-restricted funds are being disbursed in a timely manner.	T	The CFO verified this is true as of September 30.
16. Giver-restricted funds are always used for the intended purpose.	T	The CFO verified this is true as of September 30.
17. We have not borrowed any of the restricted asset balances to fund operational expenses in the last year.	F	The CFO confirms that $200,000 of cash that relates to restricted net assets has been used for operating purposes as of September 30.

[3] Read more on dashboards in Lesson 5 – "Dashboards Are Not a Secret Sauce for Sound Governance" from *More Lessons From the Nonprofit Boardroom: Effectiveness, Excellence, Elephants!* by Dan Busby and John Pearson (Winchester, VA: ECFAPress, 2019), 28–34.

TOOL #8: The Board's Annual Fundraising Audit

Use this TRUE OR FALSE annual audit as a first step in assessing if the ministry is communicating giving opportunities with integrity and accuracy—and whether or not the board understands and affirms the ministry's current fundraising practices.

From Chapter 3:
"The Role of the Board in Development"

The authors recommend that boards develop reporting, measurement, and accountability tools regarding expectations between the CEO, the board chair, and the Chief Development Officer—and set policy and budgets according to those expectations.

"By having solid reporting tools tied to your key performance metrics, you will be able to spot trouble early and respond."[1]

Excellence, Authenticity, and Great Care

A Theology of Development

Does your ministry conduct God's work with a spiritual intentionality? Here is an excerpt from a "Theology of Development" statement, by John Frank and R. Scott Rodin, which many Christ-centered boards have affirmed. The full document gives guidance to the CEO, the Chief Development Officer, and the board to ensure that all fundraising practices are in alignment with the ministry's mission, vision, values, and theology.

> Because we know the Owner
> and are called to serve the Owner,
> our desire is to be a blessing to our ministry partners
> and to carry out our work with the highest level
> of skill and excellence of which we are capable.
>
> For us this means that fundraising
> God's way
> should be conducted with
> excellence, authenticity, and great care and concern
> for those we serve.[2]

[1] John R. Frank and R. Scott Rodin, *Development 101: Building a Comprehensive Development Program on Biblical Values* (Colbert, WA: Kingdom Life, 2015), 34.
[2] Ibid., 143–48.

The Board's Annual Fundraising Audit

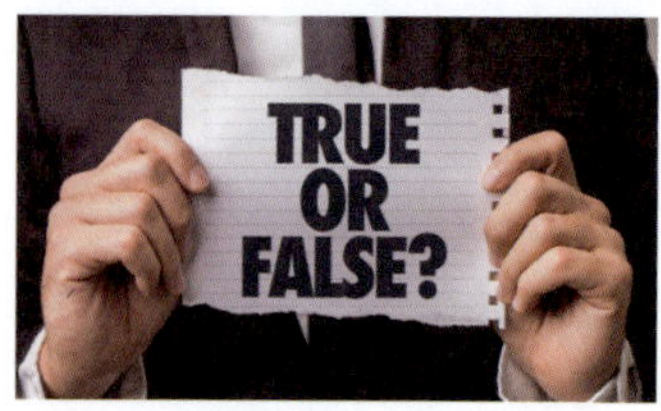

10 Statements the Board Must Address Annually

Your board should expect clarity and honesty from the CEO, the Chief Development Officer (CDO), the CFO, staff, and all of the board's committees. To provide clarity—so board members understand basic fundraising issues and fundraising trends—the information should be presented with a variety of approaches (for the diverse learning styles of your board members) and can include verbal and written reports, dashboards, and graphs. But there's another important step—an annual checklist.

TRUE OR FALSE? Here are 10 statements that can be adapted for your ministry. Ask your CFO and CDO to provide the answers for the question, "How does the board know?" Ultimately, of course, for the board to have faith and trust in the accuracy and veracity of the answers to these statements—the board will be dependent on the honesty and integrity of the CEO and the staff.

Adapt these statements for your ministry—and review the answers at least annually.

See pages 76–77 for a sample completed fundraising audit.

The Board's Annual Fundraising Audit	True/ False	How does the board know?
1. The board knows if in securing charitable gifts, all representations of fact, descriptions of the financial condition of the organization, or narratives about events are current, complete and accurate.		
2. The board understands the ministry's fundraising program relating to raising restricted donations.		
3. The board knows if statements made about the use of gifts by the ministry in its charitable gift appeals are always honored.		
4. The board is aware of communication being shared with givers concerning the potential of over-funding or under-funding of projects for which funds are being raised.		
5. If the ministry is raising funds using a matching gift approach, the board knows if the initial matching funds were "at risk."		

The Board's Annual Fundraising Audit	True/ False	How does the board know?
6. The board knows if staff or external fundraisers are being compensated on the basis of a percentage of funds raised.		
7. The board knows if the ministry always provides givers appropriate and timely charitable gift acknowledgments.		
8. The board knows if the ministry is providing a report, upon written request, including financial information on any specific project for which it has sought or is seeking gifts.		
9. The board is compiling, analyzing, and leveraging giving data to serve and support its giving base.		
10. The board is aware if the ministry provides a copy of the most recent year-end financial statements to anyone upon request.		

Boards Rank Fundraising as Their Greatest Need

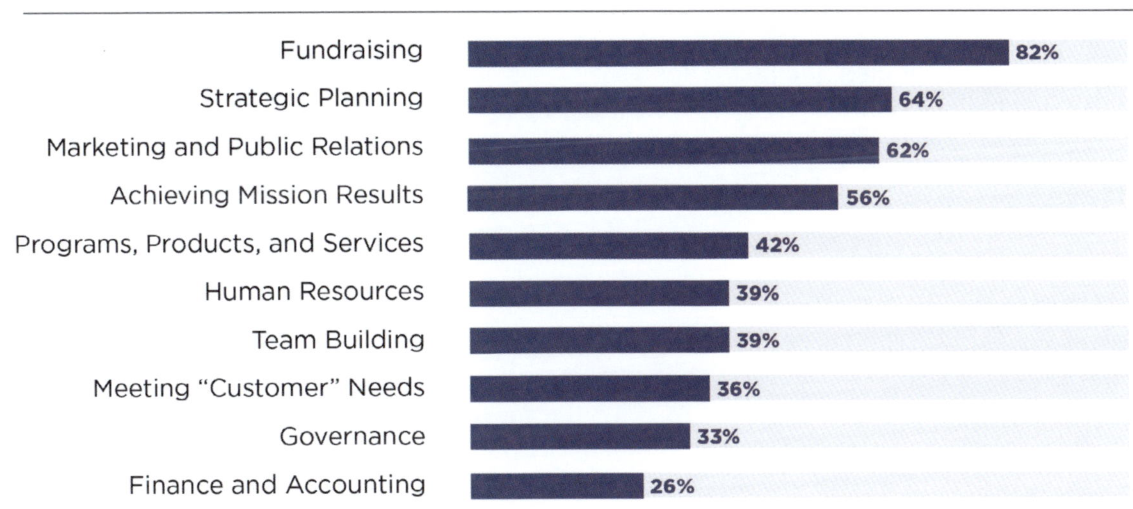

Sample completed Board's Annual Fundraising Audit[3]

The Board's Annual Fundraising Audit	True/ False	How does the board know?
1. The board knows if in securing charitable gifts, all representations of fact, descriptions of the financial condition of the organization, or narratives about events are current, complete and accurate.	T	The Chief Development Officer verified this is true in his report to the board dated September 30.
2. The board understands the ministry's fundraising program relating to raising restricted donations.	T	In the 4th quarter board meeting each year, the Chief Development Officer provides an update of the projects for which the ministry solicits restricted gifts.
3. The board knows if statements made about the use of gifts by the ministry in its charitable gift appeals are always honored.	T	The Chief Development Officer verified this is true in his report to the board dated September 30.
4. The board is aware of communication being shared with givers concerning the potential of over-funding or under-funding of projects for which funds are being raised.	F	Staff has not confirmed this information to the board.
5. If the ministry is raising funds using a matching gift approach, the board knows if the initial matching funds were "at risk."	T	The Chief Development Officer verified this is true in his report to the board dated September 30.

The Board's Annual Fundraising Audit	True/ False	How does the board know?
6. The board knows that staff and external fundraisers are not being compensated on the basis of a percentage of funds raised.	T	The Chief Development Officer verified this is true in his report to the board dated September 30.
7. The board knows if the ministry always provides givers appropriate and timely charitable gift acknowledgments.	T	The Chief Development Officer verified this is true in his report to the board dated September 30.
8. The board knows if the ministry is providing a report, upon written request, including financial information on any specific project for which it has sought or is seeking gifts.	T	The Chief Development Officer verified this is true in his report to the board dated September 30.
9. The board is compiling, analyzing, and leveraging giving data to serve and support its giving base.	F	Only giving totals are provided to the board with no breakdown of gifts by gift size.
10. The board is aware if the ministry provides a copy of the most recent year-end financial statements to anyone upon request.	T	The Chief Development Officer verified this is true in his report to the board dated September 30.

[3] Read more on dashboards in Lesson 5 – "Dashboards Are Not a Secret Sauce for Sound Governance" from *More Lessons From the Nonprofit Boardroom: Effectiveness, Excellence, Elephants!* by Dan Busby and John Pearson (Winchester, VA: ECFAPress, 2019), 28–34.

TOOL #9: The Board's Annual Evaluation of the Top Leader

Review these templates—and then customize your annual process so it fits your unique situation and your unique top leader! (One size doesn't fit all.)

Boards That Lead: When to Take Charge, When to Partner, and When to Stay Out of the Way

by Ram Charan, Dennis Carey and Michael Useem

One of the Top-10 Board Responsibilities

". . . Only One Piece of a Complicated Puzzle"

> Most chief executives are constitutionally optimistic, and since by definition their role is to surmount challenges, the tenor they bring into the boardroom is likely to be relentlessly upbeat. Taking executive overassurance into account will aid directors in detecting nascent troubles ahead, but it is only one piece of a very complicated puzzle.
>
> . . . it is useful for directors to keep a weather eye on early signs of executive deficits. Assuming that the company's central idea has been well formulated in the boardroom, three embryonic indicators, if ignored too long, often mushroom into far more:
>
> - lack of strategy,
> - failure to execute, and
> - wrong people calls.

You must read more on this—it's worth the price of the book.

Oh, my! Just when you thought you were knowledgeable in governance, along comes a 219-page poke-in-the-ribs, plus an incredible 40-page section with 18 checklists for board members, a bonus chapter on "Trends in Director Monitoring and Leading," a director evaluation worksheet, and six golden pages on "Division of Responsibilities Between the Board Leader and the CEO."[1]

---

[1] Ram Charan, Dennis Carey, and Michael Useem, *Boards That Lead: When to Take Charge, When to Partner, and When to Stay Out of the Way* (Boston: Harvard Business Review Press, 2014), 139–63.

The Board's Annual Evaluation of the Top Leader (CEO or Executive Pastor)

TOOL #9 includes:

- ❑ 1. Two Books: Two Insights
- ❑ 2. Understanding the Context for the Top Leader's Annual Assessment
- ❑ 3. One Approach for the Annual Assessment of the Top Leader (Consultant Help)
- ❑ 4. A Common Assessment Finding: "Delegation Deficiencies"
- ❑ 5. Two Resources: BoardSource Online Assessments and *CarverGuide7*
- ❑ 6. Four More Books: More Insights on Assessment of the Top Leader
- ❑ 7. "Cut-and-Paste" Template for Online Survey: Top Leader Annual Assessment

Attn: Church Boards

John Pellowe writes: "When you look to your pastor for support in times of need, it can be tough to interact with the pastor in your role as a deacon or elder. The spiritual connection may put you in a difficult situation when you have to evaluate your pastor's job performance or make a decision that goes against what your pastor thinks should be done. Hopefully you will not experience this much, but there is a potential that you could face this type of challenge as a director.

"A pastor who is insecure could play the 'God card' and justify a proposal saying, 'The Lord told me we must do this.' A fellow board member could say the same thing. What would your response be? This is another reason why you should have some level of spiritual maturity, so that you recognize spiritual abuse and so that you are comfortable with group discernment."[2]

[2] John Pellowe, *Serving as a Board Member: Practical Guidance for Directors of Christian Ministries* (Elmira, ON, Canada: Canadian Council of Christian Charities, 2012), 60–61.

▶ 1. Two Books: Two Insights

INSIGHT 1: BoardSource's "Top-10" list of board roles and responsibilities includes:

☑ "**Select the chief executive**. Boards must reach consensus on the chief executive's responsibilities and undertake a careful search to find the most qualified individual for the position."

☑ "**Support and evaluate the chief executive**. The board should ensure that the chief executive has the moral and professional support he or she needs to further the goals of the organization."[3]

INSIGHT 2: Ram Charan notes this:

☑ "There is nothing more important for a CEO than having the right strategy and right choice of goals, and for the board, **the right strategy is second only to having the right CEO.**"[4]

"What you measure improves."[5]

"If you don't know what your top three priorities are, you don't have priorities."[6]

Donald Rumsfeld

"The higher you go [in your career], the more your problems are behavioral"[7]

Marshall Goldsmith

---

[3] Excerpted from "What Are the Basic Responsibilities of Nonprofit Boards?" Accessed August 14, 2019. *BoardSource*: *https://boardsource.org/resources/board-responsibilities-structures-faqs/.*

[4] Ram Charan, *Owning Up: The 14 Questions Every Board Member Needs to Ask* (San Francisco: John Wiley & Sons, 2009), 68.

[5] Donald Rumsfeld, *Rumsfeld's Rules: Leadership Lessons in Business, Politics, War, and Life* (New York: HarperCollins, 2013), 299.

[6] Ibid., 304.

[7] Marshall Goldsmith and Mark Reiter, *What Got You Here Won't Get You There: Discover the 20 Workplace Habits You Need to Break* (New York: Hyperion, 2007), 42.

▶ 2. Understanding the Context for the Top Leader's Annual Assessment

Richard T. Ingram notes:

> In the end, although we may not be able to precisely define what outstanding leadership is, we know it when we see it! Let's admit that this very subjective process is more art than science, more human than anything else. We can and should use various objective measures or strategic indicators of the organization's progress on its financial condition, for example, as part of the assessment process—but whether a leader stays or goes so often hangs on much more subtle factors.[8]

BoardSource Resources. BoardSource provides a library of articles and other resources for conducting the annual CEO performance review/assessment. See the options in this section for BoardSource's online assessment tools that can also be customized. Chapter 3, "Support and Evaluate the Chief Executive," (pages 29-38) from the book, *Ten Basic Responsibilities of Nonprofit Boards* (Third Edition), by Richard T. Ingram (published by BoardSource) is helpful with context, philosophy, and principles of performance assessment— but it doesn't provide specific questions to ask in the performance review of the top leader.

Attn: Church Boards

As you know, most of the governance literature is not faith-based, and so the approach, the assumptions and even the process sometimes (not always) may not be grounded in a biblical context of growth, grace and mercy! And . . . while some of the assessments address character issues, many assessment tools will not adequately position the assessment in the context of the fruits of the spirit, spiritual discernment, human vision versus God's vision (Big Hairy Audacious Goals vs. Big HOLY Audacious Goals), etc. *So . . . faith-based buyers beware!*

DVD Training for Faith-Based Board Members. Canadian Council of Christian Charities provides eight training modules on DVD, *The Board's Most Important Relationship: Training for Christian Ministry Directors and Staff Leaders*, created by John Pellowe, CEO of CCCC. They include:

- ❑ 1. Theological Foundation: Four biblical principles of a God-honouring relationship (15 min.)
- ❑ 2. Considerate Boards: How boards can show consideration for the staff leader (32 min.)
- ❑ 3. Considerate Leaders: How leaders can show consideration for the board (15 min.)
- ❑ 4. Caring for the Leader: Practical ways boards can support the senior leader (31 min.)
- ❑ 5. Caring for the Board: Practical ways senior leaders can support the board (16 min.)
- ❑ 6. **Leadership Reviews: How to review the senior leader's performance** (37 min.)
- ❑ 7. Leadership Problems: Dealing with conflict, lack of trust, underperformance, and domineering leaders (15 min.)
- ❑ 8. Ending the Relationship: Retirements, resignations, and terminations (17 min.)

For more information: *www.cccc.org/microsites/board_relationship/*

[8] Richard T. Ingram, *Ten Basic Responsibilities of Nonprofit Boards*, 3d ed. (Washington, DC: BoardSource, 2015), 33.

▶ 3. One Approach for the Annual Assessment of the Top Leader (Consultant Help)

Here's just one example of a top leader assessment process—based on the approach often used by John Pearson as a consultant:

Here's what I often provided to clients. While I seek to customize annual assessments for each unique situation, I find that most of my work involves creating the first-ever assessment and then providing some tools so a client can continue to replicate the process every year. The process usually involves these three phases, and perhaps a fourth phase of coaching the top leader.

Attn: Church Boards

While this section details a CEO assessment, the process can easily be customized for the annual assessment of the senior pastor and/or executive pastor.

Phase 1: Pre-Work

- Phone call with CEO (or senior pastor) and board chair
- Development of a customized online survey using a "360" approach:
  - Every board member completes an online assessment
  - Each staff member reporting directly to the CEO (or senior pastor) completes an assessment on the top leader
  - The CEO (or senior pastor) completes a self-assessment

Phase 2: Board Meeting

- Prior to the board meeting, I meet with the CEO and board chair (same day, or sometimes with a phone call in advance)—and deliver the results.
- At the board meeting, I brief the CEO and board on the process, and then the CEO is excused for about 45 minutes. I'll often highlight the CEO's "3 Powerful S's" which include:
  - **Strengths** (from the Gallup StrengthsFinder assessment – *www.gallupstrengthscenter.com/home*)
  - **Spiritual gifts**
  - **Social styles** (drivers, analyticals, amiables, expressives)

  . . . to remind the board members that each leader is unique, and none of us have ALL the gifts and strengths!
- During the executive session of the board meeting (without the CEO or other staff in the room), I create exercises for the board members to review the confidential "360" results of all three groups (board, direct reports, CEO self-assessment). Note: At the conclusion of the Executive Session, the confidential surveys are collected and shredded. (The chair and the CEO each keep one copy.)

- During the executive session, we create a written list of affirmations and areas where improvement is needed—and ask for every board member's approval of the list. (I emphasize the wisdom from John Carver, "The board speaks with one voice, or not at all.")[9]
- The CEO is then invited back into the room and a board member reads the "draft" list to the CEO of affirmations and where improvement is needed.
- The CEO then has the option of responding then to the review, or asking for clarification, or thanking the board with a response to come later.

Phase 3: After the Board Meeting

- Within three to four days, the written notes are edited by the chair (usually, if he/she is gifted at wordsmithing), and then delivered via email to the CEO.
- Within 10-14 days, the CEO provides a written response to the chair—noting "next steps" for areas needing improvement. Example: If the board suggested that the CEO work on his/her delegation skills, the CEO might suggest one or two next steps on becoming a more effective delegator (coaching, reading a book, attending a workshop, seeking out a coach or mentor, etc.).
- The chair then closes the loop:
  - Thanks the CEO for the response.
  - Communicates the response to the full board.
  - Delegates the accountability/reporting approach.
  - Schedules the next annual CEO performance review.

Phase 4: Coaching (if needed)

Next…the coaching process begins, if helpful, and I often recommend one or more of the following books (to read my review, google the "[book title], John Pearson's Buckets Blog"):

- ❑ *The Coaching Habit: Say Less, Ask More & Change the Way You Lead Forever*, by Michael Bungay Stanier
- ❑ *What Got You Here Won't Get You There: Discover the 20 Workplace Habits You Need to Break*, by Marshall Goldsmith with Mark Reiter
- ❑ *How to Delegate*, by Alec Mackenzie (39-minute audio resource)
- ❑ *The One Minute Manager Meets the Monkey*, by Ken Blanchard and William Oncken, Jr.
- ❑ *Leadership Briefs: Shaping Organizational Culture to Stretch Leadership Capacity*, by Dick Daniels
- ❑ "The Delegation Bucket" – Visit "The Book Bucket" webpage for *Mastering the Management Buckets*, by John Pearson, for a list of books within each of the 20 core competencies, including "The Delegation Bucket." – *http://managementbuckets.com/book-bucket.*

[9] John Carver and Miriam Mayhew Carver, *CarverGuide 1: Basic Principles of Policy Governance* (San Francisco: Jossey-Bass, 1996), 2.

▶ 4. A Common Assessment Finding: "Delegation Deficiencies"

Delegation Deficiencies. In our experience when conducting (or participating in) 360 assessments of the top leader, most direct reports to the CEO or senior pastor whine that the top leader delegates too many things! Conversely, most boards rate their top leader as deficient in effective delegation. Here's a classic audio resource on delegation (just 39 minutes) which includes this 10-question assessment.

How to Delegate[10]

39-minute audio CD
by Alec Mackenzie

Alec Mackenzie, the time management guru and author of the international bestselling book, *The Time Trap: The Classic Book on Time Management*, has an **Effective Delegation Quiz** for you—and if you fail the quiz—he says you may be seriously overpaid![11]

Ten Delegation Questions:

☑ **Check if Yes**

- ❑ 1) Do you take work home regularly?
- ❑ 2) Do you work longer hours than your subordinates?
- ❑ 3) Do you spend time doing for others what they could be doing for themselves?
- ❑ 4) When you return from an absence from the office, do you find the in-basket too full?
- ❑ 5) Are you still handling activities and problems you had before your last promotion?
- ❑ 6) Are you often interrupted with queries or requests on on-going projects or assignments?
- ❑ 7) Do you spend time on routine details that others could handle?
- ❑ 8) Do you like to keep a finger in every pie?
- ❑ 9) Do you rush to meet deadlines?
- ❑ 10) Are you unable to keep on top of your priorities?

How Many Questions Were Yes?

0 to 1: You are an excellent delegator!

2 to 4: You can improve.

5 to 6: You have a serious delegation problem.

7 to 10: You are undoubtedly doing much of your subordinates' work and may be seriously overpaid!

[10] Alec Mackenzie, *How to Delegate – Audio CD* (Listen USA, 1990).

[11] Read John Pearson's review of "How to Delegate" in the April 3, 2013 edition (Issue No. 273) of *Your Weekly Staff Meeting*, archived at: *http://urgentink.typepad.com/my_weblog/2013/04/how-to-delegate-cd.html.*

▶ 5. Two Resources: BoardSource Online Assessments and CarverGuide 7

BoardSource: "ACE"

Review the CEO assessment options, demo, and pricing at:
https://boardsource.org/board-support/assessing-performance/chief-executive-assessments-ace/

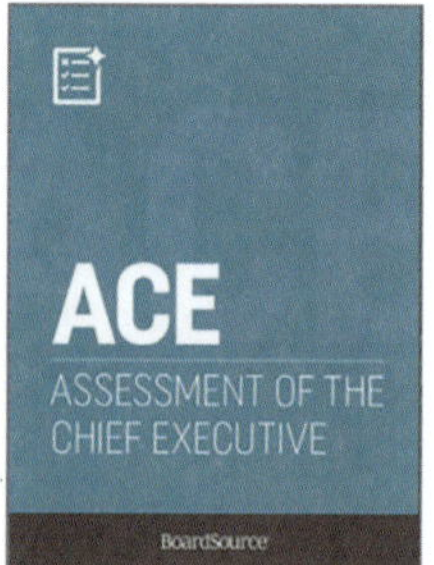

The Assessment of the Chief Executive (ACE) tool enables your board to evaluate the performance of your chief executive in four key areas:

- ☑ Annual performance goals
- ☑ Core competencies
- ☑ Leadership qualities
- ☑ Accomplishments & challenges

Sample **Questions:**

The following questions are adapted from BoardSource materials:[12]

Please indicate whether your CEO met your expectations in the following areas:

1 – Very Ineffective
2 – Ineffective
3 – Neither Ineffective nor Effective
4 – Effective
5 – Very Effective
N/A – Don't Know

☑ **Board Governance and Board Relations**	**1**	**2**	**3**	**4**	**5**	**N/A**
1. Our CEO's working relationship with our board (as defined by candor, competency, trust, and integrity) is…						
2. Our CEO's working relationship with our board chair (including all the key essentials for effective board meetings) is…						
3. Our CEO's communication with the board (including between meetings) is…						
4. Our CEO's critical role of balancing communication and information flow (including confidential information) between the board and the senior staff is…						
5. Our CEO's work in supporting the board chair and our board committees by leveraging the talent and expertise of individual board members is…						

Please add any comments about our CEO's performance related to this core competency:

[12] Adapted from "Assessment of the Chief Executive." Accessed on August 14, 2019, *BoardSource*: *https://boardsource.org/board-support/assessing-performance/chief-executive-assessments-ace/.*

CarverGuide 7: Board Assessment of the CEO

The CarverGuide Series on Effective Board Governance

CarverGuide 7
Board Assessment of the CEO
by John Carver (22 pages)

6 DON'TS!

Discuss John Carver's counsel on "What Not to Do in Your CEO Evaluation"[13]

1	"**Don't** make CEO evaluation a popularity contest, whether popularity with board members, staff, clientele, or the public."
2	"**Don't** use a prefabricated CEO evaluation form you've found in a book, workshop, or magazine."
3	"**Don't** evaluate the CEO on whether he or she accomplished her personal objectives for the year."
4	"**Don't** commission a group of citizens to evaluate your CEO for you."
5	"**Don't** ask the staff, public, customers, clients, patients, or students what they think of your CEO's performance."
6	"**Don't** ever, ever evaluate the CEO on criteria that have not been created in writing by the board ahead of time."

"Remember that the purpose of CEO evaluation is to increase the likelihood of the board's getting its job done. There are three imperative steps in accomplishing this board job that directly affects the CEO. The board must:

#1. Define what should be achieved (ends) and what should be avoided (executive limitations).

#2. Fix the point of accountability on the CEO.

#3. Check regularly that ends are achieved and limitations are not violated."[14]

John Carver

[13] John Carver, *CarverGuide 7: Board Assessment of the CEO* (San Francisco: Jossey-Bass, 1997), 17, 20.
[14] Ibid., 20.

▶ 6. Four More Books: More Insights on Assessment of the Top Leader

4 BOOK REVIEWS

How Many Board Members Does It Take to Change a Light Bulb?

Four Governance Books Reviewed by John Pearson
Your Weekly Staff Meeting eNews[15]

Issue No. 311 of *Your Weekly Staff Meeting* features mini-snippets on four governance books, along with the question: "How many board members does it take to change a light bulb?"

Serving as a Board Member – 4 Books

I'm frequently asked, "What governance book would you recommend we read before our next board and senior team retreat?"

My standard response is to ask a series of questions. What books have they read? Any new board members? Any stuck-in-a-rut board members? **Do they need the basics on governance, or a kick-in-the-behind?** Is it time for an inspirational book on decision-making and spiritual discernment? Are they readers or listeners? (Maybe a TED Talk?) Are they way too busy? Then maybe just a really, really skinny book—with big print and lots of white space? Faith-based or not?

One size doesn't fit all. So in addition to the governance books I've reviewed in past issues (visit my Board Bucket webpage at *www.managementbuckets.com/board-bucket*), here are mini-snippets from four books. Two ideas:

- Purchase all four books and ask four board members to give 5- to 10-minute reviews at your next board meeting or retreat.
- Or delegate your reading to four board members and then, based on their feedback, select one book for the entire board to read.

> ***"Lord, many of us have experienced profound personal insights by reading the right book at the right time. Some of us have even made life-altering decisions after reading significant books. So guide us in our selection of books. Amen."***[16]
>
> Dan Busby and John Pearson

[15] John Pearson, "How Many Board Members Does It Take to Change a Light Bulb?" *John Pearson's Buckets Blog* (*Your Weekly Staff Meeting*), November 6, 2014, *http://urgentink.typepad.com/my_weblog/2014/11/serving-as-a-board-member-4-books.html.*

[16] From the prayer in "Lesson 38, Great Boards Delegate Their Reading," by Dan Busby and John Pearson, *Lessons From the Nonprofit Boardroom: 40 Insights for Better Board Meetings* (Winchester, VA: ECFAPress, 2018), 201.

❑ OPTION #1: *Serving as a Board Member: Practical Guidance for Directors of Christian Ministries*

by John Pellowe (188 pages)[17]

In his foreword to this excellent book, Jim Brown, author of *The Imperfect Board Member*, notes "now it seems like 'governance consultant' is a pre-painted shingle that goes with every early-retirement, golden parachute check that gets handed out. The web is fraught with blogs and e-books on the topics of boards."

Based on a seminar, and a DVD of the same title, the book is one of the best Christ-centered governance books available. Right from the get-go in the first chapter, "Readiness to Serve," Pellowe speaks to the hearts of future board members about passion and calling:

- **"If the ministry's mission is not closely tied to your interests, your board service will be a draining experience..."**
- "The Holy Spirit can nudge us towards those good works that God has prepared for us to do (Eph. 2:10); this nudging is usually described as a call."
- "God's individual call is normally in line with the gifts that you already have."

And he's just warming up on pages 4 and 5! He adds on page 7, "You really should be able to think theologically about the mission, governance, and leadership of the ministry you are serving. If you are new to the Christian faith, you may not yet be well enough equipped for board service in a Christian ministry."

The book's format is unique with the voices of other experts blended into sidebars. Pellowe, CEO of the Canadian Council of Christian Charities since 2003, sprinkles in his personal insights and stories (like his home church board meetings!) every few pages—fascinating stuff! *Example:* His story on page 126 on the "Bad" 3 Rs: boards that waste enormous amounts of time on "Reviewing, Rehashing and Redoing."

It's tough to pick just one favorite quotation or paragraph—but this grabbed me:

> You must be diligent as a director. Make sure that you ask any questions that are on your mind. **As the saying goes, the only bad question is the one you had, but didn't ask.** You may think that since you have a banker on your board, you do not need to ask any financial questions because someone else is looking after that. It is your duty to ask these questions anyway. Do not rely on someone else to do your thinking.

[17] John Pellowe, *Serving as a Board Member: Practical Guidance for Directors of Christian Ministries* (Elmira, ON, Canada: Canadian Council of Christian Charities, 2012).

❑ **OPTION 2: *Best Practices for Effective Boards***
by E. LeBron Fairbanks, Dwight M. Gunter II, and James R. Couchenour (191 pages)[18]

Total years of board leadership and board service for these three co- authors would rival almost any other trio. The best practices have been culled from 1) a lifetime of service as a denominational education commissioner (working with 54 educational institutions in 36 countries), 2) as a board chair and business leader, and 3) as a seasoned pastor/author and board member.

➔ With almost 40 pages covering 11 documents in the appendix, you could skip the book and strike gold in every resource: "Leader Effectiveness Review Grid (22 leadership behaviors)," "Board Standing Policy Manual," "Rules of the Road for Christlike Conflict Management," and a "Board Survey" with 22 questions.

Can a book that articulates Christ-centered character standards for board members also meet the high bar of governance excellence? Yes! The guts of the book, 12 chapters, include helpful discussions on:

- "Ears In, Fingers Out" (great shorthand for the board role)
- "Take Time" (slowing decision-making down to hear from God)
- "Yes! to Missional Change" (choose your battles wisely)
- "Role Models of Generosity and Stewardship" (why board members must set the pace in generous giving and inspiring others to give)

In his chapter, "Yes! to Missional Change," Pastor Dwight Gunter asks "How many Christians does it take to change a light bulb?" His answer: **"Seven. One to change the bulb and six to resist the change."** (Insert "How many board members…" and it's just as funny.)

Co-author LeBron Fairbanks, founding director of BoardServe.org, which serves as a global intervention and coaching resource for boards, shares my favorite quotation in the book—this from a CPA firm:

**"In the long run, only integrity matters.
In fact, without integrity,
there will be no long run."**

[18] E. LeBron Fairbanks, Dwight M. Gunter II, and James R. Couchenour, *Best Practices for Effective Boards* (Kansas City, MO: Beacon Hill, 2012).

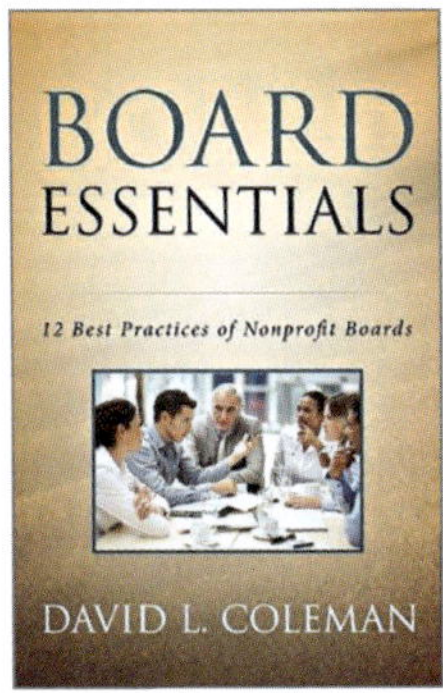

❑ OPTION 3: *Board Essentials: 12 Best Practices of Nonprofit Boards,* by David L. Coleman (109 pages)[19]

OK…here's your skinny book. Coleman has culled from dozens of resources and produced 12 best practices—short chapters, long on practical tools and wisdom. Here's a topical taste: mission, membership, definition of governance, board roles and responsibilities, the CEO's role, the CEO and the board chair, board policies ("speak with one voice"), board meetings, fiduciary responsibilities, the board development committee—and much, much more.

Coleman, though he understands nonprofit life as a former foundation grantmaker and faith-based organization leader, has crafted this short-and-sweet book that works for both Christ-centered and secular boards. My favorite quotation in the book is a Peter Drucker keeper:

> **"The first task of the leader is to make sure that everyone sees the mission, hears it, lives it. If you lose sight of your mission, you begin to stumble and it shows very, very fast."**

❑ OPTION #4: *Ten Basic Responsibilities of Nonprofit Boards* (Second Edition), by Richard T. Ingram (90 pages)[20]

The first title of six in BoardSource's "Governance Series" delivers the generally agreed-upon list of the 10 roles and responsibilities of nonprofit board members. (Christ-centered boards will likely add one or two more.) The book includes an excellent 20-point self-assessment for board members, with probing questions like:

- "Are there ways in which your talents and interests can be more fully realized at or between board or committee meetings?"
- "Have you and the board taken steps to deal with real or apparent conflicts of interest in your board service?"
- "Which aspect of your service on the board has been the least satisfying and enjoyable?"

Favorite quotation (on CEO performance reviews): "In the end, although we may not be able to precisely define what outstanding leadership is, we know it when we see it! Let's admit that this very subjective process is more art than science, more human than anything else. We can and should use various objective measures or strategic indicators of the organization's progress on its financial condition, for example, as part of the assessment process—but whether a leader stays or goes so often hangs on much more subtle factors."

[19] David L. Coleman, *Board Essentials: 12 Best Practices of Nonprofit Boards* (Tacoma, WA: BoardTrek Nonprofit Consulting, 2014)

[20] Richard T. Ingram, *Ten Basic Responsibilities of Nonprofit Boards*, 2d ed. (Washington, DC: BoardSource, 2009).

▶ 7. "Cut-and-Paste" Template for Online Survey: Top Leader Annual Assessment

Sample Template Idea:

Use the 20 core competencies from John Pearson's book, ***Mastering the Management Buckets: 20 Critical Competencies for Leading Your Business or Nonprofit***.

Read more on the 20 competences: *www.ManagementBuckets.com.*

John has customized many "360" annual CEO evaluations using this template as a starting point.

On the following pages is an example of how you might create and customize a "360" assessment for your CEO.

Thanks to Jeff Lilley, board coach, for allowing us to use an assessment example from his CEO years at Seattle's Union Gospel Mission.

You can create your own survey account at: *www.SurveyMonkey.com.*

➔ *NOTE: Permission is granted to adapt this survey for your use within your organization.*

Attn: Church Boards

Review the church resources suggested for Tool #9 before you begin customizing this survey for your senior pastor. One size doesn't fit all. And note John Carver's wisdom (see previous pages), "Don't ever, ever evaluate the CEO on criteria that have not been created in writing by the board ahead of time."

Only Two Thirds of Boards Annually Evaluate Their CEO

ECFA Research Says...

Our board conducts an **annual performance review** of the CEO. 67%

REMINDER TO READERS OF THIS BOOK

This CEO Assessment template and the Board Self-Assessment template (Tool #5) are designed to be dropped into an online survey software, such as www.SurveyMonkey.com.

On the following pages is an example of how you might create and customize a "360" assessment for your CEO.

Thanks to Jeff Lilley, board coach, for allowing us to use an assessment survey example from his CEO years at Seattle's Union Gospel Mission.

Email Cover Memo (with survey link) and Introductory Page on the Survey

Attn: Seattle's Union Gospel Mission Board of Directors

SURVEY DEADLINE: Feb. 22 – Tuesday 5 p.m.

Thank you for investing time, thought and prayer into this survey. Your insight and wisdom will help advance both the ministry of the Mission and the leadership of Jeff Lilley. Individual responses to this survey will remain ANONYMOUS and the combined results, along with all of the individual responses to the essay questions, will be shared with the Executive Committee and with Jeff at the next Executive Committee meeting. (John Pearson will be facilitating this process on that Friday.)

When you're connected to the Internet, please click on this link:

[INSERT SURVEY LINK HERE]

This is one of three online surveys. Jeff's direct reports (6 people) will also be completing a second survey and Jeff will complete a third survey: his self-assessment.

This survey was created by John and used in recent years with our previous CEO. It includes updated edits from Jeff, John and myself.

Note: The survey must be completed in one sitting. You may now pray and then begin! THANKS!

[Name]
Chair, Board of Directors

SECTION A:
Introduction to the Annual CEO Assessment Survey – Board Members

(Drop into a survey template at *www.SurveyMonkey.com*)

➤ **1.** How many years have you served on the board?

- ❑ Less than 1 year
- ❑ 1 – 3 years
- ❑ 4 – 6 years
- ❑ 7 – 9 years
- ❑ 10 – 12 years
- ❑ 13 – 15 years
- ❑ 16 or more years

➤ **2. THE BOARD'S KEY ROLE.** Effective nonprofit boards know they must encourage and inspire the organization's CEO. The board must also affirm corporate goals and then CEO goals (Standards of Performance) that are aligned with the corporate goals. Then, the board must monitor CEO performance and reward achievement. If the annual goals are clear, then performance evaluation is thoughtful and objective. If the goals are fuzzy, then the CEO performance process can become rather subjective.

So . . . check ALL that apply below:

- ❑ Seattle's UGM has clear annual corporate goals.
- ❑ The President (Jeff Lilley) has specific annual goals.
- ❑ The board has effectively monitored Jeff's performance against the approved annual goals.
- ❑ We've been in transition for a while, so I'm OK with a lack of clear annual goals, but the board needs to address this in the next 30 to 90 days.
- ❑ I'm not a big fan of annual performance reviews.
- ❑ An annual performance review of the President is an imperative!
- ❑ Other (please specify):

SECTION B:
Cause, Community, Corporation

The leadership and management functions can be described with three hats the CEO wears: The Cause, The Community, and The Corporation. Please evaluate Jeff's effectiveness in these three areas. Your evaluation should reflect his overall effectiveness for all programs and functions. You can note specific affirmations and areas needing improvement in the essay questions near the end.

➤ **3. THE CAUSE.** Please check how effective you believe Jeff has been in each of these key leadership and management areas, during the last 12 months. (Check "N/A" if you have no first-hand knowledge of his effectiveness.)

The Cause: ☑	**1** Very Ineffective	**2** Ineffective	**3** Neither Ineffective nor Effective	**4** Effective	**5** Very Effective	**N/A**
RESULTS-ORIENTED (Part 1). Identifies desired outcomes and results.						
RESULTS-ORIENTED (Part 2). Accomplishes desired outcomes and results.						
CUSTOMER-FOCUSED. Facilitates board/staff agreement on who are our primary and supporting customers (recipients, donors, volunteers, etc.).						
STRATEGY-DRIVEN. Creates and executes strategies to achieve results.						
PROGRAM-COMPETENT. Able to roll out sustainable programs that achieve agreed-upon results, that are under budget, that are within our value system, and demonstrate high quality.						

➤ **4. THE COMMUNITY.** Please check how effective you believe Jeff has been in each of these key leadership and management areas, during the last 12 months. (Check "N/A" if you have no first-hand knowledge of his effectiveness.)

The Community: ☑	**1** Very Ineffective	**2** Ineffective	**3** Neither Ineffective nor Effective	**4** Effective	**5** Very Effective	**N/A**
LEADER-LEARNER. Models life-long learning as a leader.						
LEADER-MENTOR. Coaches and mentors his key people.						
SERVANT-LEADER. Demonstrates God-honoring servant leadership.						
PEOPLE-STUDENT (Part 1). Continually improves his own people skills; effectively applies such skills to all his people interactions.						
PEOPLE-STUDENT (Part 2). Understands people styles, strengths and giftedness.						
ACHIEVEMENT-CELEBRATOR. Has a system in place to celebrate individual and team performance so staff and volunteers are rewarded, affirmed and celebrated.						
CULTURE-INTERPRETER. Understands the organization's culture and ethos and communicates it to the various constituencies (recipients, board, donors, staff, volunteers, etc.).						
TEAM-BUILDER. Creates winning teams and builds a climate for others to do the same.						
FUN-INTENTIONAL. Leads the team in enjoying work and life, having fun, creating memories and demonstrating balanced lives.						
DONOR-SMART. Creates a sustainable fundraising and development strategy.						
VOLUNTEER-PURPOSED. Builds a volunteer movement that serves both the mission of the organization and the volunteers.						
CRISIS-READY. Has crisis plans in place and the board's confidence that we're ready for most crises, if they were to hit.						

➤ **5. THE CORPORATION.** Please check how effective you believe Jeff has been in each of these key leadership and management areas, during the last 12 months. (Check "N/A" if you have no first-hand knowledge of his effectiveness.)

The Corporation: ☑	**1** Very Ineffective	**2** Ineffective	**3** Neither Ineffective nor Effective	**4** Effective	**5** Very Effective	**N/A**
BOARD-DEVELOPER. Helps facilitate a plan for the board's role and influence and works with officers and committees to serve and inspire them.						
BUDGET-PRUDENT. Creates a sustainable budget and financial plan and forecasts, achieves and reports financial info at agreed-upon dates.						
DELEGATION-SKILLED. Delegates as much as possible and focuses on what only the CEO can and should be doing.						
OPERATIONS-SYSTEMIZED. Creates operational policies and procedures and systems that serve, not hamper, progress and results.						
COMMUNICATION-ORIENTED. Understands the importance of targeted PR, marketing, branding and messaging; creates systems for evaluation and improvement.						
MEETINGS-ENHANCER. Facilitates formal and informal gatherings of UGM people (recipients, board, staff, volunteers, donors, etc.) and adds value and energy to what could be routine or mundane meetings.						

SECTION C:
President's Position Description

Position descriptions provide general guidelines of responsibilities (but not specific annual goals with metrics). However, it is helpful to review the position description each year and assess alignment.

➤ **6. PRESIDENT'S POSITION DESCRIPTION.** Based on the key responsibilities outlined in the President's Position Description, please check how effective Jeff has been in these areas in the last 12 months. (Check N/A if you have no first-hand knowledge of his effectiveness.)

President's Position Description: ☑	**1** Very Ineffective	**2** Ineffective	**3** Neither Ineffective nor Effective	**4** Effective	**5** Very Effective	**N/A**
Leadership						
Strategic planning						
Fundraising						
Board of Directors relations						
Public relations						
Maintain Customer Service standards (CARE)[21]						

➤ **7. PRESIDENT'S PERSONAL LEADERSHIP.** Based on these "softer" personal leadership elements outlined in the President's Position Description, please check how effective Jeff has been in these areas in the last 12 months. (Check "N/A" if you have no first-hand knowledge of his effectiveness.)

President's Personal Leadership: ☑	**1** Very Ineffective	**2** Ineffective	**3** Neither Ineffective nor Effective	**4** Effective	**5** Very Effective	**N/A**
Maintains a vision for the Mission.						
Maintains a public and private life that is consistent with 1 Timothy 1-6, with an indisputable reputation within the community.						
Maintains a servant's heart for both people and ministries.						

[21] Seattle's Union Gospel Mission defines customer service standards with CARE (Committed, Attentive, Responsive, Excellent).

SECTION D: Leveraging Strengths

➤ 8. **JEFF'S GREATEST STRENGTHS.** Any list is incomplete because every person (every CEO) is uniquely gifted by God. No one CEO has all the gifts! But, please list here the greatest strengths, in your opinion, that Jeff demonstrates in his leadership of Seattle's Union Gospel Mission:

➤ 9. **JEFF'S TOP-5 STRENGTHS.** According to the CliftonStrengths® assessment for Jeff, his Top-5 Strengths are:[22]

1) **"STRATEGIC®** – People especially talented in the Strategic theme create alternative ways to proceed. Faced with any given scenario, they can quickly spot the relevant patterns and issues."
2) **"INPUT®** – People especially talented in the Input theme have a craving to know more. Often they like to collect and archive all kinds of information."
3) **"LEARNER®** – People especially talented in the Learner theme have a great desire to learn and want to continuously improve. The process of learning, rather than the outcome, excites them."
4) **"INTELLECTION®** – People especially talented in the Intellection theme are characterized by their intellectual activity. They are introspective and appreciate intellectual discussions."
5) **"BELIEF®** – People especially talented in the Belief theme have certain core values that are unchanging. Out of these values emerges a defined purpose for their lives."

In your opinion, do people around Jeff help him maximize these Top-5 strengths?

❍ Yes
❍ No
❍ Other (please specify):

"While the best leaders are not well-rounded, the best teams are."[23]

Tom Rath and Barry Conchie

[22] CliftonStrengths® and each of the 34 theme names are trademarks of Gallup, Inc. To discover your top five CliftonStrengths®, please visit the Gallup Strengths Center at *https://www.gallupstrengthscenter.com/*.
[23] Tom Rath and Barry Conchie, *Strengths Based Leadership: Great Leaders, Teams and Why People Follow* (New York: Gallup Press, 2008), 2.

SECTION E:
Your Open-Ended Assessment Thoughts

Here's your chance to communicate your specific thoughts regarding Jeff's performance evaluation. (Reminder: while this is anonymous, 100 percent of your comments below WILL be included in the confidential report given to Jeff and the Executive Committee.)

➤ **10. GROWTH OPPORTUNITIES.** As you reflect on [this past year] and Jeff's [first] year of leadership at Seattle's Union Gospel Mission, identify the areas where Jeff now needs to grow in order to be a more effective leader.

➤ **11. MAGIC WAND #1.** If you could "wave a magic wand" and encourage Jeff to START doing something new or different, in his leadership role in the next 12 months, what would it be?

➤ **12. MAGIC WAND #2.** What should Jeff STOP doing in his leadership role (or style) in order to become a more effective leader for the organization?

➤ **13. THE BOARD'S ROLE.** In your opinion, what should the board do differently (if anything) to serve Jeff more effectively?

➤ **14. MEMO TO JEFF.** (Please be brief!) Here's your chance to share a thought or two with Jeff—on any concern, idea, affirmation, or even something that maybe bugs you. (Note: Everyone will read these comments also. Be discerning here. Perhaps what you need to share should be done in a one-on-one setting first with Jeff.)

➤ **15. OPTIONAL:** LAST CHANCE. Any other comments for the Executive Committee or Jeff? Thank you for investing time in this survey.

REMINDER TO READERS OF THIS BOOK

This CEO Assessment template and the Board Self-Assessment template (Tool #5) are designed to be dropped into an online survey software, such as *www.SurveyMonkey.com.*

TOOL #10: The 5/15 Monthly Report to the Board

Use this tool to keep the board informed and inspired between meetings. Once formatted, it takes just 15 minutes to write and 5 minutes to read.

In the hallways of boardrooms, perhaps the most constant whine is, **"We don't hear anything from our CEO [or senior pastor] in between board meetings.** How can I steward this ministry, if I'm not in the loop?"

Leaders also whine. "My board runs the continuum: the micro-managers want a weekly report. Others don't want email. They just call when they have a question. Frankly, I don't really bless anyone."[1]

Try This Board Reporting Tool for 90 Days

POP QUIZ! ☑ Check: True or False?

T	F	Board Members
❑	❑	Informative reports to the board from our top leader are received regularly.
❑	❑	As a board member, I'm sometimes the last to hear both good and bad news.
❑	❑	I receive way too many emails from our CEO (or senior pastor)—and I can't discern what's really important and what's really just an FYI.
❑	❑	I faithfully respond to every email or phone call from our top leader within 24 hours.
❑	❑	Our Board Policies Manual establishes the type and frequency of reports from our top leader.

T	F	CEO/Senior Pastor
❑	❑	I feel guilty that I'm not reporting adequately to the board in between meetings.
❑	❑	To be honest, I used to send more reports to the board, but no one ever read them.
❑	❑	I wish I felt more supported by the board. This is hard work. I don't think board members pray for me.
❑	❑	I have to keep the main thing the main thing. If I take time to write board reports that no one reads, it's a lose/lose.
❑	❑	Our Board Policies Manual establishes the type and frequency of reports from our top leader.

Attn: Church Boards

Invite your senior pastor and/or executive pastor to create a first draft of this tool—and then ask for suggestions at your next board meeting. Customize it for the unique needs of your church—and your senior pastor's reporting style. Once you've tested it for several months, it should require only about 15 minutes per month for the senior pastor's final touches—before it goes out to the board. Try it!

[1] Adapted from Dan Busby and John Pearson, *Lessons From the Nonprofit Boardroom: 40 Insights for Better Board Meetings*, 2d ed. (Winchester, VA: ECFAPress, 2018), 29–35. See "Lesson 6: Eliminate Hallway Whining."

The 5/15 Monthly Report to the Board

A Communication Template

"CEO's 5/15 MONTHLY REPORT TO THE BOARD"

✓ 5 Minutes to Read and 15 Minutes to Write

✓ emailed on the 15th of every month

John was blessed a few years back when Pat Clements, board chair at Christian Management Association (now Christian Leadership Alliance), introduced John to a simple, time-saving template. Like clock-work, on the fifteenth of every month, Clements, then CEO at Church Extension Plan, sent his 5/15 Report to his national board. So John borrowed his brilliant idea and customized the template for the board of CMA and sent it out—like clockwork—on the fifteenth of every month. The hallway whining stopped.

The Big Idea. Once formatted and tested, leaders can write this report in just 15 minutes each month and board members should be able to read it in just five minutes—and have a regular diet of both the good news, the new news, and the bad news. The content and frequency can be memorialized in the Board Policies Manual, by board action, so there is 100 percent board agreement on a report that serves the board's needs and expectations.

The Content. Customize the report so it meets your needs, but it will likely be five or less pages, easy to read, with a standard template. The content might include (in this order):

- Date/To/From/Subject
- Next Board Meeting (date, location, special details)
- Monthly Dashboard Report on 3-5 Board-approved Annual "SMART" Goals (Peter Drucker: "If you have more than five goals, you have none.")
- Committee Highlights (bullet points only—and only if there is new information)
- Board Nominating Committee "Pipeline Report" (the running list of confidential prospect names under consideration)
- Monthly Financial Report Summary (YTD vs. Budget for revenue and expense)
- Major Program Notes (bullet points)
- Ministry Events Calendar & Top Leader's Travel Schedule (12 to 24 months)
- A Brief Ministry Story—for the Board's Encouragement (maximum of one-half page)
- Prayer Requests
- Personal Note from the Top Leader (one brief paragraph)
- Board Meeting Schedule (12 to 24 months: dates/locations/times and 2-4 key agenda items for each meeting: audit, CEO/Senior Pastor annual performance review, budget approval, annual board self-assessment, etc.)

After you have created and tested the first draft, with feedback from the board and the senior team, it's ready to systematize and delegate to the executive assistant or another team member.

5/15 MONTHLY REPORT TO THE BOARD - SCHEDULE			
Point Person	**Task**	**Deadline**	**Done Date**
Executive Assistant	Begin Draft #1: request reports from others	7th	
Senior Staff and Committee Chairs	Submit updates for reports	10th	
CFO	Submit Monthly Financial Report Summary	12th	
Executive Assistant	Draft #2: All reports compiled	13th	
CEO/Senior Pastor	Dictate or approve "Ministry Story" and personal note; approve final draft	14th	
Executive Assistant	Email PDF of report to all board members (cc: senior team). Plus: quarterly or occasionally, also email to selected former board members.	15th	

REMINDER #1: Readers or Listeners? Not all board members are readers. Listening is the preferred learning style for some people. If possible, accommodate both styles. So for your listeners, record the information, and email the recording—but keep it to five minutes or less.

REMINDER #2: The Four Social Styles. It's important for CEOs to communicate effectively to all four social styles:

- **The Analytical Style** appreciates communication that is clear and concise.
- **The Driving Style** prefers a "just stick to the facts" report.
- **The Amiable Style** says "get to know me"—and content is often a lower priority.
- **The Expressive Style** wants you to listen to their opinions—so in your report ask for feedback and input.[2]

NEXT STEPS:

- ❑ **Step 1. Decide:** Assess the current status of between-meeting reports to the board and discern if a "5/15 Monthly Report to the Board" is worthy of a 90-day test period.
- ❑ **Step 2. Delegate:** Inspire your top leader to delegate to the executive assistant or another staff person the gathering of information.
- ❑ **Step 3. Respond:** Ask board members to respond to every monthly report—with a quick email thanks, a note, or a voicemail message.

2 For more on the four social styles, visit *http://tracom.com/social-style-training/model* or read the faith-based resource by Bob Phillips and Kimberly Alyn, *How to Deal With Annoying People: What to Do When You Can't Avoid Them* (Eugene, OR: Harvest House, 2005).

CUSTOMIZE THIS TEMPLATE TO INFORM AND INSPIRE YOUR BOARD—BETWEEN MEETINGS!

5/15 Monthly Report to the Board

5 Minutes to Read 15 Minutes to Write

- ☑ **CEOs/Senior Pastors:** Use this monthly report template and delegate the "starter" to a team member or your executive assistant.

  Then you can finish it with your unique style. Email it on the same date each month.

- ☑ **Board Members:** Feedback is the breakfast of champions. Email a quick "Thanks—I got it!"

CEOs:

The 5/15 Monthly Report template on the following pages is designed for a CEO's report to the nonprofit board.

Senior Pastors:

Download the 5/15 Monthly Report template and customize it for your church board's unique culture and reporting requirements.

> ***"Just because it's common for CEOs to ask for forgiveness rather than permission doesn't mean it's acceptable."***[3]
>
> Jim Brown

[3] Jim Brown, *The Imperfect Board Member: Discovering the Seven Disciplines of Governance Excellence* (San Francisco: Jossey-Bass, 2006), 111.

Nonprofit Template

3J Global Ministries "5/15 Report"

"5 MINUTES TO READ—AND 15 MINUTES TO WRITE"

CEO's Monthly Report to the Board of Directors

Office: (555) 123-1234 • Mobile: (555) 987-6543
P.O. Box 123 • Anytown, CA 92673
John@3JGlobalMinistries.org • www.3JGlobalMinistries.org

DATE: May 15, 2020

TO: 3J Global Ministries Board of Directors
cc: Bob Brown and Brenda Smith, Senior Team

FROM: John W. Doe, CEO

RE: CEO's 5/15 Monthly Report to the Board

Greetings. This is the first of what will now be monthly board reports to you, generally emailed on the 15th of each month. I'm calling this the "5/15 Report" – because it will take you just five minutes to read and it will take me just 15 minutes to write (with Bob's help).

This new report format will be especially helpful to show to board prospects as we brief them on the work and ministry of 3J Global Ministries.

◉ **Board Governance**

Board Meeting Schedule: Draft #1. As we confirm dates for future board meetings (calls and in-person meetings), we'll fill in the meeting grid (see attached).

Next Board Meeting. See you soon! Our next board meeting is our annual board retreat, as you know. (See the email from Bob with all the details.)

Date May 21-22, 2020

Day/Time Thursday 4:00 p.m. to Friday 4:00 p.m.

Location ABC Conference Center, Phoenix, Arizona

CEO's Annual S.M.A.R.T. Goals. Attached is the Monthly Dashboard Report and update on my 2020 CEO S.M.A.R.T. Goals.

Board Documents. I am working with Enrique, and the team, to create drafts for your consideration on the following board documents:

- Board Member Annual Affirmation Statement (& Conflict of Interest Statement)
- Board Nominating and Election Policies (tied to our bylaws and/or proposed bylaw changes)
- Board Chair and Officers Position Description (roles and responsibilities)
- Board Policies Manual and Prime Responsibility Chart
- Board Member Orientation Notebook
- ECFA Accreditation (*www.ECFA.org*)

CONFIDENTIAL!

"Prospect Pipeline" for Future Board Members. Here's an update from the Nominating Committee on the board prospects they are interviewing. See the board schedule for when board members will be elected.

No.	Prospect	Recommended by:	Status	Nom. Comm. Action
1	Jane Doe	Nominating Committee	Fully vetted	Yes
2	Billy Kim	Nominating Committee	In process	
3	Alberto Villa	CEO	Fully vetted	Yes
4	David Burry	Former Board Member	Still "dating"	
5				

- **Financial Reports**

As of April 30, 2020, we are $_____ ahead/behind of our proposed four-month budget forecast.

Financial Report	**FY2020** 12-Month Budget 1/1/20 - 12/31/20	**FY2020** 4-Month Budget 1/1/20 - 12/31/20	**FY2020** 4-Month Actual 1/1/20 - 12/31/20	**FY2020** 4-Month Variance 1/1/20 - 12/31/20
Revenue	$	$	$	$
Expense	$	$	$	$
Net Income	$	$	$	$

The full four-month financial reports and dashboards will be uploaded to the board portal by May 25, 2020.

- **2020 Major Program Notes**

Per board consensus, the following programs are updated here monthly, along with the staff's color-coding of the progress on program goals YTD.

	Program	News/Changes/Concerns
1	3J Global Ministries Forums	• Attendance is up by 30% YTD. • Revenue will hit, perhaps, 40% of annual budget.
2	Vision 2022 Initiative	• Slow start due to staff changes, but we will recover.
3	Mission Agency Partners Program	• Just exceeded our FY goal of 10 partners. PTL!
4	Local Church Ambassadors Program	• May need to postpone until next fiscal year. • Pilot program was a dismal failure, but we learned a lot!
5	Care Coaches Initiative	• Our consultant brought huge value. Client satisfaction goals of 4.2 on a scale of 1.0 to 5.0. Exceeded goal!
6	MissionFuture Capital Campaign	• Frankly, a disappointing start. May ask our Executive Committee to address our rather conservative fund development policies. • Consultant is concerned, but we just received a major unrestricted gift of $100,000. (Details at our meeting.)

GREEN on Target	YELLOW Caution!	RED Alert!

Additional Program Notes:

- **2020-2021 Calendar**

Here are our key calendar dates, our travel, speaking engagements, etc. This is listed for board members both as an "FYI" and as a prayer reminder.

Date	Event	Venue City, State	Sponsored by:
Year 2020			
Year 2021			

- **A 3J Global Ministries Story—For Your Encouragement!**

Here's a portion of an email we received from an enthusiastic volunteer!

"Headline . . . "

Insert story here . . . . .

Thank you, Board Members!

Thank you for investing your time and resources in 3J Global Ministries! (Add more here…)

Gratefully,

John

P.S. Please note our future board meeting dates on the attached pages.

2020 Board Meeting Schedule (Draft 1 as of Jan. 15, 2020)

Year 2020	Day/Time	Location	Agenda
February 20	Thursday 10:00 a.m. PDT	Telephone Conference Call	• Review FY2019 financial reports • Quarterly Update Call
May 21-22	Thursday 4:00 p.m. to Friday 4:00 p.m.	Annual Board Retreat ABC Conference Center Phoenix, AZ	• 2021-2022 Strategic Plan brainstorming • Board Governance update • Nominating Committee Report • Financial Reports (4 months) • CEO's Annual S.M.A.R.T. Goals – Review • Board Meeting Schedule approval
August 20	Thursday 10:00 a.m. PDT	Telephone Conference Call	• Review 7-month financial reports • Quarterly Update Call • CONFIDENTIAL: Prospect Pipeline Report (future board members)
November 19	Thursday 8:30 a.m. – 4:30 p.m. Optional Dinner with spouses at 6:00 p.m.	Chicago	• Welcome to New Board Members • Financial Reports (10 months) • 2021 Annual Plan, Calendar, Leading Indicators and CEO's 2021 S.M.A.R.T. Goals • 2021 Budget • Plans for CEO's Performance Review (based on 2020 S.M.A.R.T. Goals) • Board Governance Committee Report on Board Member Self-Assessment Survey (Oct.) • Appointment of Auditor

2021 Board Meeting Schedule (Draft 1 as of ________, 2020)

Year 2021	Day/Time	Location	Agenda

Note to CEOs:

Some CEOs also attach their ***Monthly Dashboard Report*** (see Tool #11) to the *5/15 Report.* Or you may prefer to email it as a separate document.

TOOL #11: Monthly Dashboard Report

Use this tool to update the board and senior team on the CEO's or senior pastor's Top-5 Annual S.M.A.R.T. Goals. (Send updates at least monthly.)

This 1-Page Color-Coded Tool Is Powerful!

Color-Code Your Dashboard Reports Red? Yellow? Green?

Does your boardroom's culture welcome bad news?

Note this leadership insight/tool from the retired CEO of Ford, Alan Mulally:

> Mr. Mulally also changed the way Ford's management team operated. He instituted a weekly meeting where each manager presented a report on his [or her] areas, coded in green, yellow or red, to show whether business was on target.
>
> After a few months, Mark Fields—now Mr. Mulally's designated successor—confessed that a vehicle program for a new sport-utility vehicle was 'red.' Mr. Mulally clapped in response, setting an atmosphere where Ford executives felt encouraged to air bad news, rather than let problems fester.[1]

"Earlier I discussed Dr. Gail Matthew's research that individuals with written goals were 39.5 percent more likely to succeed. But there's more to the story. Individuals who wrote their goals and sent progress reports to friends were 76.7 percent more likely to achieve them."[2]

Gary Keller with Jay Papasan

[1] Neal E. Boudette, Christina Rogers, and Joann S. Lublin, "Ford Chief Executive Officer Alan Mulally's Legacy: Setting Ford on a Stronger Course." Posted April 21, 2014. *The Wall Street Journal*: *www.wsj.com/articles/SB10001424052702304049904579515852823291232.*

[2] Gary Keller and Jay Papasan, *The ONE Thing: The Surprisingly Simple Truth Behind Extraordinary Results* (Austin, TX: Bard, 2012), 187.

The Monthly Dashboard Report

The Color-coded Progress Report on the Top Leader's Top-5 Annual S.M.A.R.T. Goals

When boards and their top leaders understand the awesome power of S.M.A.R.T. goals, they'll never go back to the mishmash days of unfocused work and misplaced priorities. The CEO/senior pastor and the board must agree on the Top Leader's Top-5 Annual S.M.A.R.T. Goals.

Certainly one of John's top-10 life experiences was sitting at the feet of Peter Drucker, the father of modern management, for four days in Estes Park, CO, with 30 other Christian leaders in August 1986.

> Peter Drucker shared a story at that small retreat gathering that John will never forget. Drucker talked about his consulting role with a Fortune 500 company CEO. At the end of the morning meeting, Drucker asked the CEO the $64,000 question: "This afternoon, as you know, I'm meeting with your vice president of marketing. What key result must he achieve by the end of this year?"
>
> According to Drucker, the CEO answered immediately. "That's easy," the corporate titan responded. "My VP's key result for this year must be ABC." (While I was at the four-day retreat when Drucker told this story, I don't recall the specifics, so we'll call the goal "ABC.")
>
> That afternoon, Drucker met with the VP of marketing and began, "This morning, as you know, I met with your CEO and asked him what key result you must achieve this year." The VP, like his boss, responded immediately. "That's a no-brainer. We've agreed that the key result for marketing must be XYZ!"
>
> Drucker wasn't surprised and those of us in the room all laughed because we've been there. We walk out of staff meetings, strategy meetings, and strategic planning retreats and we're absolutely convinced that the assignments and end results are crystal clear. The target on the wall is "ABC," but somehow, a vice president hears "XYZ."

What's the solution? Every team member must put in writing (repeat: put in writing) their *Top-5 S.M.A.R.T. Goals* that are reviewed, prayed over, and affirmed by the team. And the CEO/Senior Pastor must go one step further: his or her *Top-5 S.M.A.R.T. Goals* must be approved and affirmed by the board. Then the *Monthly Dashboard Report* becomes a fairly simple report—not on how busy the top leader is—but on results achieved, as God blesses.

Do this—and you'll be amazed at the awesome power of S.M.A.R.T. goals![3]

[3] John Pearson, *Mastering the Management Buckets: 20 Critical Competencies for Leading Your Business or Nonprofit* (Ventura, CA: Regal , 2008). For more on S.M.A.R.T. goals, read the Results Bucket, the Strategy Bucket, and the Meetings Bucket chapters.

S.M.A.R.T. GOALS DEFINED

Annual S.M.A.R.T. Goals must be Specific, Measurable, Achievable, Realistic, and Time-related.

S.M.A.R.T. GOALS ARE:

- ☑ **Specific.** What results will be achieved?
- ☑ **Measurable.** Is the exact target and finish line crystal clear? (You'll know when to celebrate because everyone will agree the goal was reached.)
- ☑ **Achievable.** Is it pie-in-the-sky? Has this goal ever been achieved before—by anyone?
- ☑ **Realistic.** Is the goal rooted in reality and aligned with adequate resources? Does the team agree? Has your spiritual discernment process confirmed this? Note: "The actual achievement of audacious goals is very uncommon."[4]
- ☑ **Time-related.** Is there a specific target date (not a target month)? (Instead of generalizing with "3rd Quarter," commit to "Sept. 30, 2020.")

SMART GOALS and *NOT-SO-SMART GOALS*:

GOALS	Specific	Measurable	Achievable	Realistic	Time-Related
■ ***NOT-SO-SMART GOALS***					
1) Plan the best annual meeting event on the planet!					
2) Increase the number of major donors giving $5 billion or more.	✓	✓			
3) Conduct a client satisfaction survey by Sept. 30, 2020.		✓	✓	✓	✓
4) Launch the XYZ Program as soon as possible in numerous cities.					
5) To raise $50,000, ask every donor to give an extra $10 this month.	✓	✓			✓

■ **SMART GOALS**					
1) Survey annual meeting participants on 5 key factors by May 15.	✓	✓	✓	✓	✓
2) Increase the number of major donors by 15% by Oct. 25.	✓	✓	✓	✓	✓
3) Score 4.2 or better on our client satisfaction survey by 9/25/21.	✓	✓	✓	✓	✓
4) Launch the XYZ Program in these 25 cities (see list) by 6/30/21.	✓	✓	✓	✓	✓
5) *Write a goal here:*	✓	✓	✓	✓	✓

[4] Dan Busby and John Pearson, *Lessons From the Nonprofit Boardroom: 40 Insights for Better Board Meetings*, 2d ed. (Winchester, VA: ECFAPress, 2018), 194. Read "Lesson 37: Don't Stretch Credulity With BHAGs and Stretch Goals."

SAMPLE TEMPLATE FOR A NONPROFIT MINISTRY
(Color-Code Each Monthly Progress Report)

S.M.A.R.T. Goals are: ➔ **S**pecific, **M**easurable, **A**chievable, **R**ealistic, and **T**ime-related.

ABC Ministry – CEO Monthly Dashboard Report (2020)
Annual TOP-5 SMART GOALS for Jane Doe

Monthly Update to be submitted to Board of Directors by the 15th of each month.
These FY2020 TOP-5 SMART GOALS were approved by the Board of Directors on Dec. 15, 2019.

FY 2020 – 3 Months **January 1 – March 31, 2020** *Updated on April 15, 2020 by Jane Doe*	**Target Date**	**Monthly Update** **3-Month Report** **Ending 3/31/2020**
1. **Revenue and Expenses.** Achieve the year-end net income goal of $40,000, based on revenue of $500,000 and expense of $460,000.	12/31/20	• On target
2. **Operating Reserves**. Increase operating reserves from $114,000 to $154,000 (equivalent to 4 months of the FY2020 expense budget).	12/31/20	• We are now forecasting just 2 months of reserve by year-end. Finance Comm. will review a revised "Plan B."
3. **Board Member Recruitment.** Assist the board with cultivating up to five new board prospects for terms beginning on Jan. 1, 2021.	9/30/20	• Due to the Project XX crisis, our board chair and I have not invested any time on this.
4. **Three-Year Rolling Strategic Plan:** Based on board feedback, recommend the final version of the 2021-2023 Strategic Plan to the board.	9/15/20	• Board will review at the September board meeting
5. **Vision 2025 Resource Center.** Implement the Phase 1 Pilot Program of the Vision 2025 Virtual Resource Center, including the cultivation, recruitment, orientation and engagement of 2 state coordinators, 10 area coordinators and 50 local church ambassadors.	10/31/20	• On target! Mike Pate has agreed to be our State of Hawaii coordinator! And… 17 new coordinators have also become "Level 3 Donors."

⬆ Color-code each box based on the monthly update.

GREEN **on Target**	**YELLOW** **Caution!**	**RED** **Alert!**

"Goals are over-arching and should be few in number. If you have more than five goals, you have none.

You're simply spreading yourself too thin."[5]

Peter Drucker

[5] Peter F. Drucker, Frances Hesselbein, and Joan Snyder Kuhl, *Peter Drucker's Five Most Important Questions: Enduring Wisdom for Today's Leaders* (Hoboken, NJ: John Wiley & Sons, 2015), 5–6.

6 Questions for the Board About . . .
Your CEO's (or Senior Pastor's) *Top-5 S.M.A.R.T. Goals*

❑ 1. Have we used a spiritual discernment process to discern these goals?

> ***"Just because something is strategic does not necessarily mean it is God's will for us right now."***[6]
>
> Ruth Haley Barton

❑ 2. Are our goals and budget in alignment with our mission and our theology?

> ***"One of the most important questions for nonprofit leadership is, Do we produce results that are sufficiently outstanding for us to justify putting our resources in this area? Need alone does not justify continuing. You must match your mission, your concentration, and your results. Like the New Testament parable of the talents, your job is to invest your resources where the returns are manifold, where you can have success."***[7]
>
> Peter Drucker

❑ 3. Specifically, what are the *Top-5 Goals* that the board wants our CEO/Senior Pastor to achieve this year? (Do they meet the "S.M.A.R.T." criteria?)

> ***"Goals poorly formulated are goals easily forgotten."***[8]
>
> Michael Hyatt

❑ 4. What are the *Top-5 S.M.A.R.T. Goals* each direct report to the CEO/Senior Pastor must achieve this year?

> ***"Every facet of the organization has a person assigned with accountability for ensuring goals are met."***[9]
>
> Verne Harnish

---

[6] Ruth Haley Barton, *Pursuing God's Will Together: A Discernment Practice for Leadership Groups* (Downers Grove, IL: InterVarsity Press, 2012), 99.

[7] Drucker, Hesselbein, and Kuhl, *Peter Drucker's Five Most Important Questions*, 5–6.

[8] Michael Hyatt, *Your Best Year Ever: A 5-Step Plan for Achieving Your Most Important Goals* (Grand Rapids, MI: Baker, 2018), 22.

[9] Verne Harnish, *Scaling Up: How a Few Companies Make It . . . and Why the Rest Don't – Mastering the Rockefeller Habits 2.0* (Ashburn, VA: Gazelles, 2014), 147.

❑ 5. Has the board discussed, discerned, and affirmed no more than five goals for the top leader—and are they in writing and recorded in the board's minutes?

> ***"If you have more than five goals, you have none."***[10]
>
> Peter Drucker

❑ 6. Does the board receive the *Monthly Dashboard Report* from the top leader—every month?

> ***"Boards don't need to hear how busy the CEO is — they need to hear about results."***[11]
>
> Jim Brown

Not All Boards Receive Regular Dashboard Reports

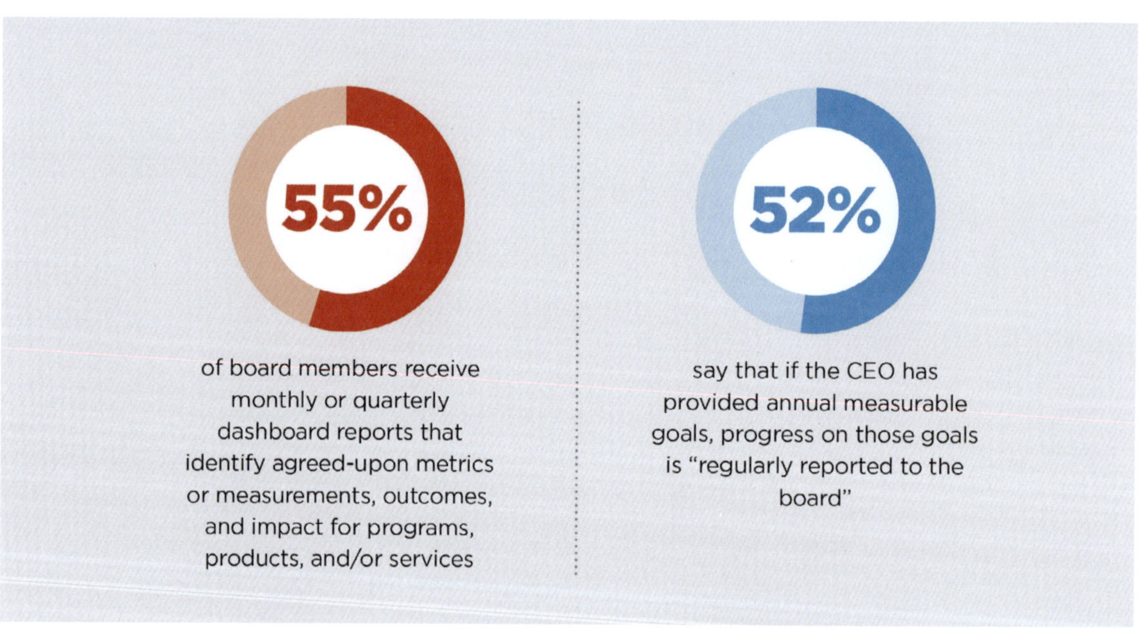

Set Measurable Goals

"Did your CEO offer 3 or more measurable goals that your board approved this year?"

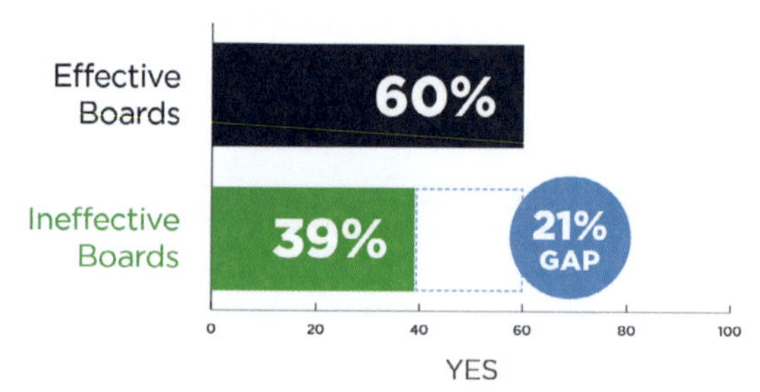

[10] Drucker, Hesselbein, and Kuhl, *Peter Drucker's Five Most Important Questions*, 63.

[11] Jim Brown, *The Imperfect Board Member: Discovering the Seven Disciplines of Governance Excellence* (San Francisco: Jossey-Bass, 2006), 85.

If you prefer "S.M.A.R.T.E.R." Goals to "S.M.A.R.T." Goals, then read this:

Your Best Year Ever:
A 5-Step Plan for Achieving Your Most Important Goals
by Michael Hyatt

- ❑ "Goals poorly formulated are goals easily forgotten."[12]
- ❑ "Dragging the worst of the past into the best of the future is another reason goals fail."[13]
- ❑ "Resources are never—and I mean never—the main challenge in achieving our dreams. In fact, if you already have everything you need to achieve your goal, then your goal's probably too small."[14]

If you prefer another definition of "S.M.A.R.T." then pick or create your own:

- ❑ Specific, Measurable, Achievable, Realistic, Timely
- ❑ Specific, Measurable, Achievable, Relevant, Time-Bound
- ❑ Specific, Measurable, Actionable, Relevant, and Timely (process metrics)
- ❑ Specific, Measurable, Appropriate, Realistic, Time-Bound
- ❑ Specific, Measurable, Attainable, Realistic, Tangible
- ❑ Specific, Measurable, Attainable, Results-oriented, Time-based
- ❑ Specific, Motivating, Achievable, Rewarding, and Tactical

Note: for more definitions of "S.M.A.R.T." goals" visit: *www.acronymfinder.com.*

"Self-assessment is the first action requirement of leadership: the constant resharpening, constant refocusing, never being really satisfied. And the time to do this is when you are successful. If you wait until things start to go down, then it's very difficult."[15]

Peter Drucker

[12] Michael Hyatt, *Your Best Year Ever*, 22.
[13] Ibid., 21.
[14] Ibid., 52.
[15] Drucker, Hesselbein, and Kuhl, *Peter Drucker's Five Most Important Questions*, 5–6.

IMPORTANT! The Monthly Dashboard Report Assumes Your Top Leader Has an Organization-Wide Communication Rhythm

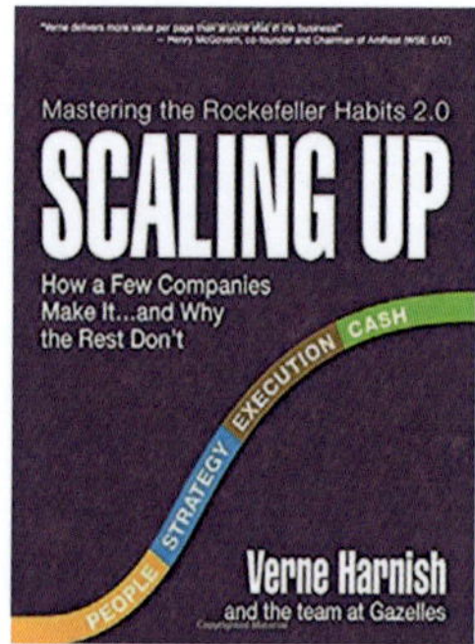

THE 10 HABITS:

"Routines that set you free!"[16]

Effective Boards Inspire Their CEOs and Senior Pastors to Create Robust Communication Flows With Their Teams:
Daily → Weekly → Quarterly → Annually

Learn More: Rockefeller Habits Checklist™

> There are 10 fundamental habits that support the successful execution of your strategy—habits that haven't changed for 100 years since John D. Rockefeller implemented them…
>
> And like the checklists that are critical to the airline industry in making sure planes stay in the air, consider these 10 habits as a 'preflight' checklist for keeping your [organization] growing and ensuring that it doesn't stall out.[17]

Example: **Rockefeller Habits Checklist™ (No. 3 of 10)**

3. **Communication rhythm is established and information moves through organization accurately and quickly.**

   - ❑ All employees are in a daily huddle that lasts less than 15 minutes.
   - ❑ All teams have a weekly meeting.
   - ❑ The executive and middle managers meet for a day of learning, resolving big issues, and DNA transfer each month.
   - ❑ Quarterly and annually, the executive and middle managers meet offsite to work on the 4 Decisions.[18]

Attn: Church Boards

Read Bill Hoyt's practical book, *Effectiveness by the Numbers: Counting What Counts in the Church*, on what should be measured in a local church. The book describes how to count attendance breadth and depth, visitor retention, market share (Saddleback Church's market share is just 4.2 percent in its neighborhood), ministry involvement, community deployment, small groups, the development of leaders, stewardship and tithing, and much more. *Bottom line:* are you measuring your church's biblical mandate of making disciples? "Your mission is what you measure," says Thomas G. Bandy in the foreword.[19]

---

[16] Harnish, *Scaling Up*, 15.

[17] Ibid.

[18] Ibid., 147.

[19] William R. Hoyt, *Effectiveness by the Numbers: Counting What Counts in the Church* (Nashville: Abingdon, 2007).

TOOL #12: Quarterly Board Meeting Agenda and Recommendations

*Use this agenda template to signal the board, seven to 10 days in advance, that this board meeting is **important**—and their insights are needed.*

Read: *Harvard Business Review*

"What Makes Great Boards Great"

by Jeffrey A. Sonnenfeld

Advance Agendas = Board Member Trust

Phone-Book-Size Board Reports?

What kind of CEO waits until the night before the board meeting to dump on the directors a phone-book-size report, that includes buried in a thicket of subclauses and footnotes, the news that earnings are off for the second consecutive quarter? Surely not a CEO who trusts his or her board. Yet this destructive, dangerous pattern happens all the time.

Another sign that trust is lacking is when board members begin to develop back channels to line managers within the company. This can occur because the CEO hasn't provided sufficient, timely information, but it can also happen because board members are excessively political and are pursuing agendas they don't want the CEO to know about.

If a board is healthy, the CEO provides sufficient information on time and trusts the board not to meddle in the day-to-day operations. He or she also gives board members free access to people who can answer their questions, obviating the need for back channels.[1]

Jeffrey Sonnenfeld says that effective boards must do five things:

- ❑ Create a climate of trust and candor
- ❑ Foster a culture of open dissent
- ❑ Utilize a fluid portfolio of roles
- ❑ Ensure individual accountability
- ❑ Evaluate the board's performance

[1] Jeffrey A. Sonnenfeld, "What Makes Great Boards Great." Posted September 2002. *Harvard Business Review*: *https://hbr.org/2002/09/what-makes-great-boards-great.*

Quarterly Board Meeting Agenda and Recommendations

Standard Template for a Nonprofit Organization

Key Elements of an Effective Board Meeting

"Frankly, I don't remember why I called this meeting."

- ❑ **ADVANCE MATERIALS.** Agenda, reports and recommendations arrive seven to 10 days in advance of the meeting.
- ❑ **ADVANCE PREPARATION.** Every meeting is important because the advance agenda and written recommendations signal this—and unexcused absences are rare. Board members prepare—and pray—in advance and come to the board meeting on time, rested, relaxed, and ready to spiritually discern God's voice.
- ❑ **BALANCED CONTENT.** There is a balance of: relational and inspirational; good news and bad news; due diligence and faith-stretching; action and policy; focus on the current year but also the BHAG and the Rolling 3-Year Strategic Plan; *and never staff or volunteer work*!
- ❑ **STRENGTHS ARE LEVERAGED.** The board chair and the CEO lead the board in leveraging the 3 Powerful S's: **S**trengths, **S**ocial styles and **S**piritual gifts.[2]
  - ✓ **S**trengths[3] - *www.gallupstrengthscenter.com/home*
  - ✓ **S**ocial Styles - *www.tracomcorp.com/social-style-training/model*
  - ✓ **S**piritual Gifts - *https://gifts.churchgrowth.org/spiritual-gifts-survey*

[2] John Pearson, *Mastering the Management Buckets: 20 Critical Competencies for Leading Your Business or Nonprofit* (Ventura, CA: Regal, 2008). See The People Bucket, The Team Bucket, The Board Bucket, and The Volunteer Bucket chapters.

[3] Dan Busby and John Pearson, *Lessons From the Nonprofit Boardroom: 40 Insights for Better Board Meetings*, 2d ed. (Winchester, VA: ECFAPress, 2018), 130. Read "Lesson 25: Align Board Member Strengths With Committee Assignments: Leverage the Three Powerful S's."

Fork-in-the-Road Decision: 2 Options to Providing Hard Copies of All Board Materials

- ❑ **Option 1: Use Board Software.** Select one of the many board portal applications, such as BoardEffect.[4]

- ❑ **Option 2: Email PDFs of Board Materials.** Email board materials in advance and offer to provide hard copies in a 3-ring binder format at every board meeting. Once you have used the PDF/hard copy option, you may be able to rely solely on PDFs or transition to the board software option (see Option 1).

Option 2

EXAMPLE – Template for a Nonprofit Organization

Quarterly Board Meeting: Table of Contents

#1. Agenda and Recommendations	**1**
#2. CEO's Report ❑ 5/15 Monthly Report to the Board ❑ CEO Annual S.M.A.R.T. Goals and Monthly Dashboard Report (color-coded)	**2**
#3. Minutes ❑ Board of Directors Minutes ❑ Committee Minutes	**3**
#4. Financial Reports	**4**
#5. Rolling 3-Year Strategic Plan: 2020 – 2022 ❑ Executive Summary ❑ Strategic Plan Placemat (1 page) ❑ Two-page Strategy Summary (per Chapter 5 in *Owning Up*, by Ram Charan)[5]	**5**
#6. Budget: FY2020 (Jan. 1 – Dec. 31, 2020)	**6**
#7. CEOs Personal & Professional Growth Plan ❑ CEO Employment Agreement (Confidential) ❑ Professional Development Plan (including any coaching this year) ❑ Annual Performance Review Process (1-page)	**7**
#8. Board of Directors Directory: Roster, Classes, Terms, Officers, Committees and Board Meeting Calendar (and StrengthsFinder Chart)	**8**
#9. Board Member Commitment Documents ❑ Board Member Annual Affirmation Statement ❑ Conflict of Interest Policies ❑ Confidentiality Policy	**9**
#10. Board Policies Manual (BPM) and Bylaws	**10**

[4] Nick Price, "Why a Board Portal Will Improve the Performance of Your Nonprofit Board." Posted Dec. 7, 2017. *BoardEffect*: *www.boardeffect.com/blog/board-portal-will-improve-performance-nonprofit-board.*

[5] Ram Charan, *Owning Up: The 14 Questions Every Board Member Needs to Ask* (San Francisco: John Wiley & Sons, 2009), 57. Question 5, "Does Our Board Really Own the Company's Strategy," recommends boards have a two-page strategy document available at every meeting to ensure new initiatives are in alignment with the strategy.

EXAMPLE – Template for a Nonprofit Organization

Quarterly Board Meeting

Agenda and Recommendations

Note: Reports and materials not included in this pre-meeting email will be distributed at the meeting (or via email in advance of the meeting).

Time Estimate	Action Requested ❑ Inform ❑ Accept ❑ Approve	Name	TAB	Topic
8:00 a.m.				***Arrive early for coffee and goodies!***
9:00 a.m.		Chair		**A. Call to Order**
9:05 a.m.		Chair		**B. Roll Call and Welcome to Board Members and Guests** ❑ Guest: ❑ Guest:
9:06 a.m.				**C. Opening Prayer**
9:10 a.m.	❑ Approve	Sec.	3	**D. Minutes of the Last Meeting (Date: __________ 2020)** ❑ [Or . . . consider a "Consent Agenda"][6]
9:15 a.m.		Chair		**E. Personal Updates** (Board and Guests) & Prayer
9:45 a.m.		Gov. Chair		**F. 10 Minutes for Governance** ❑ Discuss in teams of two: "Lesson 23: Focus on Mission Impact and Sustainability" (*Lessons From the Nonprofit Boardroom*, Second Edition, pages 117-122)
9:55 a.m.				**Break**
10:10 a.m.	**DISCERN!**	Chair	5	**G. "Heavy Lifting" for This Meeting: Our Assumptions About the Next Three Years (3 Teams)** ❑ **Pre-reading:** *Rumsfeld's Rules: Leadership Lessons in Business, Politics, War, and Life*, by Donald Rumsfeld (see the chapter on assumptions)* ❑ See Strategic Plan document, "Assumptions—Draft 2.0" on pages 11-12.
12:00 p.m.			5	**Working Lunch (3 Teams)**
1:00 p.m.	❑ Accept	CEO	2	**H. CEO's Report and Q&A**
1:25 p.m.	❑ Accept	Treas.	4	**I. Financial Reports** ❑ Jan. 1 – July 31, 2020 (7-Month Report) ❑ See Financial Dashboards on the Board Portal

[6] Jeremy Barlow, "What Is a Consent Agenda for a Board Meeting?" Posted February 6, 2016. *BoardEffect: www.boardeffect.com/blog/what-is-a-consent-agenda-for-a-board-meeting/.*

Time Estimate	Action Requested ❑ Inform ❑ Accept ❑ Approve	Name	TAB	Topic
1:35 p.m.	❑ Inform	Chair	1	**J. Committee Reports** ❑ Executive Committee (, Chair) ❑ Governance Committee (, Chair) ❑ Finance & Audit Committee (, Chair)
2:00 p.m.				**Break**
2:15 p.m.	❑ Approve	Comm. Chairs	1	**K. Recommendations** (see attached pages)
3:00 p.m.		Chair		**L. Executive Session** (without CEO, staff, or guests) ❑ Executive Session ❑ Board Meeting resumes with Executive Session summary to CEO (and time for Q&A)
3:30 p.m.		Chair		**M. New Business**
4:00 p.m.		Chair		**N. Closing Prayer and Adjournment**

*Conduct an assumptions exercise

Rumsfeld's Rules: Leadership Lessons in Business, Politics, War, and Life

by Donald Rumsfeld

Rumsfeld recommends four steps in strategic planning:[7]

Step 1: Set the Goals

Step 2: Identify Your Key Assumptions*

Step 3: Determine the Best Course of Action

Step 4: Monitor Progress Through Metrics

"The very reason for labeling them assumptions is to stress that they are not facts."[8]

"The assumptions stage of strategic planning tends to be one of the most neglected. Assumptions are often left unstated, it being taken for granted that everyone around a table knows what they are, when frequently that is not the case. The assumptions that are hidden or held subconsciously are the ones that often get you into trouble."

"It is possible to proceed perfectly logically from an inaccurate premise to an inaccurate and unfortunate conclusion."[9]

Donald Rumsfeld

[7] Donald Rumsfeld, *Rumsfeld's Rules: Leadership Lessons in Business, Politics, War, and Life* (New York: HarperCollins, 2013), 65–88.
[8] Ibid., 75.
[9] Ibid., 76.

Recommendations

(Insert "MSC" by recommendation, if approved: "Moved, Seconded, and Carried")

A. Financial

____ **Recommendation #2020-22. Financial Report.** That the board accept the unaudited financial reports for (see Tab 4):

- January 1 – July 31, 2020 (7 months)

B. Board Governance

____ **Recommendation #2020-23. Minutes.** That the board approve the minutes of the following meetings and board actions:

- May 22, 2020 – Board Meeting minutes (see Tab 3)
- July 31, 2020 – Email Ballot on XYZ Contract (see Tab 3)

"PLACEHOLDER" RECOMMENDATION FOR FUTURE USE:

____ **Recommendation #2020-___. Board Member Candidates.** That the board invite the following people to join the Board of Directors, as recommended and vetted by the Nominating Committee:

Class of 2021 to 2023:

1)____________________

2)____________________

3)____________________

C. President/CEO

____ **Recommendation #2020-24. President/CEO's Annual Performance Assessment.** That the board approve the following format and structure for the President/CEO's Annual Performance Assessment:

- November 3, 2020 Online Survey sent to the board, CEO and his direct reports
- November 14, 2020 Survey deadline
- November 20, 2020 (At Board Meeting) - Review of surveys and review of results and next steps agreed upon by Board and CEO

Recommendation #2020-25. President/CEO's Employment Agreement. That the CEO's Employment Agreement (Draft # _____, July 1, 2020) be approved for the period of _____ to_____ .

D. Strategic Plan/Annual Plan and Programs/Products/Services

____ **Recommendation #2020-26. 2021-2023 Rolling 3-Year Strategic Plan.** That the board approve the latest edits on the 2021-2023 Strategic Plan (See Tab 5), including:

- Executive Summary (Tab 5)
- Strategic Plan Placemat: Version 4.0 (Tab 5)
- Two-page Strategy Summary ("Does our board own the strategy?" per Ram Charan)

E. New Business/Recommendations*

Recommendation #2020-_____.

Recommendation #2020-_____.

Recommendation #2020-_____.

Board Meeting Resources:

Lessons From the Nonprofit Boardroom: 40 Insights for Better Board Meetings, Second Edition (2018)

by Dan Busby and John Pearson

Read:

- ❑ Lesson 19: **Never Throw Red Meat on the Board Table**. Boards need advance preparation to fully address complex issues.
- ❑ Lesson 5: **Before the Board Meeting**. Collaborate, then wisely build the board meeting agenda.
- ❑ **Blog:** *http://nonprofitboardroom.blogspot.com/*

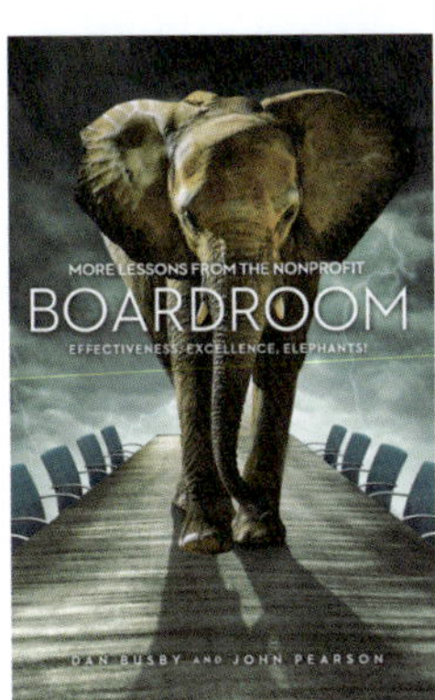

More Lessons From the Nonprofit Boardroom: Effectiveness, Excellence, Elephants!

by Dan Busby and John Pearson

- ❑ Lesson 39: **Identify Your Key Assumptions.** An inaccurate premise may lead to a colossal flop!

"Policy Development is the board's chief occupation."

Why should you include the latest version of your Board Policies Manual (BPM) in the binder (or on the board portal) for every meeting?

Boards That Make a Difference: A New Design for Leadership in Nonprofit Organizations

by John Carver

According to Policy Governance® Guru John Carver, "Governing by policy means governing out of policy in the sense that no board activity takes place without reference to policies. Most resolutions in board meetings will be motions to amend the policy structure in some way. **Consequently, policy development is not an occasional board chore but its chief occupation."**[10]

[10] John Carver, *Boards That Make a Difference: A New Design for Leadership in Nonprofit Organizations* (San Francisco: Jossey-Bass, 2006), 72.

2020 Board Meeting Schedule (Draft 1 as of Jan. 15, 2020)

Year 2018	Day/Time	Location	Agenda
February 20	Thursday 10:00 a.m. PDT	Telephone Conference Call	• Review FY2019 financial reports • Quarterly Update Call
May 21-22	Thursday 4:00 p.m. to Friday 4:00 p.m.	Annual Board Retreat ABC Conference Center Phoenix, AZ	• 2021-2023 Strategic Plan brainstorming • Board Governance update • Nominating Committee Report • Financial Reports (4 months) • CEO's Annual S.M.A.R.T. Goals – Review • Board Meeting Schedule approval
August 20	Thursday 10:00 a.m. PDT	Telephone Conference Call	• Review 7-month financial reports • Quarterly Update Call • CONFIDENTIAL: Prospect Pipeline Report (future board members)
November 19	Thursday 8:30 a.m. – 4:30 p.m. Optional Dinner with spouses at 6:00 p.m.	Chicago	• Welcome to New Board Members • Financial Reports (10 months) • 2021 Annual Plan, Calendar, Leading Indicators and CEO's 2019 S.M.A.R.T. Goals • 2021 Budget • Plans for CEO's Performance Review (based on 2020 S.M.A.R.T. Goals) • Board Governance Committee Report on Board Member Self-Assessment Survey (Oct.) • Appointment of Auditor

2021 Board Meeting Schedule (Draft 1 as of ________, 2020)

Year 2021	Day/Time	Location	Agenda

How Often Should Boards Meet?

"The Texas legislature is in session for 140 days every two years. We are working on changing that so we'll be in session for two days every 140 years!"[11]

Texas Governor Greg Abbott

[11] Texas Governor Greg Abbott interview with Neil Cavuto on "Cavuto: Coast to Coast," Fox Business Network, March 21, 2018.

TOOL #13: Board Retreat Read-and-Reflect Worksheets

Prior to your next board retreat, create a "Read-and-Reflect Worksheet" and inspire the board to read one governance book in preparation for your retreat.

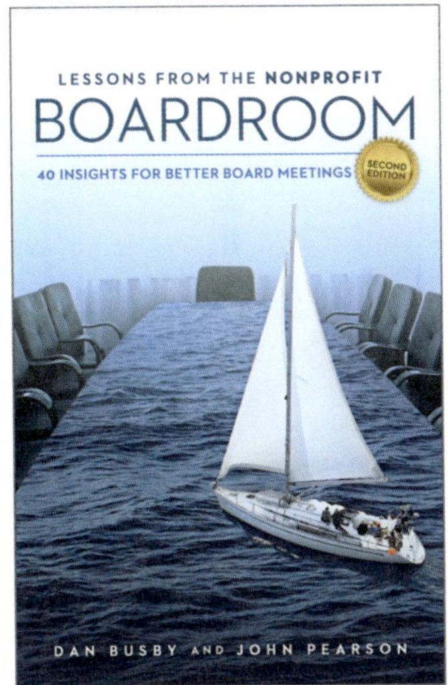

Read Lesson 38, "Great Boards Delegate Their Reading."[1]

What Would Chesterton Read?

Great Boards Read at Least One Book a Year!

"If you were marooned on a desert island and could have only a single book with you, what would you choose? Somebody once asked this question of G. K. Chesterton. Given his reputation as one of the most erudite and creative Christian writers in the first half of the twentieth Christian century, one would naturally expect his response to be the Bible. It was not. Chesterton chose *Thomas' Guide to Practical Shipbuilding*."[2]

He finally had time to develop a marketing plan.

[1] Dan Busby and John Pearson, *Lessons From the Nonprofit Boardroom: 40 Insights for Better Board Meetings*, 2d ed. (Winchester, VA: ECFAPress, 2018), 198–201.

[2] John Ortberg, *The Life You've Always Wanted: Spiritual Disciplines for Ordinary People* (Grand Rapids, MI: Zondervan, 1997), 188.

Board Read-and-Reflect Worksheets

Great Boards Read at Least One Book a Year!

7 Book Options

If you select one of these seven books for your next retreat, distribute the appropriate worksheet, with the book, to each board member. Or, select an alternate governance book and create your own customized worksheet.

❑ **Option 1:**

Owning Up: The 14 Questions Every Board Member Needs to Ask

by Ram Charan

> With the right composition, a board can create value; with the wrong or inappropriate composition, it can easily destroy value.[3]

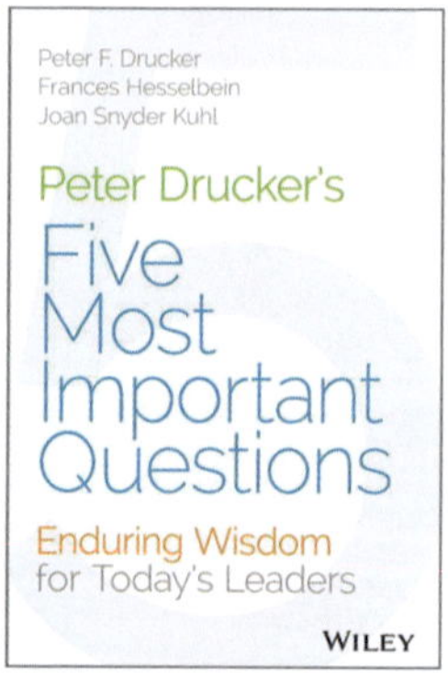

❑ **Option 2:**

Peter Drucker's Five Most Important Questions: Enduring Wisdom for Today's Leaders

by Peter F. Drucker, Frances Hesselbein, and Joan Snyder Kuhl

Question 2: Who Is Our Customer? On Uber and other disrupters: "Of course, the traditional taxi drivers are outraged, and some cities have banned Uber because it is threatening the well-oiled machine of mediocrity."[4]

❑ **Option 3:**

Called to Serve: Creating and Nurturing the Effective Volunteer Board

by Max De Pree

Effective boards do very good planning, says De Pree. He lists three planning questions and then suggests who must be involved in the planning. "…some people need to be involved, to be blunt, because they are going to pay the bill."[5]

---

[3] Ram Charan, *Owning Up: The 14 Questions Every Board Member Needs to Ask* (San Francisco: Jossey-Bass, 2009), 1.

[4] Peter F. Drucker, Frances Hesselbein, and Joan Snyder Kuhl, *Peter Drucker's Five Most Important Questions: Enduring Wisdom for Today's Leaders* (Hoboken, NJ: John Wiley & Sons, 2015), 26.

[5] Max De Pree, *Called to Serve: Creating and Nurturing the Effective Volunteer Board* (Grand Rapids, MI: Wm. B. Eerdmans, 2001), 14–15.

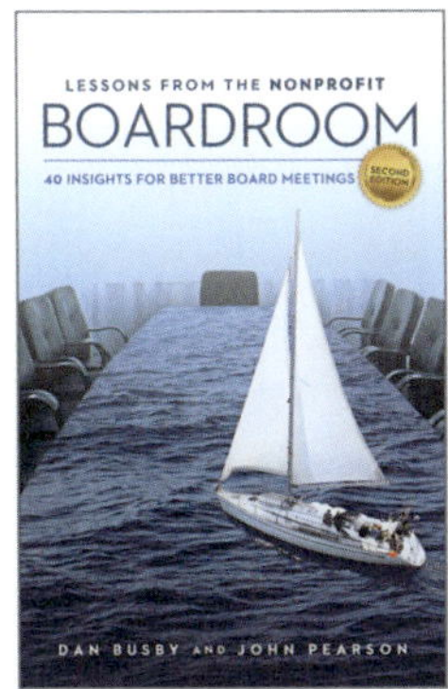

❑ **Option 4:**

Lessons From the Nonprofit Boardroom: 40 Insights for Better Board Meetings, Second Edition

by Dan Busby and John Pearson

Lesson 37: Don't Stretch Credulity With BHAGs and Stretch Goals. "The actual achievement of audacious goals is very uncommon."

❑ **Option 5:**

Lessons From the Church Boardroom: 40 Insights for Exceptional Governance

by Dan Busby and John Pearson

Lesson 14: Be Intentional About Your First 30 Minutes. "Does your board meeting need a refresh—so you experience holy moments more frequently?"

❑ **Option 6:**

More Lessons From the Nonprofit Boardroom: Effectiveness Excellence, Elephants!

by Dan Busby and John Pearson

Lesson 26: Big Rocks, Pebbles, and Sand. Ministry boards have a natural gravitational pull toward issues that should be reserved for staff.

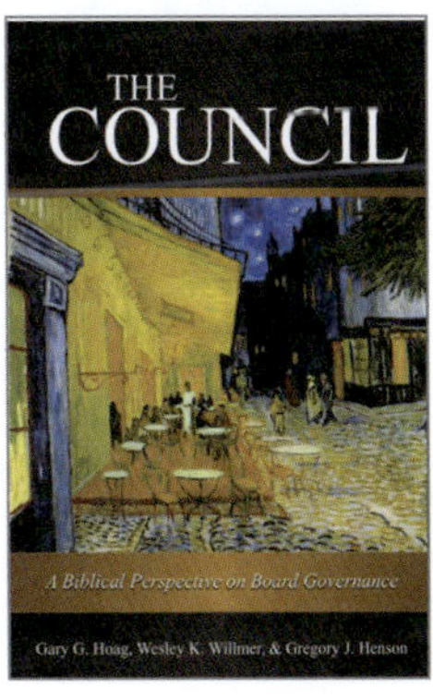

❑ **Option 7:**

The Council: A Biblical Perspective on Board Governance

by Gary G. Hoag, Wesley K. Willmer, and Gregory J. Henson

Chapter 6: Model: Spiritual Practices for Maintaining a Biblical Mindset

❑ Option 1: Board Retreat Read-and-Reflect Worksheet

Great boards read at least one book a year to improve their governance competencies!

2020 Board Retreat
XYZ Ministry
Read-and-Reflect Worksheet

MEMO

DATE: May 1, 2020

TO: Board of Directors

FROM: Jane Doe, Board Chair

RE: Preparation for Board Retreat

We are prayerfully looking forward to meeting with all of you at the 2020 Board Retreat. We want our time together to reflect the heart and spirit of Henry Blackaby's memorable comment, "Find out what God is doing…and then join Him."

This worksheet is designed to get everyone thinking in advance. We urge you to invest time in prayer and preparation BEFORE the board retreat. Please note this wisdom from Peter Drucker:

"The best way to predict the future is to create it."
Peter Drucker

✦ **Reading Assignment**

You have received the book, *Owning Up: The 14 Questions Every Board Member Needs to Ask*, by Ram Charan. We'll dig deep into this resource. And we'll heed this reminder, also from Peter Drucker: **"Plans are only good intentions unless they immediately degenerate into hard work."**

Drucker also said that "we now accept the fact that learning is a lifelong process of keeping abreast of change. And the most pressing task is to teach people how to learn." So…what can we learn that will help us with board governance?

A "Read-and-Reflect Worksheet" is attached to this memo. After you've read the book, please jot down your thoughts and then bring the worksheet with you to the board retreat. Thanks! We're looking forward to seeing how God will lead you in this process.

✦ **Why is this important?** James M. Kouzes and Barry Z. Posner note in *The Leadership Challenge*:

"Leaders must challenge the process because systems will unconsciously conspire to maintain the status quo and prevent change."

Read-and-Reflect Worksheet

XYZ Ministry • 2020 Board Retreat

→Please bring the worksheet with you to the Board Retreat

"The business landscape has changed. The game has changed. What boards do needs to change as well."

Ram Charan

From the book's website: *www.ram-charan.com*

Your world as a director has suddenly changed. You've seen members of other boards take the heat when their companies imploded. The managements of Lehman Brothers, Bear Stearns, Merrill Lynch, and Washington Mutual clearly failed, but so did their boards. Now the board of every company beset with problems is coming under scrutiny.

The pressure is on. Your board must own up to its accountability for the performance of the corporation. **Governance now means leadership**.

Boards must change their modus operandi to address the new and complex issues that are emerging. These include:

- Ensuring liquidity in the context of the global financial crisis
- Setting CEO performance targets in a very uncertain economy
- Assessing strategy and enterprise risk under extreme volatility

So what should boards do now? What should they be talking about in their meetings and executive sessions? What decisions must they make? How assertive must they be regarding company priorities and operating goals?

In *Owning Up*, business advisor and corporate governance expert Ram Charan answers these and other burning questions on the minds of directors and business leaders. He describes best practices that are emerging in boardrooms he has observed firsthand. And he provides practical recommendations on a range of issues, from compensation to dealing with external constituencies. Wisely attuned to the human side, he confronts the need for some boards to refresh their composition and for others to rebalance their board dynamics.

Directors, CEOs, general counsels, and operating executives will find here the guidance they need to meet the new and rising standards for corporate governance in this demanding business environment.

<table>
<tr><td>Reading Options</td><td>Owning Up: The 14 Questions Every Board Member Needs to Ask,
by Ram Charan

2 Options:
☑ Option 1. Read the entire book—and you may win a Chick-fil-A card!
☑ Option 2. Read these “6 Most Relevant Chapters” and scan the rest:
❑ Chapter 1: Board Composition
❑ Chapter 2: Risk Management
❑ Chapter 4: CEO Succession
❑ Chapter 5: Corporate [Ministry] Strategy
❑ Chapter 12: Board Self-Assessment
❑ Chapter 13: Micromanaging</td></tr>
<tr><td>Introductory Critical Questions:</td><td>Ram Charan makes some very strong statements at the beginning of the book. Do you agree with them?</td></tr>
</table>

Do you agree or disagree?	**Yes! Absolutely!**	**To Some Extent**	**Not at All**
1. Has the business landscape changed?			
2. Has “the game” changed?			
3. Do boards need to change?			
4. Does our board need to change?			
5. Charan says that “Governance now means leadership.” Do you agree?			

What changes, if any, should be made—and by when?

Question 1: **Board Composition** **A "Top-6 Chapter"**	Chapter 1 Question 1: Is our Board Composition Right for the Challenge? Key Thought or Question: Implication or Application for our Board:

Question 2: **Risk Management** **A "Top-6 Chapter"**	Chapter 2 Question 2: Are We Addressing the Risks that Could Send our Company Over the Cliff? Key Thought or Question: Implication or Application for our Board:

Question 3: **Crisis Management**	Chapter 3 Question 3: Are We Prepared to Do our Job Well When a Crisis Erupts? Key Thought or Question: Implication or Application for our Board:

Question 4: **Succession Planning** **A "Top-6 Chapter"**	Chapter 4 Question 4: Are We Well Prepared to Name our Next CEO? Key Thought or Question: Implication or Application for our Board:

Question 5: **Corporate (Ministry) Strategy** **A "Top-6 Chapter"**	Chapter 5 Question 5: Does our Board Really Own the Company's [Ministry's] Strategy? Key Thought or Question: Implication or Application for our Board:

Question 6: **Information Management**	Chapter 6 Question 6: How Can We Get the Information We Need to Govern Well? Key Thought or Question: Implication or Application for our Board:

Question 7: **Executive Compensation**	Chapter 7 Question 7: How Can our Board Get CEO Compensation Right? Key Thought or Question: Implication or Application for our Board:

Note: Question 8, "The Lead Director" is not included here. Few, if any, nonprofit organizations or churches create a "Lead Director" position on the board.

Question 9: **Governance Committee**	Chapter 9 Question 9: Is our Governance Committee Best of Breed? Key Thought or Question: Implication or Application for our Board:

Question 10: **Maximizing a Board Member's Time**	Chapter 10 Question 10: How Do We Get the Most Value out of Our Limited Time? Key Thought or Question: Implication or Application for our Board:

Question 11: **Executive Sessions**	Chapter 11 Question 11: How Can Executive Sessions Help the Board Own Up? Key Thought or Question: Implication or Application for our Board:

Question 12: **Board Self-Assessment Process** **A "Top-6 Chapter"**	Chapter 12 Question 12: How Can our Board Self-Evaluation Improve our Functioning and our Output? Key Thought or Question: Implication or Application for our Board:

Question 13: **Micromanaging Symptoms** **A "Top-6 Chapter"**	Chapter 13 Question 13: How Do We Stop from Micromanaging? Key Thought or Question: Implication or Application for our Board:

Note: Question 14, "How Prepared Are We to Work with Activist Shareholders and Their Proxies?" is not included here. However, you may want to add your own question about the care and feeding of major donors. For a resource, read Part 3, "The Role of the Board in Development," in *Development 101: Building a Comprehensive Development Program on Biblical Values*, by John R. Frank and R. Scott Rodin (Colbert, WA: Kingdom Life Publishing and Steward Publishing, 2015).

→ **REMINDER**: Please bring the worksheet with you to the Board Retreat

❑ Option 2: Board Retreat Read-and-Reflect Worksheet

Great boards read at least one book a year to improve their governance competencies!

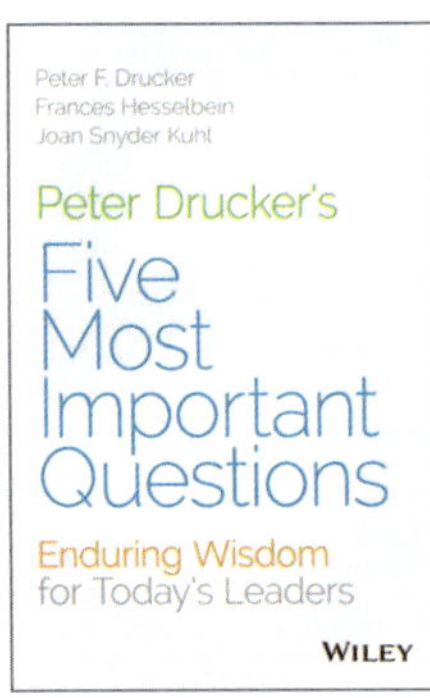

2020 Board Retreat
XYZ Ministry
Read-and-Reflect Worksheet

MEMO

DATE: May 1, 2020

TO: Board of Directors

FROM: Jane Doe, Board Chair

RE: Preparation for Board Retreat

We are prayerfully looking forward to meeting with all of you at the 2020 Board Retreat. We want our time together to reflect the heart and spirit of Henry Blackaby's memorable comment, "Find out what God is doing…and then join Him."

This worksheet is designed to get everyone thinking in advance. We urge you to invest time in prayer and preparation BEFORE the board retreat. Please note this wisdom from Peter Drucker:

"The best way to predict the future is to create it."
Peter Drucker

✦ **Reading Assignment**

You have received the book, *Peter Drucker's Five Most Important Questions*, by Peter Drucker, Frances Hesselbein, and Joan Snyder Kuhl. We'll dig deep into this resource. And we'll heed this reminder, also from Peter Drucker: **"Plans are only good intentions unless they immediately degenerate into hard work."**

Drucker also said that "we now accept the fact that learning is a lifelong process of keeping abreast of change. And the most pressing task is to teach people how to learn." So…what can we learn that will help us with board governance?

A "Read-and-Reflect Worksheet" is attached to this memo. After you've read the book, please jot down your thoughts and then bring the worksheet with you to the board retreat. Thanks! We're looking forward to seeing how God will lead you in this process.

✦ **Why is this important?** James M. Kouzes and Barry Z. Posner note in *The Leadership Challenge*:

"Leaders must challenge the process because systems will unconsciously conspire to maintain the status quo and prevent change."

Read-and-Reflect Worksheet

XYZ Ministry • 2020 Board Retreat

→Please bring the book and the worksheet with you to the Board Retreat

Peter Drucker on **Self-Assessment**:

"**Self-assessment** is the first action requirement of leadership: the constant resharpening, constant refocusing, never really being satisfied."

"The **self-assessment** process is a method of assessing what you are doing, why you are doing it, and what you must do to improve an organization's performance."

<table>
<tr><td>Reading Options</td><td>2 Options:
☑ Option 1. Read the entire book (and the commentary on each question)— and you may win a Chick-fil-A card! You'll especially enjoy the interesting color commentary by millennials in each chapter.
☑ Option 2. Read just Peter Drucker's comments on the five questions (less than 35 pages).
❑ Why Self-Assessment? (pages 1-6)
❑ Question 1: What Is Our Mission? (pages 7-11)
❑ Question 2: Who Is Our Customer? (pages 19-23)
❑ Question 3: What Does the Customer Value? (pages 35-38)
❑ Question 4: What Are Our Results? (pages 47-52)
❑ Question 5: What Is Our Plan? (pages 61-68)</td></tr>
<tr><td>Introductory Critical Questions:</td><td>Peter Drucker makes a very strong statement at the beginning of the book. (page 2) Do you agree with him?
Although I don't know a single for-profit business that is as well managed as a few of the nonprofits, the great majority of the nonprofits can be graded a 'C' at best. Not for lack of effort; most of them work very hard. But for lack of focus, and for lack of tool competence. I predict that this will change, however, and we at the Drucker Foundation [now the Frances Hesselbein Leadership Institute] hope to make our greatest impact in these areas of focus and tool competence.</td></tr>
</table>

Question 1: **What is our mission?**	Our organization's mission is to...

Is it time to re-visit our mission statement? Measure our mission statement against this "Top-10 List" below:

Top-10 Ingredients That Create an Eloquent and Arresting Mission Statement[6] **Our mission...**	**Yes! Absolutely!**	**To Some Extent**	**Not at All**
1. Is short and easily focused.			
2. Is clear and easily understood.			
3. Defines why we do what we do, why the organization exists.			
4. Does not prescribe means.			
5. Is sufficiently broad.			
6. Provides direction for doing the right things.			
7. Addresses our opportunities.			
8. Matches our competence.			
9. Inspires our commitment.			
10. Says what, in the end, we want to be remembered for.			
Bonus Question: Does our mission statement...fit on a t-shirt?			

MISSION:

Skip LeFauve: "Having a well-defined mission gives leaders a way to resolve competing interests and make better decisions."[7]

Frances Hesselbein: "Revisit the mission every three years, each time refine or amend it so that it reflects shifts in the environment and the changing needs of the customers."[8]

[6] These 10 questions are adapted from Peter Drucker, *The Five Most Important Questions Self-Assessment Tool: Participant Workbook* and Leader to Leader Institute (San Francisco: Jossey-Bass, 2010), 12.
[7] Skip LeFauve quoted in the "Leadership Tip of the Day" email from the (now-named) Frances Hesselbein Leadership Forum, June 1, 2010, *www.HesselbeinForum.org*.
[8] Frances Hesselbein quoted in the "Leadership Tip of the Day" email from the (now-named) Frances Hesselbein Leadership Forum, October 2, 2010, *www.HesselbeinForum.org*.

Question 2: **Who is our customer?**	Peter Drucker distinguishes between "primary" and "supporting" customer and says that your primary customer is "the person whose life is changed through your work." In your opinion, who is our primary customer?

Question 3: **What does our customer value?**	Research is a key part of discerning what our customers value. What would you like to know about our primary customer that we don't know today?

"It is your customers' expectations you are trying to meet, not your own."[9]

Berhnard Schroeder

[9] Berhnard Schroeder quoted in the "Leadership Tip of the Day" email from the (now-named) Frances Hesselbein Leadership Forum, October 14, 2015, *www.HesselbeinForum.org*.

Question 4: **What are our results?**	In all of his writings, Drucker talks about planned abandonment—"sloughing off yesterday." What are some of the sacred cows or dead horses we should abandon in order to make room for our most critical priorities and the achieving of God-honoring results?[10]

Question 4: **What are our results?** *Optional Homework*	John Pearson, author of *Mastering the Management Buckets: 20 Critical Competencies for Leading Your Business or Nonprofit*, begins his book (the first "bucket" or core competency) with "The Results Bucket." Optional: Visit: *http://managementbuckets.com/results-bucket* to download and read "The Results Bucket" chapter from John's book. Then . . . please jot down any insights that would apply to our present and future situation. Insights:

"Dakota tribal wisdom says that when you discover a dead horse, the best strategy is to dismount."[11]

Elmer Towns and Warren Bird

10 Read more about sacred cows and dead horses in "Lesson 23: Focus on Mission Impact and Sustainability" in *Lessons From the Nonprofit Boardroom* by Dan Busby and John Pearson.

11 Elmer Towns and Warren Bird, *Into the Future: Turning Today's Church Trends Into Tomorrow's Opportunities* (Grand Rapids, MI: Fleming H. Revell, 2000), 14.

Question 5: **What is our plan?**	Peter Drucker says that an effective plan involves five elements: • Abandonment • Concentration • Innovation • Risk taking • Analysis In your opinion, which one of the five elements (above) are we most competent in? Why? Which one element (above) needs more of our focus? Why?

Thanks for praying and preparing for our important time together!

"Is there anyone here who, planning to build a new house, doesn't first sit down and figure the cost so you'll know if you can complete it? If you only get the foundation laid and then run out of money, you're going to look pretty foolish. Everyone passing by will poke fun at you: 'He started something he couldn't finish.'"

Luke 14:28-30 (The Message)

More Drucker Resources

- ❑ **Visit:** The Drucker Bucket: *www.managementbuckets.com/drucker-bucket*
- ❑ **Read:** *Drucker & Me: What a Texas Entrepreneur Learned from the Father of Modern Management*, by Bob Buford
- ❑ **Read:** *The Practical Drucker: Applying the Wisdom of the World's Greatest Management Thinker*, by William A. Cohen

❑ Option 3: Board Retreat Read-and-Reflect Worksheet

Great boards read at least one book a year to improve their governance competencies!

Called to Serve:
Creating and Nurturing the Effective Volunteer Board
by Max De Pree

- ❑ Contrarian wisdom!
- ❑ Just 91 pages!

Do it yourself version!

- ☑ **Step 1:** Inspire a board member to create a customized "Read-and-Reflect Worksheet" that aligns with the current and specific needs of your board.
- ☑ **Step 2:** Review the worksheet formats in Option 1 and Option 2—and create your own for *Called to Serve*.
- ☑ **Step 3:** Read the book review and/or ECFA blog posts on *Called to Serve* and select various questions and emphases that address your board's unique situation.

Or…try this at your board retreat:

- ☑ **Assign** a chapter from *Called to Serve* to every board member. Sprinkle the 5-minute or 10-minute chapter reports throughout the board retreat agenda. Use a timer with a buzzer and award gift cards to those who finish on time!

"A good board will measure
the appropriate inputs as well as the outputs.
Failure to measure what matters damages our future"[12]

Max De Pree

[12] Max De Pree, *Called to Serve: Creating and Nurturing the Effective Volunteer Board* (Grand Rapids, MI: Wm. B. Eerdmans, 2001), 21.

30 Tantalizing Topics from Max De Pree's 91-page book

Called to Serve: Creating and Nurturing the Effective Volunteer Board

Source: 30 short blogs posted from Dec. 31, 2016 to Oct. 9, 2017 by John Pearson
Governance of Christ-Centered Organizations (ECFA Blog)

www.ECFAgovernance.blogspot.com

☑	POSSIBLE BOARD MEMBER PRESENTATION TOPICS AT BOARD RETREAT
	Introduction: What Will You Measure in 2017? *http://ECFAgovernance.blogspot.com/2016/12/what-will-you-measure-in-2017.html*
	2. Called to Serve: Violence and Committee Meetings!
	3. Called to Serve: Loyalty Is Never Sufficient
	4. Called to Serve: Challenged With Measurable Work
	5. Called to Serve: How to "Table" a Thank You
	6. Called to Serve: Governance Through the Prism of the Agenda
	7. Called to Serve: The Bell Curve of a Board Meeting
	8. Called to Serve: No Reading Allowed!
	9. Called to Serve: Death by Committee
	10. Called to Serve: What's More Important Than Structure?
	11. Called to Serve: Do Not Censor What the Board Receives
	12. Called to Serve: Coherence With Corrals
	13. Called to Serve: The Prospect Pipeline
	14. Called to Serve: There Are No Committee Statues!
	15. Called to Serve: SILENCE!
	16. Called to Serve: Board Member Self-Measurements
	17. Called to Serve: Be a Frantic Learner!
	18. Called to Serve: If No Progress—Skip the "Progress Report!"
	19. Called to Serve: The Phone-Book-Size Board Packet Syndrome
	20. Called to Serve: Use White Space to Practice Hospitality
	21. Called to Serve: When Your Organization Is Bleeding and Boring Board Members
	22. Called to Serve: The Ten-Foot Pole Tension
	23. Called to Serve: Board Meddling on Management's Turf
	24. Called to Serve: Max's Most Memorable Message (1924–2017)
	25. Called to Serve: What the Board Owes the CEO
	26. Called to Serve: The Error of Leadership Indifference
	27. Called to Serve: Give Space...But Plan Sparingly
	28. Called to Serve: Don't Neglect Your CEO's Growth
	29. Called to Serve: Goal No. 1—Keep Your CEO Alive!
	30. Called to Serve: No Board Detail Is Too Small (Index to 30 Blogs) *http://ECFAgovernance.blogspot.com/2017/10/called-to-serve-no-board-detail-is-too.html*

Book Review

Called to Serve:
Creating and Nurturing the Effective Volunteer Board

by Max De Pree

Your Weekly Staff Meeting eNews[13]
John Pearson, Editor/Publisher

Issue No. 352 of *Your Weekly Staff Meeting* features a "thin book" (just 91 pages) on board governance—the perfect size to inspire your board and educate your staff. And for the record— this is NOT fake news!

A Contrarian's Wisdom: Called to Serve

I tilt towards books that lean towards the contrarian quadrant. Example: former USC President Steven Sample's book, *The Contrarian's Guide to Leadership*. Before buying a book, he prefers a five-minute conversation with someone who has already read it.

So when I had a five-minute conversation with consultant and author Dave Coleman about Max De Pree's 91-page contrarian gem, it fed my board governance book-addicted soul. I love this book and the title: *Called to Serve: Creating and Nurturing the Effective Volunteer Board.*[14]

Contrarian Max De Pree writes:

- "There is a reason why this is a small book. We want it to be useful, but not a burden."
- "We believe good people need reminders and an occasional nudge, not a sermon."
- "A good board will measure the appropriate inputs as well as the outputs. Failure to measure what matters damages our future."
- "My friend Jim Beré…once told me that he would serve only on boards that had hard-working executive committees."

Commenting on board committees, De Pree notes the story of the English visitor who watched his first American football game and observed,

"The game combines the two worst elements of American culture—violence and committee meetings."

Rather than penning a 300-page snoozer, De Pree crafts a coaching conversation (a series of letters) with a young leader and his first CEO/board relationship. It's easy reading and the short epistles are extraordinary.

13 Excerpted from John Pearson, "A Contrarian's Wisdom: Called to Serve," *Your Weekly Staff Meeting* (eNewsletter), December 7, 2016, *http://urgentink.typepad.com/my_weblog/2016/12/called-to-serve-creating-and-nurturing-the-effective-volunteer-board.html.*

14 Max De Pree, *Called to Serve: Creating and Nurturing the Effective Volunteer Board* (Grand Rapids, MI: Wm. B. Eerdmans, 2001).

Board service, writes De Pree, should be "demanding in the best sense of the word." He lists three other characteristics of great boards:

- Lively
- Effective
- Fun to serve on

CEOs will appreciate every page: "...the chief responsibility of boards is to be effective on behalf of the organization." He adds, "Effective boards, in a nutshell:

- remember the long view,
- remember that the president and staff are human,
- and do the work of the board..."

Plus this:

"Most of the work of the board takes place through the implementation of an agenda."

More contrarian pokes-in-the-ribs:

- "Many high-priced consultants will tell you to have the shortest possible mission statement. I don't happen to think that is such a great idea."
- "I feel that the closer an organization comes to being defined as a movement, the closer it will come to fulfilling its potential."
- "I'm a great believer that management should be invited into the board's world but that the board should not go into management's area."
- "The chairperson should not permit anyone to read to the board."

Max De Pree served as board chair of Fuller Seminary—and get this—the seminary honored him with the establishment of the Max De Pree Center for Leadership in 1996. His day job was with Herman Miller, the office furniture company, where he served as president from 1980 to 1987 (and as a board member until 1995). His book, *Leadership Is an Art*, has sold more than 800,000 copies. (See also *Leading Without Power: Finding Hope in Serving Community.*)

Effective boards do very good planning, says De Pree. He lists three planning questions and then suggests who must be involved in the planning. ". . . some people need to be involved, to be blunt, because they are going to pay the bill."

He balances the CFO's involvement in planning with this: "Planning by the board ought always to include the chief financial officer, a bringer of necessary reality to the process. Of course, the chief financial officer should never have a role that stymies the vision. Some realities have priority over numbers."

Oh, my—I could fill a year's worth of eNewsletters with his contrarian coaching!

- "Loyalty by itself is never sufficient. You always have to link loyalty and competence."
- "When an organization demands true leadership and the results justify the time and energy, good boards respond with gusto."
- "Another crime, it seems to me, is to give really good people poor leadership."

Trust me—this book will not disappoint. All 91 pages are packed with power. Perfect snippets for your "10 Minutes for Governance" segment at every board meeting. (You do that, right?) I'll close with a story.

> Addressing the importance of creating time in the agenda for board reflection, he writes, "I remember the story, perhaps apocryphal, about President Eisenhower and his secretary of state, John Foster Dulles. Dulles was an inveterate traveler. He seemed to be on the go continuously. At one point during the discussion of a serious problem, President Eisenhower said to him,
>
> **'Don't just do something,**
> **stand there.'**
>
> Sometimes it's easier to be busy than to take the time to be reflective."

Your Weekly Staff Meeting Questions:

1. Max De Pree writes, ". . . a board can be only as good as management will help it become." *So how effective is your organization's CEO and senior team in helping the board be effective—without inappropriately doing the board's work?*
2. De Pree recommends that "Key proposals and issues like building programs or fund drives should always come to the board through its committees at least twice." *Think back for three years—has this been your practice?*

❑ Option 4: Board Retreat Read-and-Reflect Worksheet

Great boards read at least one book a year to improve their governance competencies!

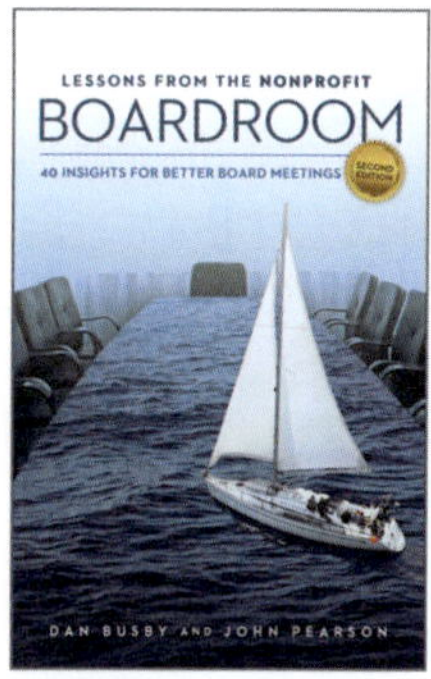

Lessons From the Nonprofit Boardroom
40 Insights for Better Board Meetings, Second Edition

by Dan Busby and John Pearson

- ❑ 40 short lessons
- ❑ 11 practical sections
- ❑ 40 guest bloggers: *www.nonprofitboardroom.blogspot.com*

Do it yourself version!

- ☑ **Step 1:** Read Lesson 38, "Great Boards Delegate Their Reading" and why you should "Deputize a 'Leaders Are Readers Champion.'"
- ☑ **Step 2:** Appoint a "Leaders Are Readers Champion" and inspire that board member to create a customized "Read-and-Reflect Worksheet" that aligns with the current and specific needs of your board.
- ☑ **Step 3:** Review the worksheet formats in Option 1 and Option 2—and create your own version of a *Lessons From the Nonprofit Boardroom* Read-and-Reflect Worksheet.
- ☑ **Step 4:** Read the book review and/or the guest blogger posts on *Lessons From the Nonprofit Boardroom* blog and select various topics and emphases that address your board's unique situation. Visit: *www.nonprofitboardroom.blogspot.com.*

"I love this quote from the U.S. Navy Seals,
'Under pressure you don't rise to the occasion,
you sink to the level of your training. That's why we train so hard.'

By being intentional about ongoing board member education,
organizations are investing in their own preparation to 'rise to the occasion'
that will inevitably emerge—at the least expected moment."[15]

Kent Stroman

[15] Quoted in "Great Boards Delegate Their Reading," by Kent Stroman, *Lessons From the Nonprofit Boardroom* (blog), Aug. 8, 2018, *http://nonprofitboardroom.blogspot.com/2018/08/lesson-38-great-boards-delegate-their.html.*

More Governance Resources: for brief reviews and discussion questions from more than a dozen "Best Board Books," visit the blog series at ECFA's *Governance of Christ-Centered Organizations* blog.

Best Board Books #1: *Boards That Lead*
http://ECFAgovernance.blogspot.com/2018/07/best-board-books-1-boards-that-lead.html

Excerpted from Lesson 38:

Great Boards Delegate Their Reading[16]

Deputize a *"Leaders Are Readers Champion."*

We've observed that there are several best practices that learning boards embrace:

- ❑ **Learning boards feature brief book reviews at every board meeting.** Great boards delegate their reading. Every board member doesn't need to read every governance book. However, with advance planning and motivation, the board chair can inspire individual board members to read and report on a helpful governance book. Some boards set the iPhone timer on the book reviewer for four or five minutes. If the reviewer concludes the report before the bell rings, he or she earns a Chick-fil-A card!
- ❑ **Learning boards inspire everyone to read the same book prior to the annual board retreat.** Select one stimulating book for everyone to read and include a "Read-and-Reflect Worksheet." Provide three options: Good—read five chapters; Better—read eight chapters; Best—read every chapter. Invite selected board members to share four-minute reviews of their assigned chapters. You'll be amazed at the preparation! *No one wants to be remembered as the unprepared presenter.*
- ❑ **Learning boards deputize a "Leaders Are Readers Champion."** Appoint one board member to keep the "leaders are readers" core value on the front burner. Provide a small budget so he or she can keep abreast of the latest trends, resources, training, books, blogs, videos, toolboxes, and websites that will help your board be lifelong learners.

So...what is "the best governance book" your board should read next? It depends, of course, on your unique situation. As you spiritually discern God's direction for your ministry, your journey can be enhanced by the books you read (or listen to). Inspire your board to read!

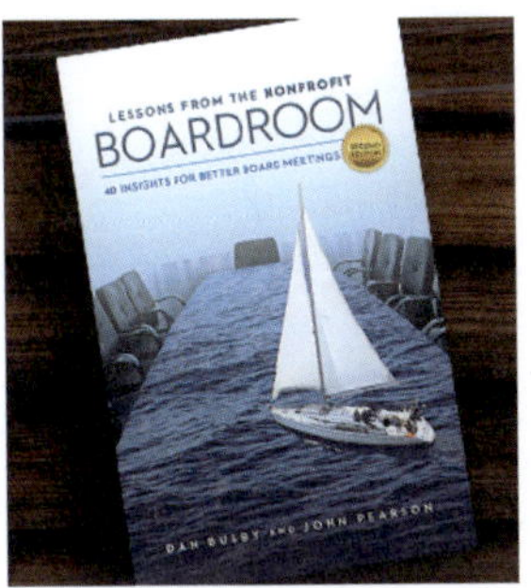

40 Governance Lessons from Dan Busby and John Pearson

Lessons From the Nonprofit Boardroom:
40 Insights for Better Board Meetings

40 guest blogger posts from November 2017 to October 2018
Governance of Christ-Centered Organizations (ECFA Blog)
www.nonprofitboardroom.blogspot.com

See next page ➜

[16] Busby and Pearson, *Lessons From the Nonprofit Boardroom*, 198–201.

☑ **Board Retreat Topics from: *Lessons From the Nonprofit Boardroom***
http://nonprofitboardroom.blogspot.com/

	PART 1: The Powerful Impact of Highly Engaged Boards
❑	1) Wanted: Lifelong Learning Board Members
❑	2) Ask the Gold Standard Question
❑	3) Break Bread, Not Relationships
	PART 2: Boardroom Tools, Templates, and Typos
❑	4) Do Unwritten Board Policies Really Exist?
❑	5) *Before* the Board Meeting
❑	6) Eliminate Hallway Whining
❑	7) Typos Matter!
	PART 3: Nominees for the Board Member Hall of Fame
❑	8) Listen to the Wisdom of Many Counselors
❑	9) Serve With Humility and Experience God's Presence
❑	10) Prioritize Prayer Over Problems
	PART 4: Epiphanies in the Boardroom
❑	11) *Tap! Tap! Tap!*
❑	12) Vision Growth Must Equal Leader Growth
❑	13) If You Need a Volunteer, Recruit a Volunteer
❑	14) If You Need a Board Member, Recruit a Board Member
	PART 5: Boardroom Bloopers
❑	15) Cut Your Losses
❑	16) Date Board Prospects Before You Propose Marriage
❑	17) Sidetrack Harebrained Ideas
❑	18) Do Not Interrupt!
	PART 6: Boardroom Time-Wasters, Troublemakers, and Truth-Tellers
❑	19) Never Throw Red Meat on the Board Table
❑	20) Apply for a Staff Position and You Can Deal With That Issue!
❑	21) Back Off the Ledge of Dysfunctional Mayhem
	PART 7: Boardroom Best Practices
❑	22) The Most Underrated Board Position
❑	23) Focus on Mission Impact *and* Sustainability
❑	24) Ministry Fundraising 101 for Board Members
	PART 8: Boardroom Worst Practices
❑	25) Align Board Member Strengths With Committee Assignments
❑	26) Spotting, Catching, or Exiting a Falling CEO
❑	27) Report Once and Report With Clarity
	PART 9: Holy Ground and Other Locations
❑	28) Slow Down and Wait on God
❑	29) Think and Pray Outside the Box—and the County!
❑	30) The Truck Driver Was No Match for the Faith-Filled Board Chair!
	PART 10: Building a 24/7 Board Culture
❑	31) Cut the Cord! Invite Board Members to Exit When They Don't Live Your Values
❑	32) Loose Lips Sink the Boardroom Ship
❑	33) "Good Is the Enemy of Great"
	PART 11: Boards That Lead and Boards That Read
❑	34) Envision Your Best Board Member Orientation Ever
❑	35) Is Your Board Color-Blind to Hazardous Conditions?
❑	36) Decrease Staff Reporting and Increase Heavy Lifting
❑	37) Don't Stretch Credulity With BHAGs and Stretch Goals
❑	38) Great Boards Delegate Their Reading
❑	39) Invest "10 Minutes for Governance" in Every Board Meeting
❑	40) A Board Prayer

❑ Option 5: Board Retreat Read-and-Reflect Worksheet

Great boards read at least one book a year to improve their governance competencies!

Lessons From the Church Boardroom
40 Insights for Exceptional Governance

by Dan Busby and John Pearson

- ❑ 40 short lessons
- ❑ 10 practical sections
- ❑ 40 guest bloggers: *www.churchboardroom.blogspot.com*

Do it yourself version!

☑ **Step 1:** Read Lesson 1, "Wanted: Lifelong Learners. Would you trust a surgeon who stopped learning?"

☑ **Step 2:** Appoint a *"Leaders Are Readers"* Champion (see "8 Ways to Use This Book at Your Church") and inspire that board member to create a customized "Read-and-Reflect Worksheet" that aligns with the current and specific needs of your church board.

☑ **Step 3:** Read the book review and/or the guest blogger posts on *Lessons From the Church Boardroom* blog and select various topics and emphases that address your board's unique situation. Visit: *http://churchboardroom.blogspot.com*

Attn: Church Boards

Review the worksheet formats in Option 1 and Option 2—and create your own version of a *Lessons From the Church Boardroom* Read-and-Reflect Worksheet, or customize the worksheet here in Option 5.

☑ **Board Retreat Topics from:** ***Lessons From the Church Boardroom***
http://churchboardroom.blogspot.com/

	PART 1: The Powerful Impact of Highly Engaged Boards
❑	1) Wanted: Lifelong Learners
❑	2) Ask the Gold Standard Question
❑	3) Guarding Your Pastor's Soul
❑	4) What Could Possibly Go Wrong?
	PART 2: Boardroom Tools and Templates
❑	5) Do Unwritten Board Policies Really Exist?
❑	6) Enhance Harmony by Clarifying Your Participant Hat Expectations
❑	7) Eliminate Fuzziness Between Board and Staff Roles
	PART 3: Nominees for the Church Board Member Hall of Fame
❑	8) Thrive With Four Kingdom Values
❑	9) Listen to the Wisdom of Many Counselors
❑	10) Prioritize Prayer Over Problems
	PART 4: Epiphanies in the Boardroom
❑	11) *Tap! Tap! Tap!*
❑	12) Looking for Consensus but Finding Division
❑	13) Caution! Understand the Governance Pendulum Principle
❑	14) Be Intentional About Your First 30 Minutes
	PART 5: Boardroom Bloopers
❑	15) Do Not Interrupt!
❑	16) The Bully in the Church Boardroom
❑	17) Don't Be Late or Annoying
	PART 6: Boardroom Time-Wasters, Trouble-Makers, and Truth Tellers
❑	18) Never Throw Red Meat on the Board Table
❑	19) Alert! The ER Factor Causes Value Extraction
❑	20) Apply for a Staff Position and You Can Deal With That Issue!
❑	21) Back Off the Ledge of Dysfunctional Mayhem
❑	22) Big Rocks, Pebbles, and Sand
	PART 7: Boardroom Best Practices
❑	23) Pastor Pay—It's About More Than Just Money
❑	24) How Many Board Members Are Present in Your Boardroom?
❑	25) Address Absentee Board Member Syndrome
❑	26) *Before* the Board Meeting
	PART 8: Boardroom Worst Practices
❑	27) Defending Risks Everywhere Is Not a Strategic Plan
❑	28) Where Two or Three Are Gathered on Social Media…
❑	29) Keeping the Boardroom Afloat
❑	30) 7 Ways to Avoid a Financial Train Wreck
	PART 9: Building a 24/7 Board Culture
❑	31) Watch Out for Boards Asleep at the Wheel
❑	32) Loose Lips Sink the Boardroom Ship
❑	33) "Good Is the Enemy of Great"
❑	34) Break Bread, Not Relationships
❑	35) Common Misconceptions of Board Members
❑	36) You Made Me Better Than I Was
	PART 10: Boards That Lead
❑	37) Is Your Board Color-Blind to Hazardous Condition Signs?
❑	38) Leverage the 80/20 Rule in the Boardroom
❑	39) Don't Stretch Credulity With BHAGs and Stretch Goals
❑	40) A Board Prayer

❑ Board Retreat Read-and-Reflect Worksheet

Great boards read at least one book a year to improve their governance competencies!

Lessons From the Church Boardroom
40 Insights for Exceptional Governance

by Dan Busby and John Pearson

Attn: Board Members

Use this worksheet as you prepare for your 10-minute presentation on your assigned lesson at our church board retreat. Limit the worksheet to one-page only and bring copies for every participant. We suggest you divide your time as follows:

- ✓ Your presentation — 3 minutes (one big idea)
- ✓ Discussion in groups of two — 3 minutes (one question)
- ✓ 30-second group reports — 4 minutes (post insights on flipchart)

You'll receive a Chick-fil-A gift card if you finish your 10-minute segment before the buzzer!

MY NAME	
Lesson Number	
Lesson Title	
Lesson Subtitle	

My favorite quotation:	
My ONE BIG IDEA or take-away from this lesson:	
Insight or implication for our church board:	
Question for groups of two discussions:	

EXAMPLE

Board Retreat Read-and-Reflect Worksheet

Great boards read at least one book a year to improve their governance competencies!

Lessons From the Church Boardroom
40 Insights for Exceptional Governance

by Dan Busby and John Pearson

Attn: Board Members

Use this worksheet as you prepare for your 10-minute presentation on your assigned lesson at our church board retreat. Limit the worksheet to one-page only and bring copies for every participant. We suggest you divide your time as follows:

- ✓ Your presentation — 3 minutes (one big idea)
- ✓ Discussion in groups of two — 3 minutes (one question)
- ✓ 30-second group reports — 4 minutes (post insights on flipchart)

You'll receive a Chick-fil-A gift card if you finish your 10-minute segment before the buzzer!

MY NAME	Gordon Kim
Lesson Number	22
Lesson Title	Big Rocks, Pebbles, and Sand
Lesson Subtitle	Church boards have a natural gravitational pull towards issues that should be reserved for the church staff.

My favorite quotation:	"Is there a 'glass ceiling' that impedes God's work in your church? Many smaller churches fail to grow because their boards are populated with pebble-pickers!"
My ONE BIG IDEA or take-away from this lesson:	Our church board must inspire every board member to address "big rocks" during board meetings—what the book calls "substantive Kingdom agenda items"—not the minutiae of "pebbles and sand." Why? Because "as churches grow, the need for boards to focus on big rocks—multiplies exponentially!"
Insight or implication for our church board:	Our board chair—and all of us—could begin to use this helpful metaphor (big rocks, pebbles, and sand) to keep us focused on the critical agenda topics that ONLY the board can address. We need to remind ourselves—frequently—that when we're tempted to be doing staff work, we may have the wrong staff in place.
Question for groups of two discussions:	QUESTION: Thinking back over our board meetings for the last 12 months, what percentage of agenda items were "big rocks" compared to pebbles and sand topics? Share one suggestion for moving us towards the big rocks.

TOOL #14: The Rolling 3-Year Strategic Plan Placemat

Roll-up your sleeves and gather the strategically-gifted board and senior staff around the table—and begin with this: "What is our strategy?"

Lessons From Bounty Paper Towels!

"Sameness Isn't Strategy. It's a Recipe for Mediocrity."

Study *Playing to Win: How Strategy Really Works*, by A.G. Lafley and Roger L. Martin, with your team and you'll appreciate the practical approach to creating a winning strategy. You'll learn what strategy is, and what strategy is all about (choice). And you'll also learn why P&G discerned that one paper towel product was inadequate for their numerous customer segments.

And this reminder also from Bob Hisrich and John Pearson:

"Give people the choice to say 'no' to a few options—yet still say 'yes.'"[1]

Read pages 4 and 5 of *Playing to Win*—and you're hooked (and convicted)! The authors list five ineffective ways that many leaders use when defining and addressing the strategy process:

- ☑ 1) "They define strategy as vision.
- ☑ 2) They define strategy as a plan.
- ☑ 3) They deny that long-term (or even medium-term) strategy is possible.
- ☑ 4) They define strategy as the optimization of the status quo.
- ☑ 5) They define strategy as following best practices."

Lafley and Martin add, "Every industry has tools and practices that become widespread and generic. Some organizations define strategy as benchmarking against competition and then doing the same set of activities but more effectively. **Sameness isn't strategy. It is a recipe for mediocrity.**"[2]

[1] John W. Pearson and Robert D. Hisrich, Ph.D., *Marketing Your Ministry: Ten Critical Principles* (Brentwood, TN: Wolgemuth & Hyatt, 1990), 98.

[2] A.G. Lafley and Roger L. Martin, *Playing to Win: How Strategy Really Works* (Boston: Harvard Business Review Press, 2013), 4–5, 36.

The Rolling 3-Year Strategic Plan Placemat (1-Page Tool)

TOOL #14 INCLUDES:

- ❑ **1. THE STRATEGIC PLAN PLACEMAT IS THE FINAL STEP, NOT THE FIRST STEP**
  The Rolling 3-Year Strategic Plan Placemat (1-Page Tool)
- ❑ **2. POP QUIZ! BOARD AND STAFF READINESS ASSESSMENT**
  The 7 Reasons Why Strategic Plans Fail
- ❑ **3. ONE PLANNING APPROACH**
  A Strategic Plan Task Force (Small Teams with Big Tasks!)
- ❑ **4. RECOMMENDED FAITH-BASED RESOURCE**
  Breakthrough: Unleashing the Power of a Proven Plan
- ❑ **5. THE G.N.O.M.E. CHART**
  Delineating the Board's Role and the Staff's Role
- ❑ **6. MORE RESOURCES ON STRATEGIC PLANNING**
  Be Strategic About Strategic Planning

Attn: Church Boards

While this template (and the example) is for a nonprofit ministry, your church's Strategic Planning Task Force can easily adapt it for use in your church. We recommend that both board and team members become familiar with a wide variety of secular resources and planning methodologies (see several mentioned in this chapter), plus these Christ-centered resources:

- ☑ *Breakthrough: Unleashing the Power of a Proven Plan*, by Randon A. Samelson (Colorado Springs, CO: Counsel & Capital, 2014)
- ☑ *Lessons From the Church Boardroom: 40 Insights for Exceptional Governance*, by Dan Busby and John Pearson (ECFAPress, Winchester, VA: 2019). See especially Lesson 38, "Leverage the 80/20 Rule in the Boardroom," and Lesson 39, "Don't Stretch Credulity with BHAGs and Stretch Goals."
- ☑ *Pursuing God's Will Together: A Discernment Practice for Leadership Groups*, by Ruth Haley Barton (Downers Grove, IL: InterVarsity Press, 2012)

❑ 1. The Strategic Plan Placemat Is the Final Step, Not the First Step

Numerous organizations have used this tool over the years—the Strategic Plan Placemat (11" x 17" in color) because it is an excellent one-page summary of their plans for the next three years. It's "rolling," because it rolls over every year—as one more year is added. So you're always looking ahead three years.

But . . . before you rush to print . . . STOP!

The Strategic Plan Placemat is the *final* step,
not the *first* step,
in your strategic planning process.

Don't skip the hard and important work
just to meet a board meeting deadline!

When you download the 11" x 17" Word document template for "The Rolling 3-Year Strategic Plan Placemat," be sure to note one approach (there are dozens) for your strategic planning process. On the following pages, you'll find helpful resources, an example of the placemat, and several excellent books.

Obviously, this one-page summary document—ultimately—is the culmination of very hard, disciplined work with both the staff and the board. **It's the end result, not the beginning.**

On the following pages, you'll see the process John often uses with clients. The CEO appoints a "Champion" for each segment (based on the champion's "3 Powerful S's: Spiritual Gifts, Strengths, and Social Style"). Then the champion works with a small team or task force of three to five others. Assignments and worksheets are provided for each team—and the champions meet once a month, or so, in person or via video conference to update each other.

These are tools that have worked for John and other facilitators—based on how God has wired them. Others have different and effective ways of discerning God's direction for the future. But note Ruth Haley Barton's reminder **"Just because something is strategic does not necessarily mean it is God's will for us right now."**[3]

"Your strategic planning consultant/facilitator/volunteer will use different tools to get you to the top of Mount Everest (a completed plan). But it's important to let your facilitator use his or her own tools!"[4]

David Schmidt

[3] Ruth Haley Barton, *Pursuing God's Will Together: A Discernment Practice for Leadership Groups* (Downers Grove, IL: InterVarsity Press, 2012), 99.

[4] Thanks to friend and colleague, David Schmidt of Wise Planning, for introducing us to the strategic plan placemat concept years ago. He knows how to get clients to the top of Mt. Everest! Visit: *https://wiseplanning.net.*

The Rolling 3-Year Strategic Plan Placemat (1-Page Tool)

See sample 11" x 17" (landscape format) strategic plan placemat example on next page →

Download the template for "The Rolling 3-Year Strategic Plan Placemat." We recommend:

- ❑ 11" x 17" landscape on high quality paper
- ❑ Full-color placemat provided to every board member and staff member
- ❑ Enlarged version displayed in boardroom and lunchroom
- ❑ Select a Bible verse that summarizes your aspirations.

XYZ International's Strategic Plan: 2020 – 2022

"Commit your actions to the Lord, and your plans will success." (Proverbs 16:3 NLT)

(Logo here)	(Slogan here)
MISSION Why we exist.	Our mission is to…
VALUES How we will treat each other and our constituents.	We value: • ____________ • ____________ • ____________
VISION What we want to be in the future.	Our vision is to…
BHAG Not achievable without God's unique blessing.	By ____, 2022, our Big HOLY Audacious Goal is to… Note: The BHAG should be written as a "SMART Goal" and be measurable, memorable, and succinct. (For balance, read *The Choice: The Christ-Centered Pursuit of Kingdom Outcomes*,[5] and Lesson 37 in *Lessons From the Nonprofit Boardroom*, "Don't Stretch Credulity With BHAGs and Stretch Goals." The actual achievement of audacious goals is very uncommon."[6]

Visionary Priorities (S.M.A.R.T. Goals)	Year 1: **2020**	Year 2: **2021**	Year 3: **2022**	Add **2023** by 11/15/2020
#1: (verb)… **TO BUILD a…**	• ______ • ______ • ______	• ______ • ______ • ______	• ______ • ______ • ______	
#2: (verb)… **TO CREATE a…**	• ______ • ______ • ______	• ______ • ______ • ______	• ______ • ______ • ______	
#3: (verb)… **TO ENRICH a…**	• ______ • ______ • ______	• ______ • ______ • ______	• ______ • ______ • ______	

Version 1.0 (Nov. 15, 2019). This Rolling 3-Year Strategic Plan Placemat is updated annually by November 15 and is ready for board approval at the year-end board meeting. **S.M.A.R.T. Goals** are: **S**pecific, **M**easurable, **A**chievable, **R**ealistic, and **T**ime-related.

[5] Gary G. Hoag, R. Scott Rodin, and Wesley K. Willmer, *The Choice: The Christ-Centered Pursuit of Kingdom Outcomes* (Winchester, VA: ECFAPress, 2014).

[6] Dan Busby and John Pearson, *Lessons From the Nonprofit Boardroom*, 2d ed. (Winchester, VA: ECFAPress, 2018), 194–97.

AMBASSADORS FOOTBALL   **FOOTBALL ◆ FAITH ◆ FUTURE**

The Rolling 3-Year Strategic Plan ▪ 2020 to 2022

MISSION	**OUR MISSION IS TO COMMUNICATE THE GOOD NEWS OF JESUS TO ALL PEOPLE THROUGH FOOTBALL.**
VISION	**OUR VISION IS THE TRANSFORMATION OF INDIVIDUALS AND COMMUNITIES THROUGH INDIGENOUS FOOTBALL OUTREACH.**
VALUES	1) **We value FOOTBALL:** We participate in football at all levels with passion, excellence and respect. 2) **We value CHURCH:** We uphold the long-term, transformative role of the Church in the world. 3) **We value TEAM:** We identify and collaborate with others in the pursuit of shared goals. 4) **We value SERVICE:** We follow the example of Jesus by leading through service and prioritising the marginalised.
BHAG	**Our Big Holy Audacious Goal**: By December 31, 20____, to…

	2020	2021	2022	2023 to be added by Nov. 15, 2020
VISIONARY PRIORITIES➔	**BUILD** (START WITH A VERB…)	**CREATE** (START WITH A VERB…)	**SUSTAIN** (START WITH A VERB…)	
GOAL #1	**#1. Enrich** ________: By Dec. 31, 2020, enrich _____ so that there are more than ______ (units) serving at least _______.	**#1. Enrich** ________: By Dec. 31, 2021, enrich _____ so that there are more than ______ (units) serving at least _______.	**#1. Enrich** ________: By Dec. 31, 2022, enrich _____ so that there are more than ______ (units) serving at least _______.	
GOAL #2	**#2. Grow** ________: By Dec. 31, 2020, grow _____ so that there are more than ______ (units) serving at least _______. ▪ Example: ____________ ▪ Example: ____________ ▪ Example: ____________	**#2. Grow** ________: By Dec. 31, 2021, grow _____ so that there are more than ______ (units) serving at least _______. • Example: ____________ • Example: ____________ • Example: ____________	**#2. Grow** ________: By Dec. 31, 2022, grow _____ so that there are more than ______ (units) serving at least _______. • Example: ____________ • Example: ____________ • Example: ____________	
GOAL #3	**#3. Research** ________: By June 30, 2020, research _____ to discern if we should launch XYZ Program in 2021. ▪ Example: ____________ ▪ Example: ____________ ▪ Example: ____________	**#3. Research** ________: By Dec. 31, 2021, research the effectiveness of ABC Program to discern if we should stop, continue or grow in 2021-22 • Example: ____________ • Example: ____________ • Example: ____________	**#3. Research** ________: By April 30, 2022, retain outside counsel to conduct a "top-to-bottom" program audit of all programs, products and services to be presented to ________ no later than Dec. 31, 2022. ▪ Example: ____________ ▪ Example: ____________ ▪ Example: ____________ ▪	

S.M.A.R.T. GOALS ARE: Specific, Measurable, Achievable, Realistic, Time-related

▶ This Rolling 3-Year Strategic Plan is updated annually by Nov. 15 and ready for board approval by Dec. 15 of each year. ◀ **"Commit your actions to the Lord, and your plans will succeed."** (Proverb 16:3 NLT)

Used by permission.

Ambassadors Football ▲ The Rolling 3-Year Strategic Plan ▲ Strategic Plan Placemat

Strategic Plan Placemat: 11" x 17" (landscape format)

EXAMPLE ONLY: The template on the previous page is just that—a template. Use the categories, if helpful, or create your own categories. If possible, begin each goal with a VERB (enrich, grow, research, engage, retain, abandon, pray, train, build, etc.). The final approved version will be the one-page summary of other documents, often including a supplementary document with 3-5 "S.M.A.R.T. Goals" for every team member. And…you're NOT done until you have created monthly "dashboard" reporting templates (See Tool #11.)

Ambassadors Football (Example Only: Used by permission.)

	Year 1: 2020
Visionary Priorities ➡	**BUILD A GLOBAL EVANGELISM MOVEMENT BY INSPIRING AND EQUIPPING 35 COUNTRIES WITH AMBASSADORS FOOTBALL EXPERTISE AND RESOURCES BY DEC. 31, 2022.**
GOAL #1	**#1. Enrich Current Country Relationships:** By Dec. 31, 2020, enrich the international work and scope of AF so that all 25 country leaders (and their indigenous boards) rate AF support and services at 4.0 on a scale of 1 to 5 (5.0 is excellent).
GOAL #2	**#2. Grow by 3 Countries:** By Dec. 31, 2020, welcome at least 3 new country relationships (for a total of 28 total countries)—and affirm that the new countries have met the criteria per the "XYZ Relationship" document, to include: • Indigenous board of at least ____ people. • Three-year sustainability plan • Partner Relationship with a current AF country
GOAL #3	**#3. Research & Teach Best Practices:** By June 30, 2020, research the best practices of AF's strongest countries and document 3 to 5 country models for effective ministry and create a 2021-2022 strategy for training these models/best practices to the other current and new countries. • Example: Case Study or Online Course or Webinars • Example: Consultant Team (of current country directors) • Example: Regional "McDonald's University" model • And…identify 2-4 other international ministry organizations that have moved from 25 to 50 countries (and how they did it).

Read more about Ambassadors Football, a unique international organization ministering through football (soccer) around the world. *www.ambassadorsfootball.org*

❑ 2. POP QUIZ! Board and Readiness Assessment The 7 Reasons Why Strategic Plans Fail

Don't assume that your organization is ready for a strategic planning process. Susan A. Waechter warns CEOs that "strategic planning often requires the board and staff to tolerate a level of vulnerability as they go through the process." She adds, "Participants should trust each other before beginning the process because negative feedback and criticism are common."[7]

Caution! The sum total of your board's and staff's prior strategic planning experiences whether in your organization or elsewhere (if negative)—may do serious damage to any future planning effort. Don't neglect what Waechter labels the "Planning to Plan" phase to assess readiness.

As part of the "Planning to Plan" introduction, perhaps at a joint board and senior team one-day offsite retreat, use this 15-minute pop quiz exercise on the next page.

POP QUIZ Steps:

- ❑ **Step 1:** Download and distribute the "Pop Quiz" page to each participant.
- ❑ **Step 2:** Invite a participant to read "Reason #1" out loud and—in teams of two—ask participants to indicate the "problem level" of this statement (1, 2, 3, 4, or 5).
- ❑ **Step 3:** Ask another participate to read "Reason #2" out loud—and repeat this process for all seven reasons (actually eight!) on why strategic plans fail.
- ❑ **Step 4 Summary:** Distribute red and green straw vote cards to each participant—and reading the statements out loud again—ask each team member to vote YES or NO on each statement, asking "Is this a major issue we will need to address before jumping in?" This will enable you to check the temperature of your organization's readiness to launch a strategic planning process.

Facilitator Suggestion: Be prepared to add your own color commentary for each of the seven reasons—after the team votes with their red and green cards. For example, you might reference this poignant wisdom from Fred Smith when discussing the importance of a written plan (noted in Bonus Reason #8):

"I learned to write, to burn the fuzz off my thinking."[8]

Fred Smith

[7] Susan A. Waechter, *Driving Strategic Planning: A Nonprofit Executive's Guide*, 2d ed. (Washington, DC: BoardSource, 2010), 12.
[8] Fred Smith, *Breakfast With Fred* (Ventura, CA: Regal, 2007), 138.

POP QUIZ! The 7 Reasons Why Strategic Plans Fail

1 – Not our problem
2 – Might be our problem
3 – This is a minor problem
4 – Yikes! This is a major problem but fixable
5 – We need a written plan to address this

No.	The 7 Reasons Why Strategic Plans Fail	Insert Problem Level
1	**EVENT THINKING:** Strategic planning is viewed as an event or a task, instead of a transformational ongoing year-round process.	
2	**TOP-DOWN EGO:** Strategic planning is created top-down and characterized by ego and arrogance, instead of humility and listening.	
3	**INTERRUPTION:** Strategic planning is seen as an "add-on" interruption to my "real work," instead of becoming absolutely core to my role.	
4	**EXTRA EXPENSE:** Strategic planning is viewed as an extra expense—with no budget line item—instead of an annual critical investment.	
5	**BINDER SYNDROME:** Strategic planning conjures up complex and time-consuming exercises and 3-ring binders, instead of being the servant to a simple and elegant plan that is grounded in the alignment between the mission, vision, values, BHAG, and S.M.A.R.T. goals.	
6	**SACRED COWS:** Strategic planning "economizes" by involving fewer and "safer" stakeholders who honor tradition, dead horses and sacred cows, versus out-of-the-box dangerous ideas!	
7	**PSEUDO PRAYER:** Strategic planning gives a wink and a prayer to holy input, versus an extraordinary process of assembling spiritually discerning people together to hear from God—who then joyfully follow His plan.	
	Bonus Reason!	
8	**VERBAL FUZZ:** Strategic planning festers in a "verbal draft" purgatory, rather than becoming a disciplined process that is both written and actually implemented!	
	Other Reasons	
9		
10		

❑ 3. One Planning Approach A Strategic Plan Task Force (Small Teams with Big Tasks!)

Here is one planning model to consider. Use this 3-ring binder table of contents to create **"The Rolling 3-Year Strategic Plan Process and Schedule."** This worksheet lists the chronological steps a task force might follow when creating the strategic plan. Small teams will address niche assignments and then share critical information and findings with the task force, culminating in the one-page Strategic Plan Placemat. See the following pages for the commentary on the small teams and their big tasks!

ABC Organization's Rolling 3-Year Strategic Plan Process and Schedule[9]
GOAL: Final Draft (Version 4.0) to Board: Sept. 15, 2020 Deadline
Updated by: Emelia Anderson on March 1, 2020

3-RING BINDER TABLE OF CONTENTS (15 tabs)

TAB	**Strategic Plan Tasks & Teams** (generally completed in this chronological order)	**Champion*** *Appointed on 12/15/19	**1st Draft Deadline**
12	**Planning to Plan: Readiness Assessment** The 7 Reasons Why Strategic Plans Fail	Facilitator	
12	**The 5 Most Important Questions You Will Ever Ask About Your Organization** (Jan. 8 session)	Facilitator	
4	Mission, Vision, Values, BHAG		
5	Our Customers and What They Value		
6A	Environmental Scan		
6B	S.W.O.T. Analysis		
6C	Trends (and Trend-Spotting Exercise)		
6D	Assumptions ("The Radar Report")		
7	Spiritual Discernment Process (ongoing: beginning to end)		
8	Three-Year Visionary Priorities (by department)		
9	Top-5 Goals for Year One		
10	Board & Senior Team S.M.A.R.T. Goals and Monthly Dashboard Reports		
11	Communicating Our Results (4 Creative Options)		
12	Appendix		
1	Introduction		
2	Organization-at-a-Glance & Historical Snapshot		
3A	Executive Summary		
3B	The Rolling 3-Year Strategic Plan Placemat		
	SUPPLEMENTARY RESOURCES:		
13	Customized Strategic Plan Versions (Board, Staff, Volunteers, Donors, etc.)		
14	***HOOPLA!*** Celebration		
15	Update of Annual Planning Calendar		

[9] Adapted from John Pearson's three-day workshop, "The Rolling 3-Year Strategic Plan Workshop: Build It. Execute It. Update It. Year After Year!" *http://managementbuckets.com/workshops.*

5 Elements

❑ **1. The Process**	Select a facilitator/consultant that has a track record for scaling Mt. Everest—and empower that person to select the methodology that has worked well for him or her in the past.
❑ **2. The People**	Board/staff task force? Staff-only task force with regular updates to the board? Either way, leverage their CliftonStrengths.®
❑ **3. The Placemat**	Wordsmith the one-page placemat with prayerful discernment and an eye to communicating the plan to multiple customers (board, staff, donors, clients, volunteers, etc.).
❑ **4. The Proclamation**	Get the plan off the shelf and into the streets! Completing the plan is just the start. Now you must sell the plan.
❑ **5. The Progress**	Monitor Results: Dashboards. Targets. Measurements. Metrics. Monthly Updates. *Make strategic planning an on-going, year-round process—not a one-time event.*

7 Steps

❑ **Step 1: Appoint a Task Force**—generally a combination of key staff and two or three board members.

❑ **Step 2: Create the Planning Calendar**—for most organizations without a written strategic plan, this process might range from three to nine months.

❑ **Step 3: Seek buy-in**—ensure that the CEO (or senior pastor), senior team, and the board agree that the time is right for a strategic planning process and that there is passion, time, and budget to accomplish the plan. (*You never have a second change to make a first impression.*)

❑ **Step 4: Appoint or retain a Facilitator or Consultant**—discern if you have internal expertise to facilitate this process or if you need to recruit a volunteer or retain a consultant.

❑ **Step 5: Appoint "Champions"** for each section of the plan (Tabs 1 to 15). If this is your first plan, the CEO may prefer to be the champion for Tab 4: Mission, Vision, Values, BHAG.

❑ **Step 6: Plan a *HOOPLA!* Celebration**—create the expectation that you will be successful and put a celebration date on the calendar and assign your best party-planner to organize the event.[10]

❑ **Step 7: Affirm the Annual Planning Calendar**—to ensure that this is a "rolling" three-year plan (that adds more one year every year—so you are always looking ahead three years), set key target dates for the next 12 months. Build strategic planning into the DNA of your organization so it's similar to your budgeting and monthly financial reporting cycle—*not a one-time annual event that provokes groans and excuses!*

View how the ProService team celebrated their achievement of a major quarterly goal, as noted in *Scaling Up.* Search *"Happy ProService"* on YouTube.[11]

[10] Read Chapter 10, "The Hoopla! Bucket" in John Pearson, *Mastering the Management Buckets: 20 Critical Competencies for Leading Your Business or Nonprofit* (Ventura, CA: Regal , 2008).

[11] Read more about ProService and quarterly themes and celebrations/rewards in Verne Harnish, *Scaling Up: How a Few Companies Make It . . .and Why the Rest Don't – Mastering the Rockefeller Habits 2.0*, (Ashburn, VA: Gazelles, 2014), 153–159.

Commentary on Strategic Plan Team Tasks
Small Teams with Big Tasks!

TAB	Strategic Plan Teams and Tasks	These tasks are generally completed in this chronological order—each task builds upon the previous team's work.
12	**Planning to Plan: Readiness Assessment** The 7 Reasons Why Strategic Plans Fail	In the first session with the board and the senior team (or perhaps the senior team and middle management), use this "pop quiz" to assess the organization's previous experience.
12	**The 5 Most Important Questions You Will Ever Ask About Your Organization:** #1. What is our mission? #2. Who is our customer? #3. What does the customer value? #4. What are our results? #5. What is our plan?	**Resources/outline for the 1- or 2-day planning retreat:** ❑ **Peter Drucker's Five Most Important Questions: Enduring Wisdom for Today's Leaders*, by Peter F. Drucker, Frances Hesselbein, Joan Snyder Kuhl (Hoboken, NJ: John Wiley & Sons, Inc., 2015) ❑ *Peter F. Drucker's The Five Most Important Questions Self-Assessment Tool: Facilitator's Guide*, Third Edition (San Francisco: Jossey-Bass, 2010) ❑ *Peter F. Drucker's The Five Most Important Questions Self-Assessment Tool: Participant Guide*, Third Edition (San Francisco: Jossey-Bass, 2010) *Required reading for all staff, board and team members.
4	Mission, Vision, Values, BHAG	**Mission:** why we exist **Values:** how we will treat each other and our constituents **Vision:** what we want to be in the future **BHAG:** our Big HOLY Audacious Goal for X years ahead
5	Our Customers and What They Value	Use the Drucker materials to discern: ❑ Our primary customer: "The person whose life is changed because of our work." ❑ Supporting customers: list the categories (donors, vendors, churches, grandparents of clients, etc.)
6A	Environmental Scan	Google "environmental scan" and document both external and internal issues that will impact your plan.
6B	S.W.O.T. Analysis	Survey stakeholders and assess: Strengths, Weaknesses, Opportunities, Threats (S.W.O.T.)
6C	Trends (and Trend-Spotting Exercise)	See Tool #15: Board Retreat Trend-Spotting Exercise
6D	Assumptions ("The Radar Report")	Identify your Top-10 assumptions that undergird your plan (example: "Giving will decrease due to aging donor base."). List the assumptions on a one-page questionnaire, "The Radar Report," and ask dozens (or hundreds) of people to evaluate if those assumptions are correct or not.

"Donald Rumsfeld on Assumptions and Planning

"It is possible to proceed perfectly logically from an inaccurate premise to an inaccurate and unfortunate conclusion."[12]

In his chapter on "Thinking Strategically," in *Rumsfeld Rules*, Donald Rumsfeld describes a military planning meeting when he served as U.S. Secretary of Defense. "The objective of the plan was straightforward enough: to defend South Korean sovereignty and defeat the North Korean threat. What I found troubling, however, was that there was no discussion of the key assumptions in which the plan was rooted."

Rumsfeld dismissed the meeting and they reconvened on the next Saturday. "That Saturday we met for hours and never discussed any of the plans, only the assumptions."[13]

TAB	Strategic Plan Teams and Tasks	These tasks are generally completed in this chronological order—each task builds upon the previous team's work.
7	Spiritual Discernment Process	This team solicits prayer requests from all the teams—and inspires all teams to discern God's voice. Some teams read Ruth Haley Barton's book, *Pursuing God's Will Together: A Discernment Practice for Leadership Groups*.
8	Three-Year Visionary Priorities (by department)	This team provides templates and instructions so each department will discern three to five "visionary priorities."
9	Top-5 Goals for Year One	After each department has submitted their visionary priorities, this team will recommend to the Task Force the Top-5 Organizational Goals for the first year of the rolling three-year plan.
10	Board & Senior Team S.M.A.R.T. Goals and Monthly Dashboard Reports	See Tool #11, "Monthly Dashboard Report," for the template for creating and reporting on three to five annual goals for the board, the CEO, and each senior team member.
11	Communicating Our Results (4 Creative Options)	Use your creativity here! Ask other organizations how they communicate results (per Drucker Question #4). Ideas: ❑ Create an "Our Results" page on your website—and update it frequently with success stories of how your plan is fostering results. ❑ Publish an annual booklet of 20-30 pages of testimonial "results" from your clients, customers, or donors. ❑ Create a video with stories of "results." ❑ Appoint a "Results Team" to scour the landscape for poignant stories of ministry results—and then how best to share them with others.

[12] Donald Rumsfeld, *Rumsfeld's Rules: Leadership Lessons in Business, Politics, War, and Life* (New York: HarperCollins, 2013), 76.
[13] Ibid., 78.

TAB	Strategic Plan Teams and Tasks	These tasks are generally completed in this chronological order—each task builds upon the previous team's work.
12	Appendix	Assign one person to the "Appendix Team" and require all teams to submit both final and early drafts of their work. In a "rolling" strategic plan process—the Appendix will be referenced year-round, year-after-year.
1	Introduction	Appoint your best writers and wordsmithers to write the introduction—once the plan is complete. Key word: brevity!
2	Organization-at-a-Glance & Historical Snapshot	Visit organizational websites to catch the flavor of how to format this "organization-at-a-glance" picture. What would a new donor, a new staff member, or a new board member find helpful? Use graphics, timelines, and photos.
3A	Executive Summary	Read executive summaries from other strategic plans. You may need several versions of the executive summary— based on who will be reading it. (Foundations? Major donors? Staff? Volunteers?)
3B	The Rolling 3-Year Strategic Plan Placemat	Reminder! This one-page, 11" x 17" document is the summary of all your hard work. Don't skimp on graphics, color, or paper quality—but keep it simple. And... proofread!
	SUPPLEMENTARY RESOURCES	
13	Customized Strategic Plan Versions (Board, Staff, Volunteers, Donors, etc.)	Consider whether your "in-house" version of the strategic plan report will be relevant to other segments. If not, create appropriate versions for other audiences.
14	***HOOPLA!*** Celebration	Read Chapter 10, "The Hoopla! Bucket" in *Mastering the Management Buckets*—and plan a celebration when the strategic plan is completed and approved by the board.[14]
15	Update of Annual Planning Calendar	This might be the most important task. Before your plan is complete, you must identify the key deadlines for the next 12 months for keeping your rolling plan—rolling! Most senior teams prefer a quarterly off-site day to review progress on the current year and then add one more year to the rolling three-year plan. (Patrick Lencioni recommends four meeting types, including the quarterly off-site meeting.)[15]

"If you have more than five goals, you have none."[16]

Peter Drucker

[14] Pearson, *Mastering the Management Buckets*, 143–55.

[15] Patrick Lencioni, *Death by Meeting: A Leadership Fable . . . About Solving the Most Painful Problem in Business* (San Francisco: Jossey-Bass, 2004), 249.

[16] Peter F. Drucker, Frances Hesselbein, and Joan Snyder Kuhl, *Peter Drucker's Five Most Important Questions: Enduring Wisdom for Today's Leaders* (Hoboken, NJ: John Wiley & Sons, 2015), 63.

❑ 4. Recommended Faith-Based Resource
Breakthrough: Unleashing the Power of a Proven Plan

Attn: Church Boards

We recommend this powerful book, based on 1 Chronicles 28-29. Use this biblical framework to enrich your church's strategic planning process.

6 Planning Steps from 1 Chronicles 28-29	WORKSHEET: Our board's insights from *Breakthrough*, by Randon Samuelson
1) Inspiring Vision	
2) A Credible Plan	
3) The Right Leader	
4) Initial Funding	
5) Going Public	
6) Sharing Credit	

Must-read!
One of the best faith-based books on strategy and strategic planning.

The Key Log Question

"Other than money, what one opportunity (or obstacle) if captured (or removed) would most advance your mission/vision?"

Author Randy Samelson helps organizations identify key opportunities or obstacles. They focus on the "Key Log."

Borrowing the perfect metaphor from Fred Smith, Sr., Samelson explains: "...in the lumber industry when trees are cut and floated down rivers, they are susceptible to log jams. Over time, the industry learned that through satellite images and computer modeling, they could identify the one key log that if blown-up would release the log jam allowing the logs to move toward their destination."

> Individuals and organizations also experience the equivalent of 'log jams.' Progress is stopped." And Samelson says there are "biblical principles that can be used to identify the key impediment and wise strategies to eliminate it."[17]

STOP!
Before you fill in your Strategic Plan Placemat, ask "The Key Log Question."

[17] Randon A. Samelson, *Breakthrough: Unleashing the Power of a Proven Plan* (Colorado Springs: Counsel & Capital, 2014), 19.

❑ 5. The G.N.O.M.E. Chart
Delineating the Board's Role and the Staff's Role in Strategic Planning

SUMMARIZE YOUR PLAN WITH A G.N.O.M.E. CHART. *This would have helped Christopher Columbus, who did not know where he was going when he left, and did not know where he had been when he returned home!*

Read Chapters 1, 2, and 3, "The Results Bucket," "The Customer Bucket," and The Strategy Bucket," in *Mastering the Management Buckets* before you begin the strategic planning process. Use this "G.N.O.M.E. Chart" (Goals, Needs, Objectives, Methods, Evaluation) to list your three to five annual "S.M.A.R.T." goals (or, if you prefer, label them "Visionary Priorities").[18]

G.N.O.M.E. CHART

Board/Staff Focus: Goals, Needs, Objectives			*Staff Focus: Methods, Evaluation	
GOALS	NEEDS	OBJECTIVES	METHODS*	EVALUATION*
1.				
2.				
3.				
4.				
5.				

*Typically, the board of directors should focus on Goals, Needs, and Objectives (Strategy)—and when the goals are crystal clear (and meet the "S.M.A.R.T." test), the board should give freedom for the staff to focus on Methods (Tactics) and Evaluation. The Evaluation column should document the process whereby the staff will evaluate and report to the board whether or not the methodology is actually achieving the goals and objectives—and if there is alignment with the vision, mission, core values, and BHAG. For more on "Needs," read "The Customer Bucket" chapter.

[18] Pearson, *Mastering the Management Buckets*, 62–64.

❑ 6. More Resources on Strategic Planning

Be strategic about strategic planning. *"Insanity is doing the same thing over and over again and expecting different results."*[19]

☑ **DELEGATE YOUR READING!** Inspire every board member and senior team member to select a book or resource from the list below (or from your staff resource library)—and share insights at your next Strategic Planning Task Force meeting.

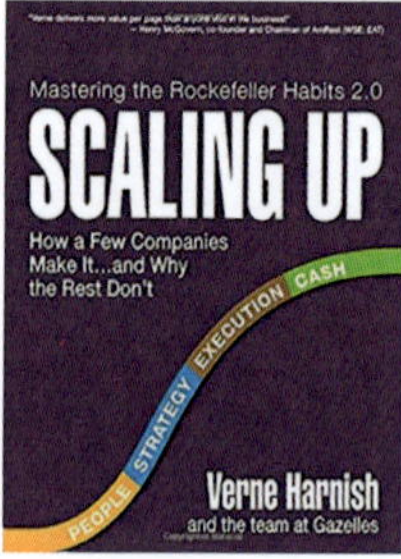

❑ ***Scaling Up:***
How a Few Companies Make It . . . and Why the Rest Don't
Mastering the Rockefeller Habits 2.0
by Verne Harnish

Recommended by Dan Busby, this book was John Pearson's 2018 "Book-of-the- Year" from his book reviews in *Your Weekly Staff Meeting* eNews.

- ❑ *Playing to Win: How Strategy Really Works*, by A.G. Lafley and Roger L. Martin
- ❑ *Little Bets: How Breakthrough Ideas Emerge From Small Discoveries*, by Peter Sims
- ❑ *How the Mighty Fall and Why Some Companies Never Give In*, by Jim Collins
- ❑ *101 Mission Statements From Top Companies: Plus Guidelines for Writing Your Own Mission Statement*, by Jeffrey Abrahams
- ❑ *Peter Drucker's Five Most Important Questions: Enduring Wisdom for Today's Leaders*, by Peter F. Drucker, Frances Hesselbein, and Joan Snyder Kuhl
- ❑ *Driving Strategic Planning: A Nonprofit Executive's Guide*, Second Edition, by Susan A. Waechter
- ❑ *The Nonprofit Dashboard: A Tool for Tracking Progress*, by Lawrence M. Butler
- ❑ *Nonprofit Sustainability: Making Strategic Decisions for Financial Viability*, by Jeanne Bell, Jan Masaoka, and Steve Zimmerman
- ❑ *5: Where Will You Be Five Years from Today?* by Dan Zadra

"Don't say you don't have enough time. You have exactly the same number of hours per day that were given to Helen Keller, Louis Pasteur, Michelangelo, Mother Teresa, Leonardo da Vinci, Thomas Jefferson and Albert Einstein."[20]

Dan Zadra

---

[19] Adapted from "The Strategy Bucket" in *Mastering the Management Buckets Workbook: Management Tools, Templates, and Tips from John Pearson*, 2d ed. (San Clemente, CA: A Pearpod Resource, 2018), 33–45.
[20] Dan Zadra, *5: Where Will You Be Five Years from Today?* (Seattle: Compendium, 2009), 3.

- ❑ *Harvard Business Review's 10 Must Reads on Strategy* (including the featured article "What Is Strategy?" by Michael E. Porter)
- ❑ "What Is Strategy?" by Michael E. Porter (*Harvard Business Review*, Nov./Dec. 1996)
- ❑ *Thinkpak: A Brainstorming Card Deck*, by Michael Michalko
- ❑ *Rumsfeld's Rules: Leadership Lessons in Business, Politics, War, and Life*, by Donald Rumsfeld
- ❑ *Illuminate: Ignite Change Through Speeches, Stories, Ceremonies, and Symbols*, by Nancy Duarte and Patti Sanchez
- ❑ *The Attacker's Advantage: Turning Uncertainty Into Breakthrough Opportunities*, by Ram Charan
- ❑ "The Big Lie of Strategic Planning," by Roger L. Martin (*Harvard Business Review*, Jan./Feb. 2014)
- ❑ *Managing Transitions: Making the Most of Change* (25th Anniversary Edition), by William Bridges

Attn: Church Boards

The following strategic planning resources will be especially helpful to church boards and church staff members.

- ❑ *Barna Trends 2018: What's New and What's Next at the Intersection of Faith and Culture*, by Barna
- ❑ *Breakthrough: Unleashing the Power of a Proven Plan*, by Randon A. Samelson
- ❑ *Effectiveness by the Numbers: Counting What Counts in the Church*, by William R. Hoyt
- ❑ *Simply Strategic Stuff: Help for Leaders Drowning in the Details of Running a Church*, by Tim Stevens and Tony Morgan
- ❑ *Well Connected: Releasing Power, Restoring Hope Through Kingdom Partnerships*, by Phill Butler
- ❑ *The Longview: Lasting Strategies for Rising Leaders*, by Roger Parrott
- ❑ *TRUST: The Firm Foundation for Kingdom Fruitfulness*, by Dan Busby
- ❑ *Visioneering: God's Blueprint for Developing and Maintaining Personal Vision*, by Andy Stanley
- ❑ *Mastering the Management Buckets Workbook: Management Tools, Templates, and Tips from John Pearson*, Second Edition, by John Pearson

Note: To read John Pearson's reviews of the above books, just google "[book title], John Pearson's Buckets Blogs," or visit *https://urgentink.typepad.com/my_weblog*. The annual update and master list of books reviewed by John, categorized within John's 20 buckets/core competencies, is posted at: *http://managementbuckets.com/book-bucket*.

Effective Boards Are Alert to Relevent Trends

ECFA Research Says...

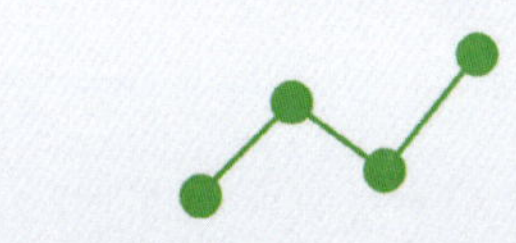

Study the Trends

"Our board devotes creative energy and board meeting time to assess risks and opportunities—and thus is well-informed about the outside forces impacting the organization."

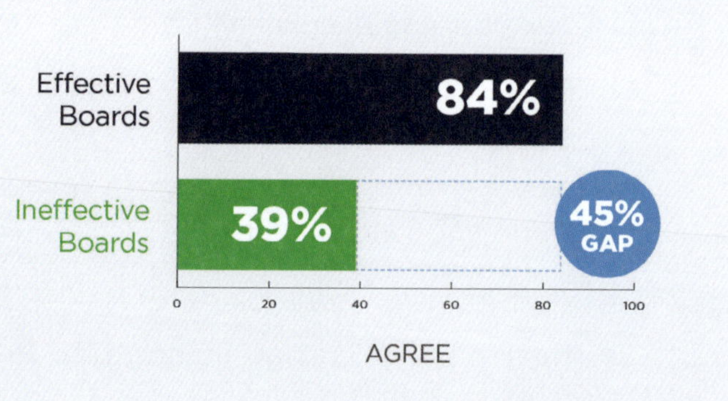

TOOL #15: Board Retreat Trend-Spotting Exercise

Use this trend-spotting template to generate insights and interaction on a key hot topic at your next retreat—each person presenting one article.

Many Important Topics Are Not Book-length!

Leverage the Media for Trend Analysis

From a 1983 (not a typo!) interview in the *Washington Post* with John Naisbitt, futurologist, on how he spots trends:

> In a word, Naisbitt analyzes a trend—say, a growing backlash to television, or the waxing of concern about crime—through the systematic reading and clipping and categorizing of millions of news items from thousands of individual copies of newspapers. Actually, content analysis is a technique as old as the hills. The news hole in a given paper on a given day is only so big, and if something comes in, then of necessity something must go out.
>
> So if you analyze what is coming in and what is going out, country-wide, on a systematic basis, you start to pick up shifts and movements, a nation's worries. Trends, John Naisbitt says, are generated from the bottom up (though fads come from the top down). That is, America changes most substantively at the grass-roots level, contrary to what Washington and New York may think. And it is at the grass roots level that our social, political and industrial organizations are undergoing massive change.[1]

John Naisbitt's 1982 book, *Megatrends: Ten New Directions Transforming Our Lives*, was on the *New York Times* bestseller list for more than two years mostly as No. 1. *Megatrends* was published in 57 countries and sold more than 14 million copies.[2]

[1] Paul Hendrickson, "Catching a Rising Trend." May 3, 1983, *Washington Post*: *www.washingtonpost.com/archive/lifestyle/1983/05/03/catching-a-rising-trend/d01c6278-b439-41d0-bf80-a53768139670/?utm_term=.abedd21abb38.*

[2] See "About Us." John and Doris Naisbitt: *http://www.naisbitt.com/about-us/.*

Board Retreat Trend-Spotting Exercise

An invigorating exercise for all 4 social styles:[3]

- ☑ Drivers
- ☑ Analyticals
- ☑ Amiables
- ☑ and *Expressives!*

5 STEPS:

- ❑ 1. Select a hot topic on trends.
- ❑ 2. Email a blank template to each board member.
- ❑ 3. Ask each board member to find a relevant article on the hot topic from: a newspaper, magazine, TED Talk, blog, professional journal, or a niche chapter in a book.
- ❑ 4. Each board member shares the article and distributes copies of the article (fill in the template, per the attached sample).
- ❑ 5. Each board member has EIGHT MINUTES MAXIMUM to share the hot topic. (Award a Chick-fil-A card if the board member is done before your iPhone alarm goes off.)

How the 4 social styles do trend-spotting in 8 minutes:

Drivers	3 memorable points and a bottom line take-away
Analyticals	17 major points, backed by research, and a 10-page handout
Amiables	1 heart-warming story
Expressives	Balloons! Food! Microphone! Big Ideas! *Maybe even vacation videos.*

"You can never do enough looking over the wall to learn how to do things. Seeing excellence in action helps individuals visualize how they can do it for themselves."[4]

James Belasco

[3] For more on the four social styles, visit: *www.tracomcorp.com/social-style-training/model/.*

[4] James Belasco quoted in the "Leadership Tip of the Day" email from the (now-named) Frances Hesselbein Leadership Forum, June 29, 2010, *www.HesselbeinForum.org.*

Trend-Spotting Presentation

2020 Board Retreat – ABC Ministry International

You have 8 minutes for your presentation:

- Retreat Hot Topic Trend: "Church or denominational trends that impact our work"
- Discussion

Your Name	
Trend: **Church or Denominational Trends**	
Publication	
Article Title/Headline	
Article Date	

Implication for our organization	

Article Options

1. "Copy" the article from a website and "paste" it here and on page 2.
2. Photocopy the original article and attach it to this sheet.
3. Bring two copies of the article: 1) Original for the file; and 2) one copy to pass around during your presentation

EXAMPLE

Trend-Spotting Presentation

2020 Board Retreat – ABC Ministry International

Theme Church or Denominational Trends

MY NAME	Hector Hernandez
Trend: **Church or Denominational Trends**	American Protestants (47 percent of the U.S. population) are increasingly identifying with nondenominational churches.
Publication	“Facts & Trends” (published by LifeWay Christian Resources of the Southern Baptist Convention®)[5]
Article Title/Headline	“What Does the Growth of Nondenominationalism Mean?” by Aaron Earls - https://factsandtrends.net/2017/08/08/what-does- the-growth-of-nondenominationalism-mean/
Article Date	August 8, 2017

Executive Summary	A study by Gallup says that the percentage of Americans who “identify” with a specific Protestant denomination **has dropped from 50 percent in 2000 to just 30 percent in 2016**. “Among Protestants, the most popular denomination is Baptist.” And according to research by Pew, “millennials seem to be more attracted to nondenominational churches than previous generations are.”

Implication for our organization	Historically, our organization has employed two full-time staff to market our church resources to denominations, generally by building relationships through the district or regional executives (and their annual meetings). Perhaps we should split our focus into two staff and volunteer teams: denominational churches and nondenominational churches?

My Recommendations	#1. Ask our CEO to conduct an analysis of our denominational relationships (sales, etc.). Is it trending up or down? #2. Ask our CEO to study the feasibility of launching a pilot program or test to nondenominational events and conferences and/or influential churches—to discern receptivity and interest in our resources.

Reminder! Attach a photocopy of the article to this worksheet.

[5] We recommend reading the 24-page PDF called *18 Important Stats in 2018: Facts & Trends* (Nashville: LifeWay, 2018).

TOOL #16: Prime Responsibility Chart

Use this tool to eliminate fuzziness between board and staff roles.

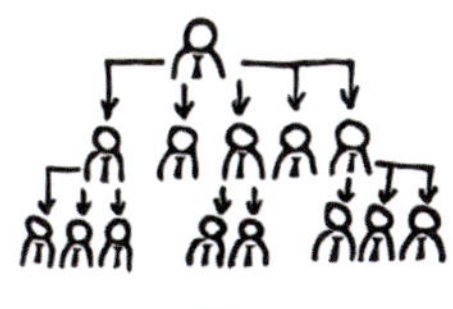

The 1-Page Tool for Fixing Fuzziness

What's the role of the board? Does everyone agree?

- ☑ **Ministering?** Listening, encouraging, and praying with ministry directors?
- ☑ **Monitoring?** Ensuring that every ministry has goals, reports, and results?
- ☑ **Meddling?** Jumping in with new ideas, fixing problems, and addressing personnel issues?
- ☑ **Micro-managing?** In the weeds, obsessing over details, and mandating lengthy reports?

Boards should relate to one just employee: the top leader. And the board must be crystal clear about the board's relationship with all other staff. There are many tools that will help clarify these relationships, such as a *Board Policies Manual* (see Tool #17).

Try this tool: the *Prime Responsibility Chart* (PRC). The PRC will help you eliminate fuzziness between board and staff roles. The PRC is short—just one page.

Roles and responsibilities are crystal clear. Based on your governance model, you may have unique approaches to some functions so the PRC can be customized to meet your unique needs.[1]

> When you're ready to graduate to a more comprehensive tool, you'll quickly see the value of *Tool #17: Board Policies Manual.*

ECFA Research Says...

Ineffective Boards Reveal a Greater Need for Outside Intervention
Board Members Who Agree They Need "Much Help" or "Major Help" with...

	Effective Boards	**Ineffective** Boards	Difference
Board/CEO/senior team clarification of roles and responsibilities	4%	41%	37%
Staff roles in board meetings	4%	19%	15%

[1] Adapted from "Lesson 7: Eliminate Fuzziness Between Board and Staff" by Dan Busby and John Pearson, *More Lessons From the Nonprofit Boardroom: Effectiveness, Excellence, Elephants!* (Winchester, VA: ECFAPress, 2019), 40–45.

Prime Responsibility Chart

The Prime Responsibility Chart Is Dynamic, Not Static

The Prime Responsibility Chart is simple and straightforward and can be revised at any time—literally at any or every meeting. Growth (or decline) in your organization, or a department, will likely impact reporting relationships, so this tool is not static—it's meant to be reviewed frequently.[2]

When the PRC is edited by board action, just make the change and update the chart with "Version 3.0" and the current date, and then email the revised PRC to board members and senior team members within 24 hours. Plus, have copies available for reference at every board meeting.

KEY PRINCIPLE: Only One Person Has "Prime Responsibility"

The most important principle: only one person has "Prime Responsibility" (P). In the absence of a Board Policies Manual (see Tool #17), this one-page chart is an excellent way to clarify board and staff roles.

NEXT STEPS:

- ❑ **Step 1. Clarify:** Ensure that your staff organizational chart is crystal clear. Verify that each staff member has just one direct supervisor. Reminder: the CEO (or senior pastor) is the only person that reports directly to the board.
- ❑ **Step 2. Create:** Inspire two or three board members (including the top leader) to customize Version 1.0 of the *Prime Responsibility Chart* and present this draft at your next board meeting. After input, edit the PRC and move to Version 2.0.
- ❑ **Step 3. Congratulate:** At the end of any lengthy discussion at a board meeting, affirm and congratulate (maybe with a Chick-fil-A card) the first board member who observes: "This is taking way too long to decide. Is it because we need to add or edit a line on our *Prime Responsibility Chart*?"

Attn: Church Boards

Inspire one or two board members to review this tool and then customize it for the unique needs of your church's board, senior pastor, and senior team. It's designed to be updated frequently as responsibilities and trust increase regularly.

[2] The "Prime Responsibility Chart" is adapted from Chapter 18: "The Operations Buckets" in John Pearson, *Mastering the Management Buckets: 20 Critical Competencies for Leading Your Business or Nonprofit* (Ventura, CA: Regal, 2008). Bill Benke, an executive at The Boeing Company, and a board member at the time at SAMBICA in Bellevue, Wash., adapted the Boeing template for use by nonprofit boards.

Important! This template is an example only. The details are not prescriptive for every board.

PRIME RESPONSIBILITY CHART

Version 1.0 (Drafted by Carlos, Jennifer and Cameron on Jan. 15, 2019)

P = Prime Responsibility **A= Assistant Responsibility** **AP= Approval Required**

BOARD AND STAFF ROLES AND RESPONSIBILITIES	Board	CEO/ Sr. Pastor	Exec.VP/ CFO/Exec. Pastor	Dept. Heads
PERSONNEL				
1) Hire and fire the top leader	P			
2) Hire and fire other senior leaders		P		
3) Hire and fire middle management		AP	P	
4) Hire and fire all other staff			AP	
5) Annual update: employee handbook	AP	AP	P	A
PLANNING				
1) Mission, vision, values	AP	P	A	A
2) Rolling 3-Year Plan Annual Update	AP	P	A	A
3) CEO/senior pastor annual goals	AP	P	A	A
4) Dept. heads annual goals		AP	AP	P
FINANCE				
1) Annual budget	AP	A	P	A
2) Quarterly financial reports			P	
3) Annual audit	AP		P	
4) Non-budgeted expenditures over $________		AP	P	A
Add additional categories, roles, and responsibilities below (as needed)				

IMPORTANT PRINCIPLE! Only one person has "Prime Responsibility" (P). In the absence of a Board Policies Manual (see Tool #17), this one-page chart is an excellent way to clarify board and staff roles. Update this chart whenever the board edits the policy and label it (for example): Version 3.0 – 4/15/2019.

"If you don't know what your top three priorities are, you don't have priorities."[3]

"What you measure improves."[4]

Donald Rumsfeld

[3] Donald Rumsfeld, *Rumsfeld's Rules: Leadership Lessons in Business, Politics, War, and Life* (New York: HarperCollins, 2013), 304.
[4] Ibid., 85.

TOOL #17: Board Policies Manual

Use this tool to create a Board Policies Manual (BPM)—and finally, you'll have all your policies in one document and always updated.

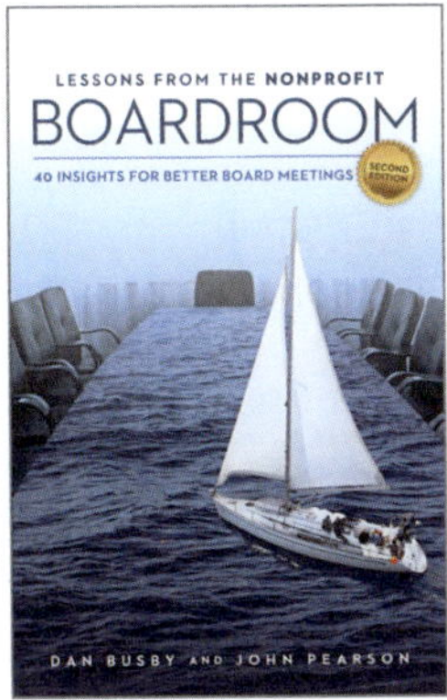

"While many organizations have written policies covering a wide range of topics, they're often filed away incoherently in the archives and no one can find them when needed.

"'Here's a fun job for a new board member,' they say. 'Please dig through 20 years of board minutes. Bring a flashlight and emergency provisions!'"[1]

The Time-Saving Tool for Organizing Policies

Bring a Flashlight and Emergency Provisions!

There are several options and approaches for creating your Board Policies Manual (BPM) if you don't have one yet. We appreciate the simplicity and clarity of the BPM template featured in the book, *Good Governance for Nonprofits: Developing Principles and Policies for an Effective Board*, by Fredric L. Laughlin and Robert C. Andringa.

Here's what Rich Stearns said, when he was CEO at World Vision (1998-2018), looking back on the development of their Board Policies Manual (BPM):

> Our attention to governance in general and the BPM in particular revolutionized our board—and I feel that I am the greatest beneficiary. I am still on a honeymoon with the board after eight years! [2]

READ MORE: To inspire your governance committee to consider developing a BPM, read Lesson 4, "Do Unwritten Board Policies Really Exist?" in *Lessons From the Nonprofit Boardroom.* (Church board members will want to read Lesson 5 in *Lessons From the Church Boardroom.*)

1 Dan Busby and John Pearson, *Lessons From the Nonprofit Boardroom: 40 Insights for Better Board Meetings*, 2d ed. (Winchester, VA: ECFAPress, 2018), 18.
2 Fredric L. Laughlin and Robert C. Andringa, *Good Governance for Nonprofits: Developing Principles and Policies for an Effective Board* (New York: AMACOM, 2007), 174.

Board Policies Manual (BPM)

A 15- to 20-page template to customize for your board's unique needs

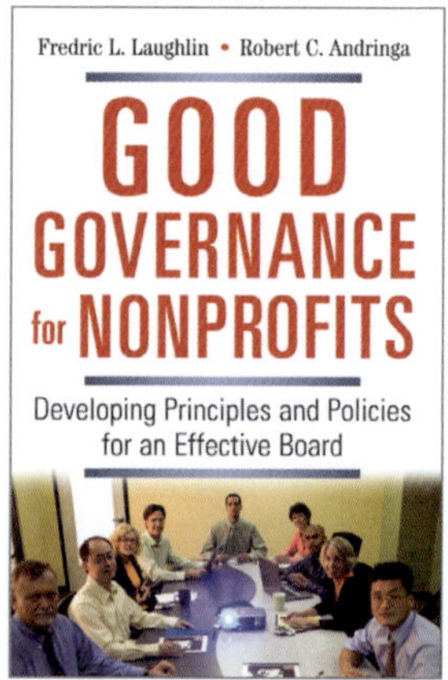

Good Governance for Nonprofits: Developing Principles and Policies for an Effective Board

by Fredric L. Laughlin and Robert C. Andringa

Wow! This book includes the brilliant template with an item-by-item color commentary on each BPM paragraph!

Just add water and stir! The book. . .

- . . . **EXPLAINS** how to use this customize the template—and build your own Board Policies Manual.
- . . . **PROVIDES** numbered color commentaries for every paragraph in the template.
- . . . **REMINDS** boards to update the BPM frequently, based on organizational needs and changing internal and external realities.
- . . . **DELIVERS** a simpler and more time-saving alternative to other policy approaches.

NOTE: Although this is not designed as a "faith-based" BPM, the context is built in so you can add the Christ-centered distinctives of your ministry. (For example, we've added the ECFA's board preamble to the BPM.)

BONUS RESOURCES:

On the following pages, you'll find the latest template from Bob Andringa and Fred Laughlin. The BPM and other helpful governance resources from The Andringa Group can also be downloaded.
Visit: *https://theandringagroup.com/resources/*

- ❑ **Board Policies Manual Template** (Microsoft Word – Updated January 2017)
  https://theandringagroup.com/resources/
- ❑ **Introduction to Board Policies Manual** (6 pages)
  https://andringatest.files.wordpress.com/2013/04/intro-to-board-policies-manual1.pdf
- ❑ **The original 2007 version** (which aligns with the color commentary in *Good Governance for Nonprofits*) can be downloaded at *www.theandringagroup.com/resources/*

Sample Template

BOARD POLICIES MANUAL (BPM)

for

"ABC Nonprofit"

This template is used by permission of the authors.

Good Governance for Nonprofits: Developing Principles and Policies for an Effective Board, by Fredric L. Laughlin and Robert C. Andringa

When Customizing This Template for your Ministry or Church . . .

...please note that the helpful Board Policies Manual template from Fred Laughlin and Bob Andringa is written for "ABC Nonprofit."

While *Good Governance for Nonprofits* is not written specifically for faith-based organizations, the recommended template can be easily adapted and customized so a faith-based organization's values and theology can be incorporated into the BPM. (*Example*: see how ECFA's board has added a "preamble" to their BPM.)

Attn: Church Boards

Leverage the practicality of this helpful template—but also customize it for your church's unique polity or denominational affiliation.

For example, you may want to replace "CEO" with "senior pastor."

Note: The Board of Directors of ECFA has customized this Board Policies Manual (BPM) for its unique use. The board added this "preamble" statement to articulate the faith values and distinctives as an evangelical Christian organization. Your board may also find value in writing a preamble for your BPM.

ECFA
Board Policies Manual (BPM)
PREAMBLE

ECFA is an evangelical Christian organization and its survival and vitality depends in large measure on how the board members guard these faith values and integrate Christianity into the work of ECFA. As a result of being an evangelical Christian organization, ECFA's board is distinct from other nonprofit boards in four ways:

1. **Common evangelical Christian faith.** The board members of ECFA are all mature Christians following Jesus Christ. These are people involved in prayerful intercession and act in faith and in integrity in all they do in their personal and professional lives.

2. **Statement of evangelical Christian faith.** ECFA has a written Statement of Faith and interpretations of Biblical truths in the Commentary of ECFA Standard 1 which board members affirm and to which member organizations agree. These faith commitments provide the values and theological framework for all decisions made by the board.

3. **Christian worldview.** As a result of the board members' common Christian faith and the organization's written Statement of Faith, the board seeks to operate from a Christian worldview. This means that board members acknowledge God as the creator and sustainer of life and that God's eternal kingdom is the ultimate purpose of our existence. The focus of ECFA, therefore, is to seek the Great Commission and its accomplishment as outlined in the Bible.

4. **Accountable to God as stewards.** As a result of the above three assumptions, ECFA and its board members are accountable to God who provides the moral authority for all that is done. With this understanding that God owns all, board members serve as stewards of God's creation and are accountable to God. The board members' actions, plans, and policies are ultimately responsible for reflecting God's will for the organization. Board members should remember that Jesus Christ is our possessor and our dispossessor. He ordains, sustains, and blesses ECFA. The organization belongs entirely to God. Prayerful deliberation then becomes the norm and not the exception.

Used by permission of Bob Andringa and Fred Laughlin, co-authors
Good Governance for Nonprofits: Developing Principles and Policies for an Effective Board
Board Policies Manual (BPM)
ABC Nonprofit

NOTE TO READERS: This template has been edited several times in minor ways since our 2007 book on this topic, *Good Governance for Nonprofits: Developing Principles and Policies for an Effective Board*. Many boards have successfully started with that book and/or this updated template to develop their own BPM. A 6-page training tool on a BPM (and other good practices) can be found at this website: *www.TheAndringaGroup.com.*

Part 1: Introduction and Administration

This Board Policies Manual (BPM) contains all of the current standing (on-going) policies adopted by the board of (insert name of organization) since the initial approval on [insert date of the board meeting when parts or the whole BPM were first approved].

1.1 Reasons for Adoption. Our reasons for adopting this BPM include:

- Efficiency of having organizing all on-going board policies in one place
- Ability to quickly orient and educate new board members and key staff about current policies
- Elimination of redundant, or conflicting, policies over time
- Ease of reviewing current policy while simultaneously considering new issues
- Opportunity to guide the Chief Executive, senior staff, and new board members through clear, pro-active policies
- A modelled approach to governance that other organizations might utilize

1.2 Consistency. Each policy in this document is expected to be consistent with the law, the Articles of Incorporation, and Bylaws, all of which have precedence over these board policies. Except for time-limited or procedural-only board decisions (approve minutes, elect an officer, etc.), which are recorded in regular board minutes, all standing policies should be included or referred in this document. Our board does not expect perfection in implementing these aspirational good practices. We do desire to advance the performance of the board and staff by constant improvement of and adherence to these policies. The CEO is responsible for developing organizational and administrative policies and procedures not inconsistent with this BPM.

1.3 Transition. Whether adopted part by part or as a complete document, as soon as some version of the BPM is voted on as the "one voice" of the board, those policies are *deemed to supersede any past policies* that might be found in old minutes or any compilation of board policies over the years, unless a prior board resolution or contract obligates the organization to a specific matter. If any actual or apparent conflict arises between the BPM and other policies or board resolutions, the Chair should resolve the matter, or the entire board as may be appropriate.

1.4 Changes. These policies are meant to be reviewed continuously, and are frequently revised and refined to reflect new wisdom. The CEO helps the board formulate new language in the BPM by distributing proposed changes in advance. We will use software that shows all changes, allowing readers to review documents easily, or, when it is recommend that certain language be deleted, it is shown in strike-through format while proposed new language is underlined. Each numbered paragraph with a proposed change will be preceded by the # sign in order to help readers quickly locate these changes. Any final change to this BPM must be approved by the full board. Any board member, as well as the CEO, may submit proposed changes. In most cases, proposed changes will be referred to and reviewed by an appropriate committee before being presented to the board for action. Whenever changes are adopted, a new document displaying these changes should be dated and quickly made available to the board and key staff. The previous version should be kept on a disk for future reference if needed.

1.5 Specificity. Each new policy will be drafted to fit in the appropriate place within the BPM. Conceptually, policies should be drafted from the "outside in," i.e., the broadest policy statement should be stated first, then the next broadest, etc. down to the level of detail that the board finds appropriate for board action, and below which management is afforded discretion as to how it implements the policies in this BPM.

1.6 Oversight Responsibility. Below are the parts, the committees primarily responsible for drafting and reviewing those parts, and the individuals given authority to interpret and make decisions within the scope of those parts:

PART	PART/CHAPTERS	OVERSIGHT COMMITTEE	IMPLEMENTATION AUTHORITY
1	Introduction	Governance Committee	CEO
2	Organization Essentials	Full board	CEO
3	Board Structure & Processes	Governance Committee	Chair
4	Board-Staff Relationship	Executive Committee	Chair/CEO
5	Executive Parameters		
SECTION			
5	Finance Parameters	Finance Committee	CEO
6	Program Parameters	Programs Committee	CEO
7	Advancement Parameters	Advancement Committee	CEO
8	Audit and Compliance	Audit & Compliance Committee	CEO
9	Miscellaneous	Any Committee	

1.7 Maintenance of Policies. The Secretary should ensure that staff members record and publish all standing policies correctly. The CEO or the CEO's designee should maintain the policies file, and provide updated copies to the board whenever the policies change, or upon request. The board will ask that legal counsel review this BPM biennially to ensure compliance with the law. Discrete documents referred to in the BPM, and listed at the end for easy tracking, will be provided to board members in digital format for their own hard drives, or kept in an online board website.

1.8 Context of Other Policies. This BPM fits into this hierarchy of policies within which *authority flows down* and *accountability flows up.*

1. Laws and Applicable Regulations
2. Parent Organization, Accreditation Requirements, etc.
3. Articles of Incorporation
4. Bylaws
5. Board Policies Manual
6. CEO-approved Organizational Policies
7. Policies Set by Managers Under the CEO

Part 2: Organization Essentials

2.1 Our **vision** is ...

2.2 Our **mission** is ...

2.3 The **values** that guide all we do are . . .

2.4 The **moral owners** to whom the board feels accountable are ... (e.g.: members, alumni, donors, taxpayers)

2.5 The primary **beneficiaries** of our services are . . .

2.6 The major general **functions**, and the approximate percentage of total effort that is expected to be devoted to each are . . .

2.7 The primary **strategies** by which we will fulfill our mission include ...

2.8 The major S.M.A.R.T. (specific, measurable, achievable, realistic, time-related) organizational **goals** and monitoring indicators for the next three years are . . .

2.9 Strategic Plans. The board is expected to think strategically at all times. The CEO is expected to develop a staff strategic plan based on the policies in this BPM, update it as necessary, link major activities in the plan to the relevant sections of this BPM, and provide copies of the plan to the board for information by [insert a date] each year (See Exhibit 1 for latest copy of the Strategic Plan).

Part 3: Board Structure and Processes

3.1 Governing Style. The board will approach its task with a style that emphasizes outward vision rather than an internal preoccupation, encouragement of diversity in viewpoints, strategic leadership more than administrative detail, clear distinction of board and staff roles, and proactivity rather than reactivity. In this spirit, the board will:

3.1.1 Enforce upon itself whatever discipline is needed to govern with excellence. Discipline may apply to matters such as attendance, respect of clarified roles, maintaining confidentialities, leaving questions regarding organizational activities and issues to the CEO, speaking to management and the public with one voice, and the self-policing of tendencies to stray from the governance structure and process adopted in these board policies.

3.1.2 Be accountable to its stakeholders and the general public for competent, conscientious, and effective execution of its plans as a whole. It will allow no officer, individual, or committee of the board to usurp this role or hinder this commitment.

3.1.3 Monitor and regularly discuss the board's own process and performance, seeking to ensure the continuity of its governance functions by the selection of capable directors, orientation and training, and evaluation.

3.1.4 Be an initiator of policy, not merely a reactor to staff initiatives. The board, not the staff, will be responsible for board performance.

3.2 Board Job Description. The job of the board is to lead the organization toward desired performance and help ensure that it occurs. The board's specific contributions are unique to its trusteeship role, and necessary for proper governance and management. To perform its job, the board will endeavor to:

3.2.1 Determine the mission, values, strategies, and major goals/outcomes, and hold the CEO accountable for developing a staff strategic plan based on these policies.

3.2.2 Determine the parameters within which the CEO is expected to achieve the goals/outcomes.

3.2.3 Monitor the performance of the organization relative to the achievement of the goals/outcomes within the executive parameters.

3.2.4 Maintain and continuously improve all on-going policies of the board in this BPM.

3.2.5 Select, fairly compensate, nurture, evaluate annually and, if necessary, terminate a CEO, who functions as the board's sole agent.

3.2.6 Ensure financial solvency and integrity through policies and behavior (including help as volunteers in fundraising).

3.2.7 Require periodic financial, legal, and other external audits to ensure compliance with the law and good practices.

3.2.8 Evaluate and constantly improve the board's performance as the governing board, and set expectations for board members' involvement as volunteers.

3.3 Board Member Criteria. In nominating members for the board, the board Governance Committee will be guided by the board-approved profile. (See Addendum A).

3.4 Orientation. Prior to election, each nominee will be given this BPM along with adequate briefings on the role of the board, officers, and staff, and an overview of programs, plans, and finances. Soon after election, each new board member will be given additional comprehensive orientation material and training.

3.5 Chair's Role. The job of the Chair is, primarily, to maintain the integrity of the board's process. The Chair "manages the board." The Chair is the only board member authorized to speak for the board, with the exception of certain rare and specifically board-authorized instances.

The Chair ensures that the board's behavior is consistent with its own rules, and those legitimately imposed upon it from outside the organizations. The content of meeting discussions will focus on those issues that, according to board policy, clearly belong to the board to decide.

The Chair's authority consists only of making decisions on behalf of the board that fall within, and are consistent with, any reasonable interpretation of board policies in Parts III and IV of this BPM. The Chair has no authority to make decisions beyond policies created by the board. Therefore, the Chair also has no authority to supervise or direct the CEO's work, but is instead expected to maintain close communication, offer advice, and provide encouragement to the CEO and staff on behalf of the board.

3.6 Board Meetings. Board events will often include time for guest presenters, interaction with staff and beneficiaries, board training, committee meetings, social activities, and plenary business sessions. Policies that are intended to improve the process for planning and running meetings are as follows:

3.6.1. The schedule for board meetings will, ideally, be set two years in advance.

3.6.2. The CEO will work with the Chair and committee chairs in developing agendas, which, along with background materials for the board and committees, monitoring reports, the CEO's recommendations for changes in the BPM, previous minutes, etc. should be mailed (or emailed) to all board members approximately two weeks prior to board meetings, or be placed on the board's website.

3.6.3 Minutes and the updated BPM should be sent to board members within X days of board meetings (or be placed on the board's website).

3.6.4 Regular board meetings will normally be held __ times a year in the months of ____, _____, and _____, preceded by a reminder notice approximately ___ days in advance of the meeting date. The ___ meeting normally will include a review of the planning and budgeting for the upcoming year. The ___ meeting normally will include a review of the performance of the CEO, and the organization for the past year. Special meetings of the board can be called according to the Bylaws [if not in the Bylaws, define that process here].

3.6.5 The Governance Committee is expected to prepare a meeting evaluation survey for completion by each board member who attends the board meeting. The completed surveys will be reviewed, analyzed, and summarized by the Governance Committee, which will then report the results of the meeting evaluation to the board members within two weeks after that meeting.

3.7 Standing Committees. Committees help the board be effective and efficient. They speak "to the board" and not "for the board." Unless authorized by the whole board, a committee may not exercise authority that is reserved to the whole board by the Bylaws, or by the laws of [name of state] governing not-for-profit organizations. Committees are not created for the purpose of advising or exercising authority over staff. Once the board creates committees, the board Chair will recommend committee chairs and members for one-year terms, subject to board approval. The board Chair and the CEO are ex officio members of all committees except the Audit and Compliance Committee. The CEO will assign one senior staff to assist with the work of each committee.

3.7.1 **Governance Committee.** This committee recommends policies to the board pertaining to governance issues and processes, including: the orientation and training of new board members, the evaluation and improvement of the contributions of individual board members and officers, and the recommendation of Bylaw changes. The committee will also develop a roster of potential board members based on the board profile, and nominate all board members and officers.

3.7.2 **Finance Committee.** This committee develops and recommends to the board those financial policies, plans, and courses of action that provide for mission accomplishment and organizational financial well-being. Consistent with this responsibility, it reviews the annual budget, and submits it to the board for its approval. In addition, the committee makes policy recommendations with regard to the levels and terms of indebtedness, cash management, investment policy, risk management, financial monitoring and reports, employee benefit plans, signatory authority for expenditures, and other policies for inclusion in this BPM that the committee determines will aid in effective financial management.

3.7.3 **Audit and Compliance Committee.** This committee oversees the organization's internal accounting controls; recommends external auditors for board approval; reviews the external auditors' annual audit plan; and reviews the annual report, management letter, and the results of the external audit. The committee, or its delegate, should have an annual private conversation with the auditor, and, as appropriate, legal counsel, all of whom may be contacted by the committee chair directly. In addition, the committee provides oversight of regulatory compliance, policies and practices regarding corporate responsibility, and ethics and business conduct-related activities, including compliance with Federal, state, and local laws governing tax-exempt entities. The committee oversees written conflict of interest policies and procedures of directors and officers and staff.

3.7.4 **Advancement Committee.** This committee studies and recommends policies relating to communications and public relations, as well as policies relating to raising financial and other resources for the organization.

3.7.5 **Programs Committee.** This committee studies and recommends board-level policies relating to programs and services of the organization.

3.7.6 **Executive Committee.** This committee includes the Chair, other officers, and the chairs of the other committees in Section 3.7. Except for the actions enumerated below, it has authority to act for the board regarding all matters, so long as the Executive Committee determines that it would be imprudent to wait for the next board meeting to take such actions. With respect to any action taken on behalf of the board, (1) the Executive Committee is required to report the action to the board within 10 days, and (2) the board may ratify the action at the next board meeting.

The Executive Committee is not authorized to make decisions with respect to the following matters: (Note: many State statutes enumerate limitations on committees as well, so it would be wise to check.)

3.7.6.1 Dissolving the corporation

3.7.6.2 Hiring or firing the chief executive

3.7.6.3 Entering into major contracts or suing another entity

3.7.6.4 Making significant changes to a board-approved budget

3.7.6.5 Adopting or eliminating major programs

3.7.6.6 Buying or selling property

3.7.6.7 Amending the Bylaws

3.7.6.8 Changing any policies the board determines must be changed only by the board.

3.7.7 [Other Committees and their areas of responsibility as determined by board]

3.8 Advisory Groups, Councils, and Task Forces. To increase its knowledge base and depth of available expertise, the board supports the utilization of groups, councils, and task forces of qualified advisers. The term "task force" refers to any group appointed by the CEO or the Chair to assist him or her in carrying out various time-limited goals and responsibilities. Although either the Chair or the CEO may form a task force, he or she should notify the board of the formation, purpose and membership within 10 days of its formation. The CEO may assign a senior staff member to serve advisory groups. The board has established the following advisory groups and/or task forces that are currently active:

3.8.1 (Name, membership, function, etc. of any advisory group the board creates.)

3.9 Board Members' Code of Conduct. The board expects ethical and businesslike conduct of itself and its members. Board members must represent unconflicted loyalty to the interests of the entire organization, superseding any conflicting loyalty such as those to family members, a business, advocacy or interest groups and membership on other boards or staffs. Board members must avoid any conflict of interest with respect to their fiduciary responsibility. There must be no self-dealing or any conduct of private business or personal services between any board member and the organization except as procedurally controlled where openness is assured, there exists competitive opportunity, and there exists equal access to "inside" information.

Board members will make no judgments of the CEO or staff performance except as the performance of the CEO is assessed against explicit board policies and agreed upon personal performance objectives.

Each board member is expected to complete and sign an Annual Affirmation and Conflict of Interest Statement (See Addendum B), which covers, inter alia, board conflicts of interest that are in accordance with the laws of [the State] governing not-for-profit organizations, and other expectations of board members.

3.10 Board Finances. Every board member is expected to be a donor of record in the first quarter of each calendar year. Expenses incurred to fulfill board activities normally can qualify as individual tax deductions; however, any board member may submit for reimbursement any expenses incurred in order to attend board or committee meetings.

Part 4: Board – CEO/Staff Relationship

4.1 Delegation to the Chief Executive (CEO). While the board job is generally confined to establishing high-level policies, implementation and subsidiary policy development is delegated to the CEO.

4.1.1 All board authority delegated to staff is delegated through the CEO so that all authority and accountability of staff—as far as the board is concerned—is considered to be the authority and accountability of the CEO.

4.1.2 Organizational Essentials policies (Part II) direct the CEO to achieve certain results. Executive Parameters policies (Part V) define the acceptable boundaries of prudence and ethics within which the CEO is expected to operate. The CEO is authorized to establish all further policies, make all decisions, take all actions, and develop all activities as long as they are consistent with laws and regulations and any reasonable interpretation of the board's policies in this BPM.

4.1.3. The board may change its policies during any meeting, thereby shifting the boundaries between board and CEO domains. Consequently, the board may change the latitude of choice given to the CEO, but so long as any particular delegation is in place, the board and its members will respect and support CEO choices. This does not prevent the board from obtaining information in the delegated areas.

4.1.4 Except when a person or committee has been authorized by the board to incur some amount of staff time and/or expense for the study of an issue, no board member, officer, or committee has authority over the CEO or the CEO's employees. Only officers or committee chairs may request information, but if such request—in the CEO's judgment—requires a material amount of staff time or funds or is disruptive, it may be refused until the Chair determines that the work is critical for board operations, and should be completed.

4.2 CEO Job Description. As the board's single official link to the operating organization, CEO performance will be considered to be synonymous with organizational performance as a whole. Consequently, the CEO's job contributions can be stated as performance in two areas: (a) organizational accomplishment of the major organizational goals in Section 2.8, and (b) organization operations within the boundaries of prudence and ethics established in board policies on Executive Parameters in Part V.

4.3 Communications and Counsel to the Board. With respect to providing information and counsel to the board, the CEO is expected to keep the board informed about matters essential to carrying out its policy duties. Accordingly, *the CEO is expected to*:

4.3.1 Inform the board of relevant trends, anticipated adverse media coverage, material external and internal changes, particularly changes in the assumptions upon which any board policy has previously been established, always presenting information in as clear and concise formats as possible.

4.3.2 Relate to the board as a whole, except when fulfilling reasonable individual requests for information, or responding to officers or committees duly charged by the board.

4.3.3 Report immediately any actual or anticipated material noncompliance with a policy of the board, along with suggested modifications to this BPM for the future.

4.4 The purpose of monitoring is to determine the degree to which the mission is being accomplished and board policies are being fulfilled. Information that does not do this shall not be considered monitoring. Monitoring will be as automatic as possible, using a minimum of board time so that meetings can be used to affect the future rather than to review the past. A given policy may be monitored in one or more of three ways:

4.4.1 **Direct board inspection:** Discovery of compliance information by a board member, a committee, or the board as a whole. This includes board inspection of documents, activities, or circumstances that allows a "prudent person" test of policy compliance.

4.4.2 **External report:** Discovery of compliance information by a disinterested, external person or firm who is selected by and reports directly to the board. Such reports must assess executive performance only against legal requirements or policies of the board, with suggestions from the external party as to how the organization can improve itself, including changes to this BPM.

4.4.3 **CEO Reports:** The CEO is expected to help the board determine what tracking data are suitable for measuring progress/outcomes in order to achieve the mission and other goals, and to comply with board policies. Currently, the board requests these regular monitoring reports, in addition to any specific reports requested in other sections of the BPM:

4.4.3.1 **Monthly:** Informal CEO reports on achievements, problems, board notices, etc.

4.4.3.2 **Quarterly:** (A) One or two-page "dashboard" report showing agreed upon key indicators that track designated financial and program outcomes over a three-year period in graphic form; (B) Other summary reports as the board may define in this BPM.

4.4.3.3 **Semi-Annually:** (A) Expense and revenue against budget report with comparison to previous year; (B) Balance sheet; (C) Cash flow projections; (D) ______statistics.

4.4.3.4 **Annual:** Within 45 days of the end of the fiscal year, with respect to that year: (A) End of year expense and revenue against budget; (B) Balance sheet; (C) Staff organization chart (or whenever major changes are made); (D) Other reports that the board may define in this BPM.

4.5 Annual Performance Review. A performance evaluation task force, comprising the board Chair, Vice Chair, and the Chair of the Governance Committee, is expected to oversee a formal evaluation of the CEO annually, focused on achievement of organizational goals, and on any other specific goals the board and CEO have agreed upon in advance, as well as the CEO's own written self-evaluation along with invited comments from all board members after they have viewed the self-evaluation. The Chair will typically serve as chair of the task force. After meeting with the CEO, the task force will report on its review to the board, including recommendations regarding the CEO's compensation, which the Executive Committee, or the board, will then act upon.

During this process, the CEO and the board will agree on any specific, personal performance goals for the year ahead. These goals should be documented in a letter to the CEO from the board Chair, and will become the primary basis for assessing the CEO's performance at the end of the next year. At least every three years, the task force may consider inviting other input in a carefully planned "360" review, including feedback from staff, peers in our sector, and individuals outside the organization who have interacted with the CEO.

4.6 Staff Compensation. The CEO is expected to hire, train, motivate, compensate, and terminate staff in a professional and caring fashion. Salaries will be set within between X% and Y% of the mean for salaries of organizations of similar size, budget, and location according to well-respected and relevant survey data. Benefits will include. . . . The CEO is expected to (A) develop and maintain an employee manual that is reviewed periodically by competent legal counsel, and (B) provide copies to the board for information around April 1 of each year.

4.7 Staff Treatment. With respect to treatment of paid and volunteer staff, the CEO should build a climate of trust, and determine policies based on competent legal counsel.

4.8 CEO Transitions. At any time, the Chair may appoint a succession/transition task force to explore options and propose strategies and board policies related to succession and transition of the CEO, and to facilitate any special needs of the outgoing and incoming CEOs and their families. The incumbent CEO should give the board, if possible, a ___-month notice of intent to leave that office. Any need for an acting or interim CEO will be considered and determined by the board. At this time, the board designates _______ to serve in an Acting CEO role whenever there is an immediate need. The board Chair is authorized, as soon as a vacancy or scheduled departure of the CEO is known, to appoint a search committee and committee chair. The search committee may include up to ___ people not on the board, including ________. The committee is expected, within 30 days of its appointment, to recommend a position announcement for board approval, a recommendation on any search consultant, the appointment of a search secretary, and a budget for the search. The search committee should present one or two qualified candidates to the full board for selection. A special task force appointed by the Chair will, at the time of selection, negotiate the new CEO's compensation and service agreement, and give both the incumbent and successor CEO any special performance priorities from the board. After he/she leaves the organization, the outgoing CEO may be given a paid role, but only with the approval of the new CEO in consultation with the officers.

4.9 Accessing Board Documents. The CEO is expected to develop and maintain a system that makes all key board documents accessible at any time by any board member. Initially, this could be a system whereby every board member would create 6-10 "folders" on a home computer hard drive, into which various documents are kept. A Board Reference Book may be maintained with all pertinent documents to which board members might wish to refer during board and committee meetings (e.g.,

Articles, Bylaws, organization chart, recent minutes, committee roster, list of key volunteers and consultants, board documents referenced in this BPM, etc.) . . . unless the better alternative of a secure website can be developed for such documents. When and if such a website is created, the CEO is expected to notify board members whenever key new information is posted to.

Part 5 – Executive Parameters

The purpose of Part 5 (with its several sections) is to detail those Executive Parameters that will guide the CEO and the staff as they work to accomplish the mission. These parameters are intended to free the CEO and staff to make timely decisions without undue board directives. For convenience, we have numbered the major sections below according to the primary functions of our organization and our committee structure, understanding that we may choose to add, merge or delete such sections in the future.

Overall, the board expects that the CEO will do nothing that is illegal, unethical, or imprudent. Beyond that, the board details its Executive Parameters in the following sections.

Section 5. Finance Parameters

5.1 Finance General. The CEO must ensure that the financial integrity of the organization is maintained at all times; that proper care is exercised in the receiving, processing, and disbursing of funds; and that financial and non-financial assets are appropriately protected.

5.2 Financial Controls. The CEO must exercise care in the accounting for and protecting of the financial assets of the organization. To the end, the CEO is expected to follow generally accepted principles of accounting and internal controls in the financial systems present within the organization. In addition, the CEO may not:

5.2.1 Receive, process, or disburse funds under insufficient controls to meet the board-appointed auditor's standards.

5.2.2 Approve an unbudgeted expenditure or commitment of greater than $________ without approval of the full board.

5.2.3 Approve an unbudgeted expenditure or commitment of $________ without approval of the Finance Committee.

5.3 Asset Protection. The CEO may not allow assets to be unprotected, inadequately maintained, or unnecessarily risked. Accordingly, the CEO may not:

5.3.1 Fail to insure against theft and casualty losses to at least 80 percent replacement value and against liability losses to board members, staff, or the organization itself beyond the minimally acceptable prudent level.

5.3.2 Allow non-bonded personnel access to material amounts of funds.

5.3.3 Subject office and equipment to improper wear and tear or insufficient maintenance.

5.3.4 Unnecessarily expose the organization, its board, or staff to claims of liability.

5.3.5 Make any major purchase of over $__________ without sealed bids or other demonstrably prudent acquisition of quality goods, or any purchase of over $_________ without written record of competitive prices, or any purchase wherein normally prudent protection has not been given against conflict of interest.

5.3.6 Acquire, encumber, or dispose of real property without board approval.

5.4 Investment Principles. The CEO may not invest or hold operating capital in insecure instruments, including uninsured checking accounts and bonds of less than AA rating, or in non-interest bearing accounts except where necessary to facilitate ease in operational transactions.

Section 6. Program Parameters

In general, the CEO is expected to establish, maintain, and eliminate programs and services as will best achieve the mission and goals in the most effective and efficient manner.

6.1 New programs should be projected to serve at least _____ people.

6.2 New programs with an expected budget exceeding $_______ must be approved by the board. Those programs now approved include: [fill in]

6.3 Programs with costs of more than $____ should be assessed for effectiveness by an outside evaluator at least every ___ years, with a written report made available to the board.

6.4 Any program executed in partnership with another organization should be ________.

Section 7. Advancement Parameters

The various efforts to represent the organization to the public (media, public relations, fundraising, new member recruitment, etc.) are expected to be integrated sufficiently so that the organization's brand/position in the external world is positive and effective.

7.1 Fundraising Strategy. The CEO is expected to develop and maintain a fundraising plan that, at a minimum, includes direct mail, major donor initiatives, planned giving, and webbased giving. Such plan should be provided to board members for review each March, along with results for each initiative. Total direct and indirect expenses for fundraising are not expected to exceed ___% of the total budget.

7.2 Donor Bill of Rights. The CEO is expected to develop and provide for board review the latest version of a Donor Bill of Rights which should include, inter alia, the following restrictions: the CEO may not allow the names of donors to be revealed outside the organization; represent to a donor that an action will be taken that violates board policies; fail to honor an enforceable restriction from a donor; or fail to confirm receipt of a donor's contribution and send him/her an annual summary of donations. The CEO is expected also to ensure that we attempt to honor donors' requests and statements of desire so long as applicable circumstances allow, provided that those donors are adequately informed that their requests and statements of desire do not ordinarily constitute binding obligations on the organization, and that the organization retains ultimate discretion and control over use of their non-designated donations. (See Exhibit X.)

7.3 Training. The CEO should provide for periodic board and staff training in new fundraising techniques and budget for such expenses.

7.4 Public Affairs. The CEO is expected to exercise care in representing that we are a charitable, mission-centered, listening organization, and develop policies and procedures for communicating with primary stakeholders and the public at large in a way that reinforces that image.

7.5 Communications Plan. The CEO is expected to develop and maintain a communications plan, shared with the board as appropriate, that describes how the organization will communicate with its various stakeholders. The plan should identify the stakeholder segments, and how the organization will both speak and listen to each segment.

7.6 Communications Restrictions. To preserve our image in the community, the CEO and any designee are the only spokespersons authorized to speak for the organization and the Chair the only spokesperson for the board. None of the spokespersons may represent the organization in any way inconsistent with the policies in Part II of this BPM; make statements that may be perceived as supporting a political party or platform; author an article, book, or publication that includes classified or sensitive information about the organization; or engage in lobbying activities at any governmental level without prior permission from the board.

Section 8. Audit and Compliance

The CEO is expected to take the necessary steps to ensure that the integrity of our systems and procedures comply with all pertinent legal, regulatory, and professional requirements, and to report to the board any material variations or violations.

8.1 Annual External Audit. An independent auditor will be hired and supervised by the Audit and Compliance Committee, after a careful selection and annual evaluation. The CEO will work with the auditor in order to gain a clean opinion of the annual financial statements and respond in detail to items in the auditor's management letter concerning opportunities to improve systems and procedures related to financial controls.

8.2 Internal Compliance. The CEO is expected to meet all requirements for complying with federal, state, or local laws and regulations. The CEO should maintain a list of compliance actions and reports that are required of nonprofit organizations, or recommended by the IRS as reflected in questions contained in the Form 990 report, and periodically submit the list for inspection by the Audit and Compliance Committee. The CEO is encouraged to contract with competent legal counsel every ____ years to compare our policies, procedures and contracts with pertinent laws and regulations to ensure we remain in essential compliance. Reports of such reviews must be made available to the Audit and Compliance Committee who, in turn, will report to the board on the overall status of the organization with respect to compliance matters.

Section 9. Miscellaneous

9.1 [available for policies that do not fit naturally in other chapters]

•••••

BPM Addendums (Board documents referenced in this BPM) are:

#	BPM Ref.	Title	Status
A	3.3	Board Profile	
B	3.9	Conflict of Interest/Annual Affirmation	
C			

BPM Exhibits (CEO/Organization documents referenced in this BPM are:

#	BPM Ref.	Title	Status
1	2.9	Strategic Plan	
2			

Any questions about this Board Policies Manual should be directed to: ___________ [often the executive assistant to the CEO, who updates the BPM immediately following each board meeting and distributes it to all who should have it].

Special Note to ECFA-Accredited Organizations and ECFA-Certified Churches:

Separate from the Board Policies Manual (BPM) provided by Laughlin and Andringa, ECFA members will want to note the following suggested edits, additions, and commentary regarding several sections in the BPM:

Section	Title	ECFA Comment
3.7	Standing Committees	While this BPM lists several suggested standing committees (Finance Committee, Audit and Compliance Committee, etc.), some boards find it prudent to combine several committee functions (Example: Finance & Audit Committee, etc.).
3.09	Board Members' Code of Conduct	ECFA's Board of Directors has edited this section to read as follows: ECFA desires to be an exemplary organization that demonstrates best practices in the nonprofit world. An important part of this example setting starts with the quality and commitment of individual ECFA board members. Board members assume ultimate legal, moral and spiritual accountability for the work of ECFA. Individual board members are committed to and have a passion (both on a personal and professional level) for the doctrinal distinctives of the evangelical faith. As a result, all that board members do is carried out through the lens of the Christian worldview, and they realize that they are ultimately accountable to God. The board responsibilities are incorporated as Appendix B to this BPM. Each board member is expected to complete and annually sign an Affirmation of Service (Appendix C). At the beginning of each board meeting, each board member is expected to sign a Covenant of Confidentiality (Appendix D).
5	Finance Parameters	The president must ensure that the financial integrity of the organization is maintained at all times; that proper care is exercised in the receiving, processing, and disbursing of funds; and that financial and nonfinancial assets are appropriately protected.
6	Program Parameters	In general, the president is expected to establish, maintain, and eliminate programs and services to achieve the organization's mission and goals in the most effective and efficient manner.

TOOL #18: Job Descriptions for the Top Leader and Board Chair

Review these sample job descriptions for the Board Chair and the CEO (or Executive Pastor) and then use these insights to refresh your documents.

"The term of the Rotator chair is usually as short as a year or two. The idea is that the ministry can survive incompetence for a short period of time."[1]

S.O.A.R With Inspired Job Descriptions!

The Number One Hiring Mistake

You're Not the Person I Hired!
A CEO's Survival Guide to Hiring Top Talent

The Number One hiring mistake: "Inadequate job descriptions drove the hiring process; these focused solely on experience and skills, not company expectations. A staggering 93 percent of searches that resulted in new executive failure made this mistake at the outset."

The solution: eliminate tired-out, traditional job descriptions and instead, create measurable expectations around four S.O.A.R. areas: Substantial Departmental Goal, Obstacles, Action, Results. [Three cheers for authors who focus on the Results Bucket!]

"The harsh reality is, when you *define* a job in mediocre terms, you tend to *attract* and *interview* mediocre people."[2]

Book Reviews:

- ❑ ***You're Not the Person I Hired*** (Janet Boydell, Barry Deutsch and Brad Remillard) *http://urgentink.typepad.com/my_weblog/2009/11/youre-not-the-person-i-hired.html*
- ❑ ***Call of the Chair: Leading the Board of the Christ-Centered Ministry*** (David McKenna) *http://urgentink.typepad.com/my_weblog/2017/06/call-of-the-chair.html*
- ❑ ***The Ideal Team Player: How to Recognize and Cultivate the Three Essential Virtues*** (Patrick Lencioni) *http://urgentink.typepad.com/my_weblog/2016/06/the-ideal-team-player.html*

[1] David L. McKenna, *Call of the Chair: Leading the Board of the Christ-Centered Ministry* (Winchester, VA: ECFAPress, 2017), 17.

[2] Janet Boydell, Barry Deutsch, and Brad Remillard, *You're Not the Person I Hired! A CEO's Survival Guide to Hiring Top Talent* (Bloomington, IN: Author House, 2006), 63–70. Read Chapters 5 and 6 for more insights.

Job Descriptions for the Top Leader and Board Chair

"The board chair-CEO relationship is like a pair of chopsticks. One is much more effective with the support of the other."[3]

☑ **Assess Your Current Job Descriptions and S.M.A.R.T. Goals (see Tool #11):**

Position	Job Description Is Current	Job Description Needs Work	SMART* Goals Are Current	SMART* Goals Need Work
Board Chair				
CEO or Senior Pastor				

***S.M.A.R.T. Goals are: Specific, Measurable, Achievable, Realistic, Time-Related (See Tool #11).**

Job Descriptions Resources:

- ❑ ECFA Knowledge Center – *www.ECFA.org/KnowledgeCenter*
- ❑ BoardSource – *www.BoardSource.org*
- ❑ Board Policies Manual (see Tool #17)

Note: For a contrarian view of job descriptions, read the "People" chapters in *Scaling Up: How a Few Companies Make It...and Why the Rest Don't – Mastering the Rockefeller Habits 2.0*, by Verne Harnish. "We are not big fans of job descriptions and prefer Topgrading's Job Scorecards."[4]

"Like a one-stringed banjo player, the chair will always sound the note reminding the members that the board's role is policy, not execution."[5]

David McKenna

[3] Michael Naufal, *The Chair-CEO Relationship: Ten Commitments for a Better Partnership* (Ottawa, Canada: Ray & Berndtson, 2005).

[4] Verne Harnish, *Scaling Up: How a Few Companies Make It . . . and Why the Rest Don't – Mastering the Rockefeller Habits 2.0* (Ashburn,VA: Gazelles, 2014), 51.

[5] McKenna, *Call of the Chair*, 63.

The Board Chair Job Description

The Board Chair's Role

Review the role of the board chair as described in the Board Policies Manual (Tool #17) from:

Good Governance for Nonprofits
Developing Principles and Policies for an Effective Board

by Fredric L. Laughlin and Robert C. Andringa

The Board Chair's Role (Section 3.5) – "The Chair Manages the Board"

See Tool #17: Board Policies Manual (BPM)

3.5 Chair's Role. The job of the Chair is, primarily, to maintain the integrity of the board's process. The Chair "manages the board." The Chair is the only board member authorized to speak for the board, with the exception of certain rare and specifically board-authorized instances.

The Chair ensures that the board's behavior is consistent with its own rules, and those legitimately imposed upon it from outside the organizations. The content of meeting discussions will focus on those issues that, according to board policy, clearly belong to the board to decide.

The Chair's authority consists only of making decisions on behalf of the board that fall within, and are consistent with, any reasonable interpretation of board policies in Parts III and IV of this BPM. The Chair has no authority to make decisions beyond policies created by the board. Therefore, the Chair also has no authority to supervise or direct the CEO's work, but is instead expected to maintain close communication, offer advice, and provide encouragement to the CEO and staff on behalf of the board."[6]

From the "color commentary" on Section 3.5 in *Good Governance for Nonprofits*

In describing the chair, we have heard board members use terms like *dynamic, lazy, control freak, hands-off leader, overbearing, timid, committed, blasé, confident,* and *self-centered.* Seldom do we hear that the chair is a 'good manager.' Yet, as described in Section 3.5, that is the chair's role—to be a good manager of the board.[7]

> ***"For every hour spent on creating and maintaining a Board Policies Manual, at least three hours of board and committee meetings will be saved before too long. It's a 'living document,' always reflecting the latest wisdom of the board."***[8]
>
> Robert C. Andringa

[6] Fredric L. Laughlin and Robert C. Andringa, *Good Governance for Nonprofits: Developing Principles and Policies for an Effective Board* (New York: AMACOM, 2007), 95.

[7] Ibid.

[8] Robert C. Andringa, "Do Unwritten Board Policies Really Exist?" *Lessons From the Nonprofit Boardroom* (blog), December 13, 2017, *http://nonprofitboardroom.blogspot.com/2017/12/lesson-4-do-unwritten-board-policies.html.*

ECFA Knowledge Center
www.ECFA.org

Used by Permission

Sample Board Chair Position Description

Authority for Electing the Board Chair

The bylaws of [Name of Ministry] stipulate that the board of directors shall annually elect a Board Chair. (Note: The bylaws may provide for an election cycle other than an annual election.)

Qualifications

Completed two years of board membership term and have an understanding of parliamentary procedures.

Term

The Chair is elected by the board for a one-year term in accordance with the bylaws.

Requirements:

- Commitment to the work of the ministry;
- Knowledge and skills in one or more areas of board governance: policy, finance, programs, and/or personnel;
- Regular attendance at periodic board meetings;
- Prepare for, and participate in, the discussions and the deliberations of the board;
- Foster a positive working relationship with other board members and the organization's staff; and
- Be aware of, and abstain from, any real or perceived conflicts of interest

Major Duties:

- Be the primary spokesperson for [Name of Ministry] to the media and the community at large;
- Chair the Executive Committee (if there is one);
- Report to the board on the status of major programs;
- Signing authority on behalf of the board for financial and legal purposes;
- Provide leadership and direction to the board;
- Arrange for Vice Chair to chair meetings when absent;
- In conjunction with the CEO, set the periodic board meeting agenda;
- Ensure board members receive agenda and minutes in a timely manner; and
- Adhere to general duties outlined in the board member job description

Do-It-Yourself Board Chair Job Descriptions

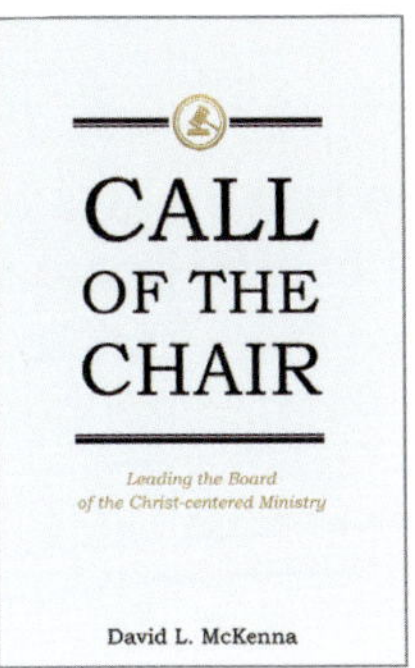

Wordsmith your own job description from "McKenna's 9 M's"

Call of the Chair:
Leading the Board of the Christ-Centered Ministry
by David L. McKenna

Read the review:
http://urgentink.typepad.com/my_weblog/2017/06/call-of-the-chair.html

No.	McKenna's 9 Ms	Per McKenna, the "distinctive role of the board chair for the Christ-centered ministry" is answered this way:
1	Missionary	
2	Model	
3	Mentor	
4	Manager	
5	Moderator	
6	Mediator	
7	Monitor	
8	Master	
9	Maestro	

Bonus Resources for Church Boards

Attn: Church Boards

Church boards (including churches that have elder boards) recognize that there is a wide variety of governance models for churches. Identify a person on your church board who is a "Learner," according to the StrengthsFinder assessment from Gallup (see Tool #20). Then inspire that person to always be on the lookout for helpful resources for both the board chair and the church board.

Lessons From the Church Boardroom
40 Insights for Exceptional Governance
by Dan Busby and John Pearson

- ❑ 40 short lessons
- ❑ Blog: *http://churchboardroom.blogspot.com/*

The New Elder's Handbook
A Biblical Guide to Developing Faithful Leaders
by Greg R. Scharf and Arthur Kok

- ❑ This resource provides church leaders a model for an elder development pipeline, including vision, recruitment of elders to carry out that vision, and specific, biblical training for developing faithful elders for God's people.

Best Practices for Effective Boards
by E. LeBron Fairbanks, Dwight M. Gunter II, and James R. Couchenour

- ❑ Authored by a pastor, an educator, and a business person/board member
- ❑ Insights and wisdom for both church and nonprofit boards
- ❑ See Appendix 7: "Rules of the Road for Christlike Conflict Management"

In his chapter, "Yes! to Missional Change," Pastor Dwight Gunter asks **"How many Christians does it take to change a light bulb?"** His answer: "Seven. One to change the bulb and six to resist the change." *(Insert "How many board members…" and it's just as funny.)*[9]

[9] E. LeBron Fairbanks, Dwight M. Gunter II, and James R. Couchenour, *Best Practices for Effective Boards* (Kansas City: Beacon Hill, 2012), 178–79.

Top Leader Job Descriptions – CEO/Senior Pastor

CEO Job Description

Review the job description for the CEO as described in the Board Policies Manual (Tool #17) from:

Good Governance for Nonprofits
Developing Principles and Policies for an Effective Board

by Fredric L. Laughlin and Robert C. Andringa

CEO Job Description (Section 4.2) – "Performance in Two Areas"

See Tool #17: Board Policies Manual (BPM)

4.2 CEO Job Description. As the board's single official link to the operating organization, CEO performance will be considered to be synonymous with organizational performance as a whole. Consequently, the CEO's job contributions can be stated as performance in two areas: organizational accomplishment of the major organizational goals in Section 2.8, and (b) organization operations within the boundaries of prudence and ethics established in board policies on Executive Parameters in Part V.[10]

From the "color commentary" on Section 4.2 in Good Governance for Nonprofits

We have seen job descriptions that are as short and simple as the one in our BPM template and others that are three pages of bullet points. Often CEO job descriptions are drawn up and closely followed during the recruiting process, but then are seldom consulted after the CEO is hired. Once the CEO is on board, the framework for the CEO/board relationship is less one of listing all the functions in the CEO's job description and more about how well the mission is being accomplished. Accordingly, the board normally looks at the CEO's "job" as being responsible for carrying out the mission of the organization while staying within the stated board policies. As a practical matter, of course, there are many factors that may complicate this simple equation, including the maturity of the organization, external influences, and other factors that are beyond the CEO's control. Accountability must be balanced with fairness as you lay out the relationship between the board and your CEO.[11]

"Recall that BPM Section 2.8 lists the current goals of the organization and therefore of the CEO. The board and the CEO mutually agree upon these, and they become the basis of the CEO's evaluation. They should be measurable and linked to the strategic plan. Therefore, even though the board is looking to the CEO to accomplish the mission in a broad sense, it must translate that overarching statement into fair and reasonable goals against which the CEO can be evaluated."[12]

Fredric L. Laughlin and Robert C. Andringa

[10] Laughlin and Andringa, *Good Governance for Nonprofits*, 123.
[11] Ibid., 124.
[12] Ibid.

Do-It-Yourself CEO Job Descriptions

Available in print or PDF at www.BoardSource.org

The Nonprofit Chief Executive's
Ten Basic Responsibilities, Second Edition

Rick Moyers

	10 Basic Responsibilities of Nonprofit CEOs[13]	☑ If this is included in your current CEO position description. ☒ Note any action steps required.
1	Commit to the mission	
2	Lead the staff and manage the organization	
3	Exercise responsible financial stewardship	
4	Lead and manage fundraising	
5	Follow the highest ethical standards, ensure accountability, and comply with the law	
6	Engage the board in planning and lead implementation	
7	Develop future leadership	
8	Build external relationships and serve as an advocate	
9	Ensure the quality and effectiveness of programs	
10	Support the board	

Download the book's "Table of Contents" and "Introduction" here:
https://boardsource.org/wp-content/uploads/2016/10/Nonprofit-CEO-Ten-Basic-Responsibilities-TOC-1.pdf

[13] Rick Moyers, *The Nonprofit Chief Executive's Ten Basic Responsibilities,* 2d ed. (Washington, DC: BoardSource, 2013).

CEO Job Description Homework:

We would add these additional basic responsibilities—based on our history, our culture, our faith-based convictions, the season/cycle we're in, and other factors:

	Additional Basic Responsibilities of *Our* Nonprofit CEO	
11		
12		
13		
14		
15		

IMPORTANT! Job descriptions are helpful, but you'll find the most helpful document for effective CEO/board relationships (and the growth of your organization) will be when you have agreement on the CEO's 3 to 5 Annual S.M.A.R.T. Goals. (See Tool #11.)

Ten Questions for Nonprofit CEOs

Question 6:
Do you know who your next board chair is likely to be?

- ❑ Yes
- ❑ No
- ❑ **Are you kidding?**[14]

[14] Ibid., 60.

Sample CEO Job Description

Nonprofit organizations exist in all sizes with an emphasis on an array of causes. Regardless of size, or whether the organization's staff is made up of volunteers or employees, every nonprofit should have one person who is the effective leader that guides the organization.

The Nonprofit Board Answer Book expresses agreement with this principle: "Every nonprofit organization should designate one person to function as its operational leader. That person's title does not have to include the words *chief executive* or *chief executive officer*, but the bylaws and other policy documents should identify which position carries the authority and responsibility to run the organization day-to-day and reports to the board of directors. The following are some reasons why:

- A board needs one point of accountability.
- Staff members need to know where the buck stops.
- Donors need to identify the leader.
- Other external constituents need to know who's in charge.
- Planning needs a facilitator.
- The organization needs one spokesperson."[15]

As noted above, it is essential for an organization to have one leader that the board and staff can look to for guidance. Proverbs 11:14 says, "Where there is no guidance, the people fall. But in abundance of counselors, there is victory." Without an executive to provide counsel and guidance, the organization is more likely to encounter hindrances. However, with a leader in position, an organization is able to flourish and grow, ultimately furthering The Great Commission.

Below is a sample job description of an Executive Director/CEO. The sample is provided as an illustration of broad guidelines for the position and should be tailored to best fit the organization using it.

CEO

Summary/Objective

The CEO is responsible for providing strategic leadership for the ministry by working with the Board and other management to establish long-range goals, strategies, plans and policies.

The CEO is the direct executive representative in the management of the corporation, and is responsible for the organization's consistent achievement of its mission and financial objectives.

Qualifications

[Tailor qualifications to fit the specific organization's function and demands of the top leadership position.]

[15] BoardSource, *The Nonprofit Board Answer Book: A Practical Guide for Board Members and Chief Executives*, 2d ed. (San Francisco: Jossey-Bass, 2007), 231–32.

Essential Functions

Reasonable accommodations may be made to enable individuals with disabilities to perform the essential functions.

1. Commit to the organization and its mission and ensure that the organization has a long-range strategy which achieves its mission, and toward which it makes consistent and timely progress.
2. Follow the highest ethical standards, ensure accountability, and comply with the law.
3. Provide leadership in developing program, organizational and financial plans with the Board of Directors and staff, and carry out plans and policies authorized by the board.
4. Implement plans and decide or guide courses of action in operations by staff. Oversee and manage organization programs and projects.
5. Exercise responsible financial stewardship.
6. Determine the financial needs of the organization, submit proposals to donors and maintain the fundraising records.
7. Oversee fundraising planning and implementation, including identifying resources, requirements, researching funding sources, establishing strategies to approach funders, submitting proposals and administrating fundraising records and documentation.
8. Manage human resources of organization, including the recruitment, employment, and release of all personnel, both paid staff and volunteers, in conformity with current laws and regulations.
9. Assist in the selection and evaluation of board members.
10. Support and advise the board, making recommendations and engaging the board in planning and the implementation of projects.
11. Build external relationships and serve as an advocate of the organization, in and around the community. Establish sound working relationships and cooperative arrangements with community groups and organizations. Maintain a positive image with the public regarding the nonprofit organization.
12. Ensure that the board is kept fully informed on the condition of the organization and all factors influencing it. Maintain knowledge and update the staff and board of significant developments and trends in the field.
13. Act as an interface between Board and employees, and between the organization and community.

Attn: Church Boards

Caution! "One size doesn't fit all." A senior pastor position description and "S.M.A.R.T. Goals" for the top leader at First Church may not be adequate (or relevant) for the senior pastor of Anytown Community Church. As you collaborate with your senior pastor on a position description, review relevant resources, such as *Wisdom From Lyle E. Schaller* and other books and websites.

Before You Create the Senior Pastor Description: Caution! "One Size Doesn't Fit All"

Wisdom from Lyle E. Schaller
The Elder Statesman of Church Leadership
Second Edition

by Warren Bird, Editor

What is the senior pastor's role: Shepherd or Rancher?

On the senior pastor's role in leading a church that functions as a "congregation of congregations" versus "one big family"...

"This effort can be reinforced if the senior minister's basic role is seen not as being a shepherd spending most of the day with one flock and considerable time with individual sheep, but as being a rancher or bishop. . . . The rancher or bishop's responsibility is to delegate to others and to trust the people to whom specific responsibilities have been delegated."[16]

Tribal Church: Lead Small, Impact Big

by Steve Stroope with Kurt Bruner, Foreword by Rick Warren

How should a senior pastor invest his or her time?

"The larger the church, the greater the need for more tribes of leaders who can lead their own tribes."[17]	**Early Ministry Season**	**Middle Ministry Season**	**Later Ministry Season**
Doing ministry	60%	30%	10%
Leading those doing ministry	30%	40%	30%
Leading those who are leading those doing ministry	10%	20%	30%
Resourcing leaders of leaders	0%	10%	30%
Total time	**100%**	**100%**	**100%**

16 Warren Bird, ed., *Wisdom from Lyle E. Schaller: The Elder Statesman of Church Leadership* (Nashville: Abingdon, 2012), 76.
17 Steve Stroope with Kurt Bruner, *Tribal Church: Lead Small, Impact Big* (Nashville: B&H, 2012), 84–85.

Sample

BONUS: Executive Pastor Job Description

Overview

The Executive Pastor is to provide vision, support, and coordination of all ministries. This person will function as the chief administrator of multiple staff. This person is responsible for the establishment of priorities and the orderly implementation of approved activities and plans. This person is a voting member of the elder board and is a member of the Pastoral Leadership Team.

Responsibilities

Administration

- Primarily responsible for leading the search for unfilled staff and volunteer positions.
- Serves as supervisor for all staff, with the exception of the Pastoral Leadership Team.
- Serves as supervisor for all non-pastoral staff to ensure that their efforts cohere with the mission of the church and that they have the share of resources they need.

Coordination

- Coordinates all seminars and conferences related to the further development for church leaders and staff.
- Oversees budget planning and monitors financial performance to insure that expenses stay within budget.
- Coordinates all activities associated with growth of all ministries and facility expansion.
- Coordinates communication of plans and vision to the congregation.
- Coordinates any ministries that do not have direct pastoral oversight.

Implementation

- Serves as a member of the Pastoral Leadership Team (PLT), which provides vision planning for all Staff led and Board approved actions.
- Oversees the implementation of the PLT actions so that communication, harmony and faithfulness to the vision prevail.
- Mentors the appropriate staff as necessary to assure staff cooperation, unity, effectiveness and efficiency.
- Monitors the appropriate staff expectations, goals and training.
- Assures that all financial reports and activities are managed properly and in a timely manner.

Reporting and Reviews

The Executive Pastor is accountable to the Senior Pastor.

Qualifications

Beliefs

- Knows Christ as personal Savior and Lord and is willing to testify accordingly.
- Agrees with the Statement of Faith, the Church Covenant, and the Biblical Principles for Christian Living as written in the Constitution.

Character

- Has unchallenged mature Christian character.
- Has demonstrated ability to work with many different types of people.
- Has the ability to communicate with sensitivity.
- Has relationships with his family, associates and friends that honor the Lord.

Competency

- A strong organizer
- A good people manager
- Detailed in follow through
- Able to motivate others, both staff and volunteers.
- Able to coordinate many ministries to maximize their effectiveness
- Self motivated
- Able to develop professional skills in others
- Accountable

Education and Experience

Must have prior full time ministry experience in a local church. An advanced degree from an acceptable seminary or educational institution is preferred.

Job Description Resources: CEO

☑ **ECFA Knowledge Center**

www.ECFA.org/KnowledgeCenter

Job Descriptions

ECFA's Knowledge Center provides access to hundreds of documents including policies, procedures and a wealth of research on topics such as charitable gifts, expense reimbursements, board governance, fringe benefits, and much more.

☑ **BoardSource**

www.BoardSource.org

ePolicy Sampler – Chief Executive (Word Doc)

Level 201

BoardSource offers Downloadable Policy Samplers in 10 different topic areas to help you create specific policies for your organization. Each Downloadable Policy Sampler covers several subtopics and includes an introduction to the subtopic area, key elements, practical tips, suggested resources, and several dozen sample policies.

The Chief Executive Sampler includes 17 samples on the following:

❑ Chief Executive Job Descriptions

❑ Chief Executive Performance Evaluation

❑ Executive Compensation

❑ Executive Transition

"There are three roles of the CEO: selecting the right people, allocating capital resources, and spreading ideas quickly." [18]

Jack Welch

[18] Jack Welch quoted in the "Leadership Tip of the Day" email from the (now-named) Frances Hesselbein Leadership Forum, June 4, 2015, *www.HesselbeinForum.org*.

Job Description Resources : Executive Pastor

Attn: Church Boards

Here are several organizations and websites that may help you in creating or revising your senior pastor's job description and S.M.A.R.T. goals.

ECFA KNOWLEDGE CENTER
www.ECFA.church/KnowledgeCenter

The Knowledge Center provides access to hundreds of documents including job descriptions, policies, procedures and a wealth of research on topics such as charitable gifts, expense reimbursements, board governance, fringe benefits, and much more.

LEADERSHIP NETWORK
http://leadnet.org/downloads/

According to Leadership Network, they have more experience in helping churches than anyone else. They help strategic pastors, staff and teams move ideas to implementation to impact.

XPASTOR
www.xpastor.org/staffing/job-descriptions/

The mission of XPastor is to "equip, coach and lead" those who lead and manage the church. XPastor's "tribe" is church leaders—Executive Pastors, Senior Pastors, Pastors, Finance Personnel and Board Members. The link above will lead you to senior pastor and lead pastor job descriptions for varying sizes of churches.

"A pastor friend, 'Carlos,' once told me, 'I don't have the spiritual gift of board meetings.' He expressed what many pastors feel.

"No church board is perfect, but the best boards set a high standard for board service. When the right people—with the right motives and God-honoring character—serve graciously together, there will be a minimum amount of dysfunction and a maximum amount of spiritual fruit and impact. Board members and pastors will thrive in board meetings as the Holy Spirit deploys their spiritual gifts and their God-designed personalities and strengths."[19]

Dan Busby and John Pearson

[19] Dan Busby and John Pearson, *Lessons From the Church Boardroom: 40 Insights for Exceptional Governance* (Winchester, VA: ECFAPress, 2018), 44–45.

Read *The One Thing*... Before You Write or Revise Your Board Chair and Top Leader Job Descriptions

This book will help you focus on the ONE thing you must do every week.

BOOK REVIEW

The ONE Thing:
The Surprisingly Simple Truth Behind Extraordinary Results
by Gary Keller with Jay Papasan

Your Weekly Staff Meeting eNews

John Pearson, Editor/Publisher

Issue No. 342 of *Your Weekly Staff Meeting* features 10 quotable quotes (all Twitter-worthy) from a hot contender already for my 2016 book-of-the-year. Gary Keller says that to focus on *The ONE Thing*, you must examine your to-do lists. He notes: "To-do lists inherently lack the intent of success."

10 Tweetable Quotations

Never done this before! Right there—on page 117—was a stunner-of-a-statement that went immediately from the book to my brain, to my laptop, to my printer, and now it's big and bold on my office door:

**"Until my ONE Thing is done—
everything else is a distraction."**

I've just read a powerful book, *The ONE Thing: The Surprisingly Simple Truth Behind Extraordinary Results*, by Gary Keller with Jay Papasan. This bestseller will certainly be on my Top-10 book list for 2016 and is already a contender for my 2016 book-of-the-year.

But first—an apology. *The ONE Thing* waited patiently on my overflowing "books-to-read" shelves for three years. Then recently, it popped back onto *The Wall Street Journal* business bestsellers list. (OK. OK. I'll read it!) But I apologize because you (and I) could have been much more productive over these last three years. So sorry—but better late than never.

Gary Keller, chairman of the board and cofounder of Keller Williams Realty, Inc., the largest real estate company in the U.S., has seen his share of failures and successes—and that's how he discovered *The ONE Thing*.

He writes, "Where I'd had huge success, I had narrowed my concentration to one thing, and where my success varied, my focus had too."

Here's Keller's big idea:

**"What's the ONE Thing
you can do this week such that by doing it
everything else would be easier or unnecessary?"**

Read his chapter titles and you're hooked. The first section highlights six lies that mislead and derail us:

- Lie #1: Everything Matters Equally
- Lie #2: Multitasking
- Lie #3: A Disciplined Life
- Lie #4: Willpower Is Always on Will-Call
- Lie #5: A Balanced Life
- Lie #6: Big Is Bad

The second section addresses the focusing question, the success habit (66 days), and the path to great answers. The final section motivates with unusual clarity on the four thieves of productivity:

- Thief #1: Inability to Say "No"
- Thief #2: Fear of Chaos
- Thief #3: Poor Health Habits
- Thief #4: Environment Doesn't Support Your Goals

Well…I promised you 10 tweetable quotations. (I know—somewhat ironic that I have over 20 quotations in a book review about *The ONE Thing*.) On a short plane ride, I winnowed hundreds of PowerPoint-worthy insights down to just 35—just before I landed. I've given you three already—and here are 20 more (but who's counting?). Tweet your 10 favorite!

On rabbits, to-do lists, and irrelevancy:

- "If you chase two rabbits, you will not catch either one." (Russian proverb)
- "Instead of a to-do list, you need a success list—a list that is purposefully created around extraordinary results."
- " . . . it turns out that high multitaskers are suckers for irrelevancy."

On a "balanced life" and productivity:

- "A 'balanced life' is a myth—a misleading concept most accept as a worthy and attainable goal without ever stopping to truly consider it."
- "'Don't put all your eggs in one basket is all wrong.' I tell you 'put all your eggs in one basket, and then watch that basket.'" (Dale Carnegie)
- "Productivity isn't about being a workhorse, keeping busy or burning the midnight oil. . . . It's more about priorities, planning, and fiercely protecting your time." (Margarita Tartakovsky)

On goal-setting, accountability, and coaching:

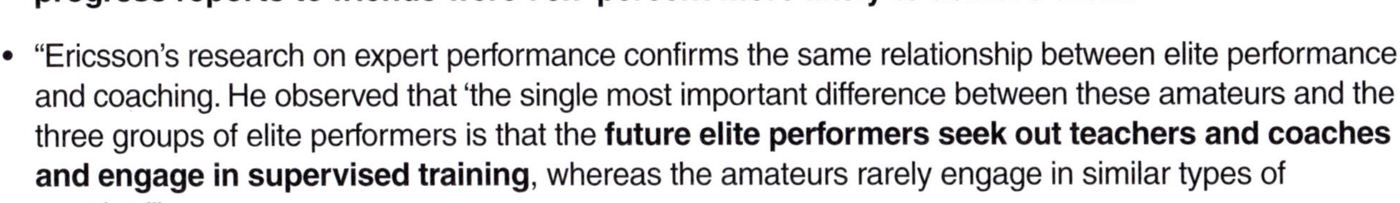

- "Accountable people receive results only others dream of."
- "When Arthur Guinness set up his first brewery, he signed a 9,000-year lease."
- "Earlier I discussed Dr. Gail Matthew's research that individuals with written goals were 39.5 percent more likely to succeed. But there's more to the story. **Individuals who wrote their goals and sent progress reports to friends were 76.7 percent more likely to achieve them.**"
- "Ericsson's research on expert performance confirms the same relationship between elite performance and coaching. He observed that 'the single most important difference between these amateurs and the three groups of elite performers is that the **future elite performers seek out teachers and coaches and engage in supervised training**, whereas the amateurs rarely engage in similar types of practice.'"

On saying no:

- "Someone once told me that one 'yes' must be defended over time by 1,000 no's."
- In the two years after Steve Jobs returned to Apple in 1997, "**he took the company from 350 products to 10**. That's 340 no's, not counting anything else proposed during that period."

On time-blocking and buckets to focus on The ONE Thing:

- "Build a bunker. Turn off your phone, shut down your email, and exit your Internet browser. Your most important work deserves 100 percent of your attention."
- "**My recommendation is to block four hours a day**. This isn't a typo. I repeat: four hours a day. Honestly, that's the minimum. If you can do more, then do it."
- "If your time-blocking were on trial, would your calendar contain enough evidence to convict you?"
- "The people who achieve extraordinary results don't achieve them by working more hours. They achieve them by getting more done in the hours they work."
- "Paul Graham's 2009 essay, 'Maker's Schedule, Manager's Schedule,' underscores the need for large time blocks."
- "Graham divides all work into two buckets: maker (do or create) and manager (oversee or direct)."
- "To experience extraordinary results, be a maker in the morning and a manager in the afternoon. Your goal is 'ONE and done.' But if you don't block each day to do your ONE Thing, your ONE Thing won't become a done thing."

On books:

"One of the reasons I've amassed a large library of books over the years is because books are a great go-to resource. Short of having a conversation with someone who has accomplished what you hope to achieve, in my experience books and published works offer the most in terms of documented research and role models for success."

Warning!

Keller: "After my wife, Mary, read this book, I asked her to do something. She turned to me and you know what she said? 'Gary, that's not my ONE Thing right now!' We laughed, high-fived, and I got to do it myself!"

Ready, set, TWEET!

John Pearson's 2016 Book-of-the-Year

Of the 24 books that John Pearson read and reviewed in 2016 in his eNews, *Your Weekly Staff Meeting*, he named *The ONE Thing* his "2016 Book-of-the-Year."[20]

Note: John's reviews of more than 400 books are archived at: *https://urgentink.typepad.com/my_weblog/*

Subscribe: *http://managementbuckets.com/enews*

[20] Gary Keller and Jay Papasan, *The ONE Thing: The Surprisingly Simple Truth Behind Extraordinary Results* (Austin, TX: Bard, 2012).

TOOL #19: Ten Minutes for Governance

Use this tool at every meeting to enhance lifelong learning.

Read Lesson 39: "Invest '10 Minutes for Governance' in Every Board Meeting."

Lessons From the Nonprofit Boardroom: 40 Insights for Better Board Meetings[1]

Just 10 Minutes Will Enrich Your Governance

The Big Idea

In every board meeting, we want to remind board members that good governance does not happen by osmosis. It happens only with intentionality, training, and keeping critical governance topics (like focusing on policy, not operations) on everyone's radar.

To get started, create a master list of possible topics (board policies, recruiting board members, understanding financial reports, ten basic responsibilities of nonprofit boards, the distinctives of Christ-centered governance, etc.). You might also find helpful topics using selected tools and templates from this book.

Teachers often learn more than their students, so rotate the leadership of this segment. Give board members advance notice when asking them to prepare a presentation. Suggest that each 10-minute segment include at least four to five minutes of interaction and dialogue.

Example: 'In groups of two, read these ten listening guidelines and identify the one guideline that is most difficult for you.' (Use a timer that buzzes at ten minutes.)

In addition to assigned reading prior to board retreats, and inspiring board members to read at least one governance book a year, you'll discover that a '10 Minutes for Governance' segment at every meeting will keep Christ-centered governance on the front burner.[2]

1 Dan Busby and John Pearson, *Lessons From the Nonprofit Boardroom: 40 Insights for Better Board Meetings*, 2d ed. (Winchester, VA: ECFAPress, 2018), 202–6.

2 Ibid., 204–5.

Example: Here's the one-page "Ten Minutes for Governance" template used by the board of directors at Christian Community Credit Union, which meets monthly. Note: In most cases, we recommend that boards meet four to six times a year (not monthly), but regulatory requirements for credit unions in California require a monthly board meeting.

Ten Minutes for Governance: *Lifelong Learning for Board Members*

Facilitator: Rick Jones

Date: March 22, 2020

Assignment: Read pages 115-119 before the meeting and check out the blog: ***40 Blogs. 40 Wednesdays.*** http://nonprofitboardroom.blogspot.com/

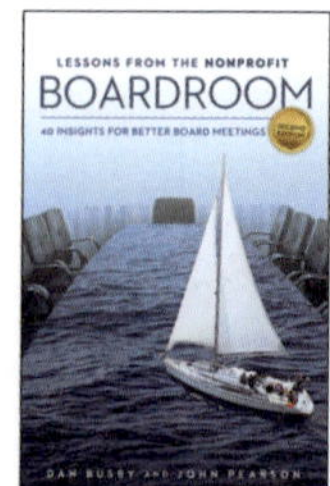

LESSON 23: Focus on Mission Impact *and* Sustainability

The "dual bottom line" equips boards to address dead horses and sacred cows (or goats). "Dakota tribal wisdom says that when you discover you are riding a dead horse, the best strategy is to dismount." (Elmer Towns and Warren Bird)

More on the book at: *www.ECFA.org/LessonsNonprofitBoardroom/*

Questions – Discuss in groups of two or three
#1. With our leadership succession changes, the developing technologies, and increasing competition in the marketplace, what "dead horses, sacred cows and goat programs" are keeping us from doing the "Star" programs (per Lesson 23) we could and should be doing? And what is keeping us from identifying them?
#2. How is the balance between business and ministry? Do we lean more toward Heart or Money Tree programs? How do we move towards the "All-Stars?"

Month	Facilitator	Lesson	Topic
December	Dale Bee	1	Wanted: Lifelong Learners *Would you trust a surgeon who stopped learning?*
January	Dave Matlock	18	Do Not Interrupt! *Don't Assume Board Members Know How to Listen*
February	Mike Barrett	12	Vision Growth Must Equal Leader Growth *Caution! Vision-casting often backfires.*
March	Rick Jones	23	Focus on Mission Impact *and* Sustainability *The "dual bottom line" equips boards to address dead horses and sacred cows (or goats).*
April	Tom Torry	9	Serve With Humility and Experience God's Presence *One board chair creates a holy moment for his CEO search committee.*
May	Cathy Barton	17	Sidetrack Harebrained Ideas *Some motions should never gain unmerited oxygen!*
June	John Pate	19	Never Throw Red Meat on the Board Table *Boards need advance preparation to fully address complex issues.*
July	Mark Roe	2	Ask the Gold Standard Question *A "pruning moment" can improve your board meetings.*

Example: for another "Ten Minutes for Governance" segment, view the short video on conflicts of interest and provide each board member with the *Read-and-Engage Viewing Guide*.[3] (See all four toolbox topics at *www.ECFA.org/Toolbox*.)

Ten Minutes for Governance: *Why do we need governance insights?*

"We are blind to the obvious and blind to our blindness!"

ECFA Governance Toolbox Series No. 3: *Addressing Board and Organizational Conflicts of Interest:* *Avoiding Trouble, Trouble, Trouble with Related-Party Transactions*

www.ECFA.org/Toolbox

Self-Assessment: Board and Organizational Conflicts of Interest

How strongly do you agree . . . or disagree with the following statements?	1 Strongly Disagree	2 Disagree	3 Undecided	4 Agree	5 Strongly Agree
Our organization has a written policy on "Conflicts of Interest and Related-Party Transactions."	○	○	○	○	○
Every board member is required to annually sign a certification document affirming that he or she has read and understands the organization's "Conflicts of Interest and Related-Party Transactions" policy.	○	○	○	○	○
Every board member that has real or apparent conflicts of interest, per our policy, is required to declare this information annually in a signed disclosure statement.	○	○	○	○	○
Our top leader (CEO or senior pastor) and other senior staff are also required to read and understand our conflicts of interest policy—and annually sign a certification document.	○	○	○	○	○
In the video, "Patricia" noted that the board "finally, finally had an executive session (without any staff members in the room)." Agree or disagree: "The frequency of our executive sessions is about right."	○	○	○	○	○
Also in the video, "Jamell" remarks: "Policies should never trump relationships. That's just not biblical." Do you agree or disagree?	○	○	○	○	○
In my opinion, our organization is "crystal clear" and "squeaky clean" in addressing board and organizational conflicts of interest—and "We're being as careful in our reputation with the public as in our reputation with God." (2 Cor. 8:21)	○	○	○	○	○

[3] See Board Member Read-and-Engage Viewing Guide, *ECFA Governance Toolbox Series No. 3: Addressing Board and Organizational Conflicts of Interest* (Winchester, VA: ECFAPress, 2015), 9.

Different Views Surface on the Amount of Future Focus

ECFA Research Says...

If you divide board meeting agendas, in terms of time spent, into a **future focus** vs. reviewing the present or past, CEOs say that in board meetings less agenda time focuses on the future than what others say. (Policy setting/review falls under a future focus.)

CEOs Don't Experience a "Future Focus" as Much as Board Members Do

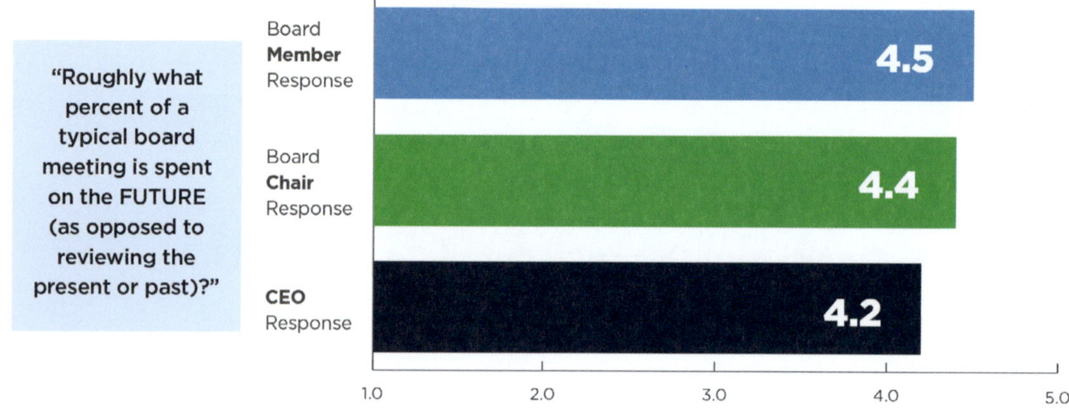

TOOL #20: Tent Cards and Tools for Leveraging Board Member Strengths

Inspire your board to complete the online CliftonStrengths® assessment and then create tent cards and tools to leverage strengths at every board and committee meeting!

Imagine! Committee Assignments by Strength

"While the Best Leaders Are Not Well-Rounded, the Best Teams Are."[1]

Tom Rath and Barry Conchie: "The odds of an employee [or a board member] being engaged are a dismal 1 in 11 (9%). But when an organization's leadership focuses on the strengths of its employees, the odds soar to almost 3 in 4 (73%)."[2]

Leadership is nothing without followers and this book describes the four basic needs of followers: trust, compassion, stability and hope. "The chances of employees being engaged at work when they do not trust the company's leaders are just 1 in 12."[3]

This is not dry, academic stuff. Four leaders—and their extremely diverse strengths—are profiled, using what the authors describe as the four domains of leadership strength:

- Executing
- Influencing
- Relationship Building
- Strategic Thinking[4]

For more on the CliftonStrengths® assessment, visit: *www.gallupstrengthscenter.com.*

[1] Tom Rath and Barry Conchie, *Strengths Based Leadership: Great Leaders, Teams and Why People Follow* (New York: Gallup Press, 2008), 2.
[2] Ibid., 83.
[3] Ibid., 2.
[4] Ibid., 43.

Leverage Your Board Members' Strengths: 4 Tools

Imagine! What if everyone on your board received committee assignments that leveraged their strengths? Each book below includes a unique access code for an online assessment at *www.gallupstrengthscenter.com.* After you complete the 20- to 30-minute online assessment, you will receive a list (and commentary) of your Top-5 strengths. Many boards compile these strengths into a chart so that committee assignments and volunteer work are delegated according to a person's strengths. Each book includes mini-descriptions of each of the 34 talent themes.

Strengths Based Leadership:
Great Leaders, Teams and Why People Follow
by Tom Rath and Barry Conchie

According to the Gallup Organization, over 18 million people worldwide have discovered their CliftonStrengths®—their top-five of 34 strengths/talent themes. Yet . . . **75 percent of the workforce do not leverage their strengths at work every day. *Yikes!*** Instead, many supervisors, bosses and boards focus incorrectly on a leader's weaknesses—instead of his or her strengths. This book also includes four "case studies" of four CEOs from each of the four domains of leadership strength: Executing, Influencing, Relationship Building, and Strategic Thinking.[5]

StrengthsFinder 2.0
Discover Your CliftonStrengths®
by Tom Rath

". . . our studies indicate that people who do have the opportunity to focus on their strengths every day **are six times as likely** to be engaged in their jobs and more than three times as likely to report having an excellent quality of life in general."[6]

Living Your Strengths:
Discover Your God-Given Talents and Inspire Your Community
by Albert L. Winseman, Donald O. Clifton, and Curt Liesveld

Recommended for Church Boards

A board member: "After serving almost four years on the church board, I had yet to fully know or understand those with whom I was working. The extent of our personal knowledge about one another went little beyond being asked to 'share your favorite movie.' At the initiation of a new church board chair and a new executive pastor, we underwent strengths coaching, both individual and team. Everyone engaged in the process, and I learned more about my teammates in one evening than in all my previous years on the board. It was the most meaningful and significant times we've spent together."[7]

[5] Rath and Conchie, *Strengths Based Leadership*, 24.

[6] Tom Rath, *StrengthsFinder 2.0* (New York: Gallup Press, 2007), iii.

[7] Albert L. Winseman, Donald O. Clifton, and Curt Liesveld, *Living Your Strengths: Discover Your God-Given Talents and Inspire Your Community*, 3d ed. (New York: Gallup Press, 2008), 56.

☑ STRENGTHS TOOL #1: Wallet-Size Cards

Laminate *and Leverage* Your Strengths!

After your board has completed the CliftonStrengths® assessment, prepare wallet-size laminated cards for each person—as a reminder to "leverage your strengths!"

OPTION 1:

JOHN PEARSON ✦ MY TOP-5 STRENGTHS[8]

1. "**FOCUS**® – People exceptionally talented in the Focus theme can take a direction, follow through and make the corrections necessary to stay on track. They prioritize, then act."
2. "**RESPONSIBILITY**® – People exceptionally talented in the Responsibility theme take psychological ownership of what they say they will do. They are committed to stable values such as honesty and loyalty."
3. "**SIGNIFICANCE**® – People exceptionally talented in the Significance theme want to be very important in others' eyes. They are independent and want to be recognized."
4. "**BELIEF**® – People exceptionally talented in the Belief theme have certain core values that are unchanging. Out of these values emerges a defined purpose for their lives."
5. "**MAXIMIZER**® – People exceptionally talented in the Maximizer theme focus on strengths as a way to stimulate personal and group excellence. They seek to transform something strong into something superb."

OPTION 2

DAN BUSBY ✦ MY TOP-5 STRENGTHS[9]

LEARNER®
ACHIEVER®
CONNECTEDNESS®
IDEATION®
BELIEF®

"I praise you because I am fearfully and wonderfully made; your works are wonderful, I know that full well."

Psalm 139:14 (NIV)

MORE RESOURCES:

- ❑ **Gallup Strengths Center:** *www.gallupstrengthscenter.com*
- ❑ **One-minute YouTube videos of all 34 strengths:** *www.youtube.com/user/GallupStrengths*

[8] CliftonStrengths® and each of the 34 theme names are trademarks of Gallup, Inc. To discover your top five CliftonStrengths®, please visit the Gallup Strengths Center at *www.gallupstrengthscenter.com/*.
[9] Ibid.

☑ STRENGTHS TOOL #2: Tent Cards

Enrich your board and committee meetings with 8 ½" x 11" tent cards—highlighting the strengths of each person.

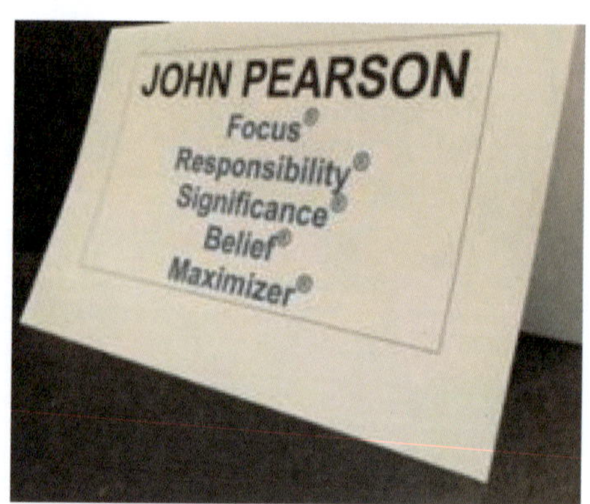

Easy-to-print! Prepare on 8 ½" x 11" card stock, print on BOTH sides, and fold in half.[10]

"A leader needs to know his strengths as a carpenter knows his tools, or as a physician knows the instruments at her disposal. What great leaders have in common is that each truly knows his or her strengths—and can call on the right strength at the right time. This explains why there is no definitive list of characteristics that describes all leaders."[11]

Donald O. Clifton

---

[10] Ibid.

[11] Rath and Conchie, *Strengths Based Leadership*, 13.

☑ STRENGTHS TOOL #3: Chart

Download the color-coded templates (8.5" x 11" and 11" x 17" landscape version for larger boards).

Our Board's Top-5 Strengths from CliftonStrengths®[12]

Names	Rick	Mike	Cathy	Mark	Maria	
Strength #1						
Strength #2						
Strength #3						
Strength #4						
Strength #5						
EXECUTING						
Achiever®						
Arranger®						
Belief®						
Consistency®						
Deliberative®						
Discipline®						
Focus®						
Responsibility®						
Restorative®						
INFLUENCING						
Activator®						
Command®						
Communication®						
Competition®						
Maximizer®						
Self-Assurance®						
Significance®						
Woo®						
RELATIONSHIP BUILDING						
Adaptability®						
Connectedness®						
Developer®						
Empathy®						
Harmony®						
Includer®						
Individualization®						
Positivity®						
Relator®						
STRATEGIC THINKING						
Analytical®						
Context®						
Futuristic®						
Ideation®						
Input®						
Intellection®						
Learner®						
Strategic®						

Chart Concept: John Pearson

[12] CliftonStrengths® and each of the 34 theme names are trademarks of Gallup, Inc. To discover your top five CliftonStrengths®, please visit the Gallup Strengths Center at *www.gallupstrengthscenter.com/*.

Our Board's Top-5 Strengths From CliftonStrengths® – *EXAMPLE*

Names	Rick Burton	Mike Porter	Cathy Jones	Mark Owens	Maria Lopez
Strength #1	Belief	Woo	Strategic	Connectedness	Relator
Strength #2	Positivity	Empathy	Maximizer	Woo	Belief
Strength #3	Developer	Positivity	Activator	Belief	Arranger
Strength #4	Connectedness	Communication	Command	Maximizer	Achiever
Strength #5	Strategic	Arranger	Relator	Learner	Focus
EXECUTING					
Achiever®					Achiever
Arranger®		Arranger			Arranger
Belief®	Belief			Belief	Belief
Consistency®					
Deliberative®					
Discipline®					
Focus®					Focus
Responsibility®					
Restorative®					
INFLUENCING					
Activator®			Activator		
Command®			Command		
Communication®		Communication			
Competition®					
Maximizer®			Maximizer	Maximizer	
Self-Assurance®					
Significance®					
Woo®		Woo		Woo	
RELATIONSHIP BUILDING					
Adaptability®					
Connectedness®	Connectedness			Connectedness	
Developer®	Developer				
Empathy®		Empathy			
Harmony®					
Includer®					
Individualization®					
Positivity®	Positivity	Positivity			
Relator®			Relator		Relator
STRATEGIC THINKING					
Analytical®					
Context®					
Futuristic®					
Ideation®					
Input®					
Intellection®					
Learner®				Learner	
Strategic®	Strategic		Strategic		

Chart Concept: John Pearson

↑Recommendation! Download the Strengths chart template.
Download the 11" x 17" color-coded blank template and add the Top-5 strengths for each board member. The completed template will visually show how "well-rounded" your board is in the four domains of leadership strength (Executing, Influencing, Relationship Building, and Strategic Thinking).[13]

☑ STRENGTHS TOOL #4: Coffee Mugs!

Present a personalized Strengths mug to every board member!

(Photo courtesy of Scott Mackes, Strengths Mugs, *www.strengthsmugs.com*)

Order at:
www.strengthsmugs.com

[13] The four domains of leadership strength (Executing, Influencing, Relationship Building, and Strategic Thinking) are described in Tom Rath and Barry Conchie, *Strengths Based Leadership: Great Leaders, Teams and Why People Follow,* (New York: Gallup Press, 2008).

TOOL #21: Board Member Annual Affirmation Statement

Share this document with board prospects to communicate your high commitment and generosity standards. Plus, require re-commitments annually from all board members.

Pursue Discipleship!

Sustaining Motivation

"Sustaining motivation is better understood as a by-product as opposed to a goal of itself. It is my experience that if you pursue discipleship with volunteers [and board members], motivation will follow. If volunteers see the fulfillment of their role as 'obeying and serving God' rather than serving you or your [organization], it will cause motivation to swell."[1]

NOTE! Two templates are available for Tool #21.

- ❑ **Nonprofit Boards**:

  TOOL #21A: Board Member Annual Affirmation Statement

  This tool is also included on the following pages.

- ❑ **Church Boards**:

  TOOL #21B: Church Board Member Annual Affirmation Statement

  This tool is only available online.

[1] Al Newell, "Sustaining Volunteer Motivation: One Principle, Five Tips" (Concord, NC: Newell & Associates, 2007), published on the High Impact Volunteer Ministry Development website in 2007 but no longer available online. Used by permission of the author, Al Newell, at *www.newellandassociates.com.*

Board Member Annual Affirmation Statement

Attn: Church Boards

The Church Board Member Annual Affirmation Statement is available online at *www.ECFA.church/Content/Church-Board-Member-Annual-Affirmation-Statement.*

A resource to supplement the materials in the

ECFA Governance Toolbox Series No. 2: Balancing Board Roles

Understanding the 3 Board Hats: Governance • Volunteer • Participant

www.ECFA.org/toolbox or ***www.ECFA.org/Content/Board-Member-Annual-Affirmation-Statement-NP***

"With crystal clarity, we explain the 3 distinct hats of board service: Governance, Volunteer and Participant."[2]

How to use this document:

Begin by asking your board members to answer three questions:

How strongly do you agree or disagree with these statements?

1 – Strongly Disagree
2 – Disagree
3 – Neither Agree nor Disagree
4 – Agree
5 – Strongly Agree

How effective is our board at establishing written criteria and qualifications for board members?	**Circle Your Answer**				
We have a "Board Member Annual Affirmation Statement" (or similar document) that summarizes the roles and responsibilities of board members, including future board meeting dates—and the board member's affirmation that he or she will be in attendance.	**1**	**2**	**3**	**4**	**5**
With crystal clarity, we explain the three distinct hats of board service: ✓ The Governance Hat ✓ The Volunteer Hat ✓ The Participant Hat	**1**	**2**	**3**	**4**	**5**
We are also crystal clear about a board member's charitable giving expectations (if any).	**1**	**2**	**3**	**4**	**5**

Use this template to create your own "Board Member Annual Affirmation Statement" so current board members, and board prospects, understand—with crystal clarity—their roles and responsibilities.

[2] See "Board Member Read-and-Engage Viewing Guide," in *ECFA Governance Toolbox Series No. 1: Recruiting Board Members* (Winchester, VA: ECFAPress, 2012), 11. Visit *ECFA.org/Toolbox.*

Introduction

Your Logo and Contact Information Here

Board Member Annual Affirmation Statement

(Approved by the Board on _____, 2020)

"Any enterprise is built by wise planning, becomes strong through common sense, and profits wonderfully by keeping abreast of the facts."

Proverbs 24:3-4 (The Living Bible)

OUR GOVERNANCE VISION. It is our expectation and hope that in future years, the members of the Board of Directors of XYZ Ministries will sense such a high calling to their roles and responsibilities—and have such a vision for the potential of serving others—that they would give the highest priority (as defined by our Board Policies Manual) in the use of their charitable time and resources to XYZ Ministries during their three-year term of service on the board.

The Roles and Responsibilities of Board Members

The full description of board member roles is listed in our Board Policies Manual. In summary, we desire to make *spiritually discerning governance and policy decisions* in these key areas:

1) **People.** We are accountable for the hiring, inspiring, guiding, evaluating, and the supporting of our CEO.
2) **Policies.** We focus on governance (as defined in the Board Policies Manual) and our stewarding and accountability process for the ministry (and our board) in the key areas of mission, vision, values, B.H.A.G. (Big HOLY Audacious Goal), strategy, strategic plan (at least three years), and the annual organizational goals; plus the CEO's three to five "Annual S.M.A.R.T. Goals" (which are Specific, Measurable, Achievable, Realistic and Time-related).
3) **Strategy.** We agree with Ram Charan's statement in *Owning Up: The 14 Questions Every Board Member Needs to Ask*, that we want our board to *own* the strategy, but not necessarily create it. He writes, "There is nothing more important for a CEO than having the right strategy and right choice of goals, and for the board, the right strategy is second only to having the right CEO."[3]
4) **Legal and Financial Due Diligence.** We take very seriously our fiduciary, legal and spiritual responsibilities as trustees of the ministry and we ensure that we are in compliance with all legal, financial, and governmental requirements, as described in our Board Policies Manual. These include, but are not limited to, policy oversight of the annual budget, cash flow, cash reserves, risk management, audits, ECFA-accreditation standards, CEO compensation, and other areas.
5) **Generous Giving.** We invite spiritually discerning and qualified men and women to serve on our board who are already in the "Generous Givers Circle," as defined in our Board Policies Manual—and who through example and influence, will encourage others to give generously to our ministry.

This document will be used two ways:

1) We will ask *current board members* to review and sign this—and affirm their commitment to XYZ Ministries annually.
2) We will ask *prospective board members* to review this in advance of their commitment to serve—and then upon their election, to sign the affirmation annually.

[3] Ram Charan, *Owning Up: The 14 Questions Every Board Member Needs to Ask* (San Francisco: Jossey-Bass, 2009), 68.

The 3 Hats of a Board Member

☑ GOVERNANCE HAT

All board members wear their "Governance" hats at board meetings. Here we seek to spiritually discern God's voice together as we steward the direction of the ministry in God-honoring ways.

☑ VOLUNTEER HAT

Contrary to what your experience may have been on other boards, here we affirm that "volunteering is optional—and is gifts-based and passion-driven." If your primary reason for serving on our board is to expand your current volunteer role or a future volunteer role, you might be more fulfilled giving more time and energy to that volunteer role—and not serve on the board. We see these two hats as distinct and separate.

When a board member does wear a volunteer hat (remember—it's optional), we remind that person to leave his or her "Governance" hat back in the boardroom! We know you won't "power up" as a board member when you're volunteering—and that you will respect the volunteer lines of authority by working with the appropriate staff or volunteer supervisor. And, of course, we know you will also refrain from bringing volunteer issues into the board meeting so other board members won't be tempted to micromanage staff functions and neglect board functions.

☑ PARTICIPANT HAT

The "Participant" hat (as you'll note in this document) includes those events in our calendar year that we expect board members to attend. While you may be introduced as a board member here, these events are not board meetings and so, once again, it would be inappropriate for you to wear your "Governance" hat at these events. In advance, we may ask for your help in some way at an event and so you might be called upon to also wear your "Volunteer" hat. Thanks!

For more information on the 3 Board Hats, download and view:

ECFA Governance Toolbox Series No. 2: Balancing Board Roles
Understanding the 3 Board Hats: Governance, Volunteer, Participant

www.ECFA.org/toolbox

Your Name: ____

XYZ MINISTRIES
Board Member Annual Affirmation Statement

MY COMMITMENT

- ❑ Yes! I affirm my high commitment and generous use of my *time, talent and treasures* for the purposes of kingdom advancement through the work of XYZ Ministries. I believe God has called me to serve and I accept these roles, responsibilities and privileges with joy and enthusiasm.

Term of office: January 1, 2020 to December 31, 2022 (3 years)

Board Members Wear 3 Hats:

- ☑ Governance Hat
- ☑ Volunteer Hat (based on your strengths, social style and spiritual gifts)
- ☑ Participant Hat (participation at ministry events and fundraising dinners, etc.)

✦ GOVERNANCE HAT:

Circle: Yes or No

Yes No 1. I affirm the XYZ Ministries Statement of Faith.

Yes No 2. I affirm I will serve faithfully on the XYZ Ministries Board of Directors, confident that I have the enthusiastic affirmation of my family (and my employer, if required) along with their understanding of the commitments I am making in the use of my time, talent and treasure.

Yes No 3. I affirm I will pray regularly for XYZ Ministries, the CEO, the staff, and the Board of Directors.

Yes No. 4. I affirm I am *highly committed* to attending the scheduled meetings of the board and committees and understand that the cost of transportation, hotel, and non-scheduled meals will be my responsibility. I will also participate in the regularly scheduled telephone conference calls. (*See the attached list for future board meetings.*)

Yes No 5. I affirm that during my three-year term on the board I will arrange my giving priorities so that I am able to be a generous giver to XYZ Ministries, recognizing that major donors, foundations and other donors have the expectation that the XYZ Ministries Board of Directors will be part of the "most highly committed" group of donors.

> *Note:* "Generous giving" does not mean that our board members must be wealthy. Instead, when at all possible, we encourage each board member to prioritize XYZ Ministries so it is one of the "Top-3" ministries for an individual's annual giving. (*See the Board Policies Manual for more details.*)

Yes No 6. I affirm that, as I'm able, I will seek to influence my colleagues, my organization/company, major donors and foundations to be generous givers to our ministry.

Yes No. 7. I affirm that I am an active attender and participant in my local church and am committed to a spiritual journey of becoming a fully devoted follower of Christ.

Yes No 8. I affirm that I will carefully consider opportunities for service on various board committees and will accept such assignments, as I am able. Note: Current standing committees of the board are:

a) Executive Committee

b) Finance & Audit Review Committee

c) Governance Committee

Yes No 9. I affirm that if I am unable or unwilling to continue to serve, prepare for and attend meetings, and execute my responsibilities as a member of the Board of Directors of XYZ Ministries, I will resign my position so that the board may have the benefit of the full support and committed time, talent and treasure of an active board member.

Yes No 10. Other:

✦ VOLUNTEER HAT:

Circle: Yes or No

Yes No 1. I understand that while I am encouraged to serve as a volunteer of XYZ Ministries, *such service is separate from my roles and responsibilities as a board member.* I understand that volunteer service is optional, but should I volunteer, the organization will seek to place me in a volunteer role that leverages my spiritual gifts, strengths and social styles.

Yes No 2. I affirm that should I serve as a volunteer, I will respect the lines of authority and accountability and not inappropriately bring my "Volunteer" hat ideas, suggestions, issues or recommendations to the board—but I will work directly with the staff person or volunteer that supervises or coordinates my volunteer work.

Yes No 3. As a XYZ Ministries volunteer, I affirm I will prayerfully consider other opportunities for volunteer service, including:

- Representing the organization at meetings and events
- Serving at an event
- Serving on an ad hoc task force or committee
- Joining the CEO in meetings with potential donors
- Other:

Yes No 4. Other:

✦ PARTICIPANT HAT:

Circle: Yes or No

Yes No 1. I understand that as a board member, I am expected to attend selected events each year as a participant—and that, as much as possible, those calendar dates will be announced a year in advance. I also understand that married board members will be highly encouraged to involve their spouses in many of these events.

Yes No 2. I affirm I will aggressively encourage others to become involved with XYZ Ministries and invite at least [circle: 3, 5, 10, ___] people new to the ministry to participate in one or more events each year, when possible.

Yes No 3. I will seek to participate in at least one major ministry event each year (such as the Annual Workshop) at my own expense. I understand that board members will receive a ___% discount on registration fees for this event. I also understand I may be asked to volunteer at this event.

Yes No 4. Other:

1 Corinthians 4:2 reminds us that to be a steward it is required that one be found trustworthy. Before God, it is my desire to be faithful in stewarding the important work of XYZ Ministries!

Signed: ______________________________ **Date** ____________

Print name: ____

2021 "Participant Hat" Expectations for Board Members (Updated: _______, 2020)

Date	**Day/Time**	**Location**	**Event** (*Required Attendance)
			*
			*
			(Optional)
			(Optional

Conflicts of Interest Disclosure Policy and Questionnaire

☑ **Two Options:**

- ❑ 1. Visit the ECFA Knowledge Center, *www.ECFA.org/Content/Conflicts-of-Interest-Sample-Policy*, for a conflict of interest template.
- ❑ 2. Download and view:

ECFA Governance Toolbox Series No. 3: Conflicts of Interest - Addressing Board and Organizational Conflicts of Interest

Avoiding Trouble, Trouble, Trouble with Related-Party Transactions

www.ECFA.org/Content/Governance-Toolbox-Series-3

ECFA Standard 6 calls for members to handle conflicts of interest and related-party transactions with excellence and integrity. Conflicts can be avoided most easily when the organization has a stated conflicts of interest policy and annually asks the Board of Directors and key administrative personnel to document potential conflicts.

The following are sample conflicts of interest policies and questionnaires. ECFA does not endorse any particular document but is providing these samples to help you (in conjunction with legal counsel and other professional advisors) develop the documents appropriate for your ministry.

Sample Conflicts of Interest Policy

All trustees, officers, agents, and employees of this organization shall disclose all real or perceived conflicts of interest that they discover or that have been brought to their attention in connection with this organization's activities.

"Conflicts of interest" occur when a person is responsible for promoting the interest of the ministry at the same time he or she is involved in a competing personal interest (financial, business, personal, or relational).

"Disclosure" shall mean providing properly, to the appropriate person, a written description of the facts comprising real or apparent conflicts of interest. An annual questionnaire shall be distributed to trustees, officers, and certain identified agents and key employees to assist them in considering such disclosures, but disclosure is appropriate and required at any time conflicts of interest may occur. The completed questionnaires shall be filed with the CEO or such other person designated by the CEO to receive such notifications. At the meeting of the top governing body, all disclosures of real or perceived conflicts of interest shall be noted for the record in the minutes.

An individual trustee, officer, agent, or key employee who believes that he or she or an immediate member of his or her immediate family might have real or perceived conflicts of interest, in addition to filing a notice of disclosure, must abstain from

(1) participating in discussions or deliberations with respect to the subject of the conflict (other than to present factual information or to answer questions),

(2) using his or her personal influence to affect deliberations,

(3) making motions,

(4) voting,

(5) executing agreements, or

(6) taking similar actions on behalf of the organizations where conflicts of interest might pertain by law, agreement, or otherwise.

At the discretion of the top governing body or a committee thereof, a person with real or perceived conflicts of interest may be excused from all or any portion of discussion or deliberations with respect to the subject of the conflict.

A member of the top governing body or a committee thereof, who, having disclosed conflicts of interest, nevertheless shall be counted in determining the existence of a quorum at any meeting in which the subject of the conflict is discussed. The minutes of the meeting shall reflect the individual's disclosure, the vote, and the individual's abstention from participation and voting.

The CEO and Board Chair shall ensure that all trustees, officers, agents, employees, and independent contractors of the organization are made aware of the organization's policy with respect to conflicts of interest.

Conflicts of Interest Questionnaire

I have read the organization's Conflict of Interest Policy and in signing this certificate, I have considered the literal expression of the Policy, but also its intent. I hereby certify that, **except as hereinafter stated**, to the best of my knowledge, I do not have any relations or interests whatever conflicting with the interests of the organization.

The exceptions are:

____

____

____

I have business relationships with the following board members:

____

____

If any situation should arise in the future which I think may involve me in a conflict of interest, I will promptly fully disclose the circumstances to the top leader or the board chair.

Furthermore, I agree to abide by the statement of confidentiality as contained in the foregoing organization's Conflict of Interest Policy.

Printed Name ____

Signed ________________________________ Date ________________

Read Lesson 31 in *More Lessons From the Nonprofit Boardroom*, "Where Two or Three Are Gathered on Social Media," and learn more about the four critical steps when considering significant transactions involving related parties:

1. Exclude
2. Compare
3. Determine
4. Document

And note: "Even when the ministry takes those four essential steps, it may still be in the best interest of the ministry to avoid the related-party transaction."[4]

[4] Dan Busby and John Pearson, *More Lessons From the Nonprofit Boardroom: Effectiveness, Excellence, Elephants!* (Winchester, VA: ECFAPress), 169.

2021 Board Meeting Schedule (Updated: November 15, 2020)

Year 2021	Day/Time	Location	Agenda
Meeting #1 Date: ______	Tuesday 2:00–4:00 p.m.	Telephone Conference Call	• 2020 Financial Reports/Budget Review • 2021 Financial Reports (2-months) • 2021 Budget (final review) • Committee Reports • Executive Director's "State of the Organization" report for 2020 • Strategic Plan update
Meeting #2 Date: ______	Thursday 12:00 noon – Lunch 1:00 – 5:00 p.m. 5:30 p.m. Optional Dinner (spouses invited)	TBD	• Financial Reports (4 months) • Committee Reports • Executive Director's S.M.A.R.T. Goals update • Leading Indicators update • Nominating Committee Report
Meeting #3 Date: ______	**BOARD RETREAT** **Thursday 4 p.m. to Friday 2 p.m.**	TBD	• Financial Report (7 months) • Strategic Plan (2022–2024) – Draft 1 (BHAG, Primary Customer, Mission, Strategies, Business Model, Development Plan, etc.) • Nominating Committee recommendations on board prospects
Meeting #4 Date: ______	Thursday 12:00 noon – Lunch 1:00 – 5:00 p.m. 5:30 p.m. Dinner (spouses invited)	TBD	• Welcome to New Board Members • Financial Reports (10 months) • 2022 Annual Plan, Calendar, Leading Indicators and Executive Director's 2022 S.M.A.R.T. Goals • 2022 Preliminary Budget • Executive Director's Performance Review (based on 2021 S.M.A.R.T. Goals) • Board Governance Committee Report • Appointment of Auditor

2022 Board Meeting Schedule (Updated: ________, 2020) – Proposed

Year 2022	Day/Time	Location	Agenda

Resources:

NOTE! Two templates are available for Tool #21.

- ❑ **Nonprofit Boards:**

  Tool #21A: Board Member Annual Affirmation Statement –
  http://www.ECFA.org/Content/Board-Member-Annual-Affirmation-Statement-NP

- ❑ **Church Boards:**

  Tool #21B: Church Board Member Annual Affirmation Statement –
  http://www.ECFA.org/Content/Church-Board-Member-Annual-Affirmation-Statement

To download these templates, refer to page ii of this book for the website.

For more help on using this tool, order:

ECFA Governance Toolbox Series No. 1: Recruiting Board Members
Leveraging the 4 Phases of Board Recruitment
Cultivation • Recruitment • Orientation • Engagement

ECFA.org/Toolbox

Engage Your Board at Every Meeting
With More Governance Help and Resources!

Visit *ECFA.org/Toolbox* to order additional titles in the ECFA Governance Toolbox Series

ECFA

440 West Jubal Early Drive, Suite 100
Winchester, VA 22601 USA

Telephone: (540) 535-0103
information@ECFA.org
www.ECFA.org

TOOL #22: **Straw Vote Cards**

Use red and green straw vote cards to discern if you have consensus or division on big and small issues—and save valuable time!

A Quick and Courteous Way to Give Every Board Member a Voice

If you are ready to vote, hold up your green card.

Finding consensus on challenging boardroom issues requires deft handling and a flexible approach by the board chair. Many boards use red and green straw vote cards to "check the pulse" of the board before a vote is taken.

> Determining if there is consensus on a particular agenda item before a vote is taken is often an excellent approach. After adequate discussion, the chair asks, "Is there consensus that it's time to vote?"
>
> This is a signal: If you have more to add, speak up! At times, a red or green straw vote card may be used to indicate consensus.
>
> "If you are ready to vote, hold up your green card; if not, hold up your red card."[1]

[1] Dan Busby and John Pearson, *More Lessons From the Nonprofit Boardroom: Effectiveness, Excellence, Elephants!* (Winchester, VA: ECFAPress, 2019), 93. For more insights, read Lesson 16, "Looking for Consensus, But Finding Division."

Add Some Fun to Your Board Meetings!

At every meeting, provide green and red straw vote cards (green means "yes" and red means "no"). Any board member can ask for a straw vote at any time. Sometimes the loudest, longest-talking board member is the only one holding up a red card—and the instant feedback will help her see she's not convincing anyone!

We were introduced to this time-saving tool by our friend and colleague, Bob Andringa, who notes: "The cards save time by testing the group's leanings early on in what could otherwise be unnecessarily long discussions.

"The straw vote cards allow everyone, even the most extreme introverts, to have a 'voice' by going visual. And when anyone can ask to test an idea by a show of cards, they help keep board members more alert to the dialogue. And they can add some fun to your meetings!"[2]

USE STRAW VOTE CARDS to help your board "reach decisions peacefully, thoughtfully, fairly and openly." Read more on the three approaches for finding boardroom consensus:

- **A consent agenda.** Routine items can be grouped under one agenda item, termed a consent agenda. Agenda items upon which the board is unlikely to quickly reach consensus should not be included in a consent agenda.
- **Unanimity.** It is rare for boards to require unanimity (100% agreement) on all actions. The danger in requiring unanimity is that one person can block an action and allow a decision to simply be endlessly kicked down the road.
- **Simple or super-majority.** Most boards make decisions by simple majority. A so-called super-majority usually requires a two-thirds or three-fourths affirmative vote of the board.[3]

[2] From an email communication to the authors on July 20, 2019. For more governance resources from Bob Andringa, visit *https://theandringagroup.com/resources/*.

[3] Busby and Pearson, *More Lessons From the Nonprofit Boardroom*, 94.

"I'd like to ask for a straw vote—before we vote on the motion."

When should a board member call for a straw vote? Almost any time!

In hundreds of board meetings over the years, we've observed board members ask for a show of red cards or green cards hundreds of times.

Show your green card if you agree, or show your red card if you disagree:

- ❑ That we ask the Governance Committee to research the benefits of moving from 12 board meetings per year to just six.
- ❑ At our last meeting, we noted Dr. John J. Medina's wisdom: **"Multitasking, when it comes to paying attention, is a myth."**[4] So because we need everyone's focused attention on today's agenda—show your green card if you agree that we ask everyone to turn their phones off and place them in the center of the table until we adjourn.
- ❑ Before we vote on this motion, show your green card if you agree our esteemed chair of the Nominating Committee should receive a Chick-fil-A gift card for her tremendous work on this year's slate of nominees!
- ❑ Mr. Chairman, we've been discussing this topic for over an hour—**but not every board member has weighed in yet.** Could we do a quick show of cards to see if most agree—or disagree—with the motion on the table?
- ❑ Whew! I've counted no less than a dozen emails—related to the 2020 Vision Campaign—just in the last 24 hours from strongly-opinionated board members! I'm not sure what anyone believes! Would it be helpful to ask everyone to show their red or green cards if you're leaning toward a Yes or a No on this motion?
- ❑ Yikes! This discussion is getting a bit contentious, and I need to apologize for the first volley that prompted it. Would you join me in raising your green cards—if you agree we should stop for 15 minutes of silent prayer? We need God's help.

[4] Dan Busby and John Pearson, *Lessons From the Nonprofit Boardroom: 40 Insights for Better Board Meetings* (Winchester, VA: ECFAPress, 2018), 13.

BONUS

5 Facilitation Techniques to Engage Board Members at Every Meeting

On the drive home from your board meetings, you want every board member to reflect: "Was I needed at this meeting? Did others engage both my heart and my head—or do they have low or no expectations that I can add value?"

If your board meetings are long on talking heads (featuring boring CEO reports and excessively detailed financial reports) and short on energetic and engaged dialogue—then consider these five ways to facilitate lively value-added discussions:

- ❑ 1. **THE FIRST 30 MINUTES.** One of my board meeting rules of thumb is to ensure that every board member shares an insight in the first 30 minutes of the meeting. It's simple. Just write a thought-provoking question on the flipchart. (Example: "What are the three greatest threats to our future ministry?") Divide the board into groups of two—and start the clock (three to five minutes only). Ask each team of two to give a 60-second report. And...presto: every board member in the room has shared an opinion or insight. ("How was the meeting tonight, Dear?" Response: "Fantastic! They really liked one of my ideas.")[6]
- ❑ 2. **STAND AND DECLARE.** If two or three board members tend to do all the talking, call a time-out and do a "Stand and Declare." Ask everyone to stand up around the table. Then ask each person to share one insight on the agenda topic in 30 seconds or less. Go around the table, one-at-a-time, and after a person speaks, he or she should be seated. In about five to seven minutes you've heard from everyone—not just the talkers.
- ❑ 3. **STRAW VOTE CARDS.** At every meeting, provide green and red straw vote cards (green means "yes" and red means "no"). Any board member can ask for a straw vote at any time. Sometimes the loudest, longest-talking board member is the only one holding up a red card—and the instant feedback will help her see she's not convincing anyone!
- ❑ 4. **STOP AND PRAY.** Are you facing a difficult fork-in-the-road decision? Stop and pray! (While you likely pray at the beginning and end of your board meetings, it's not illegal to actually pray during the board meeting!) To engage everyone, break into groups of two or three—so everyone can pray.
- ❑ 5. **CHICK-FIL-A GIFT CARDS!** Provide your board chair with two or three Chick-fil-A gift cards per meeting. Award board members for insightful questions and/or observations. After the first card is awarded, the energy level will be raised—as others vie for gift card-worthy input.

[5] Adapted from "5 Ways to Engage Board Members at Every Meeting," by John Pearson, *RESCUE magazine*, July/August 2014, 10. Published by Association of Gospel Rescue Missions, now known as Citygate Network.

[6] Busby and Pearson, *More Lessons From the Nonprofit Boardroom*, 86–90. Read Lesson 15: "Be Intentional About Your First 30 Minutes."

RESOURCES AND WORKSHEETS

**"If you want to teach people a new way of thinking,
don't bother to teach them.
Instead, give them a tool,
the use of which will lead to new ways of thinking."[1]**

R. Buckminster Fuller

[1] Verne Harnish, *Scaling Up: How a Few Companies Make It . . . and Why the Rest Don't – Mastering the Rockefeller Habits 2.0* (Ashburn, VA: Gazelles, 2014), 1.

5 Ways to Leverage These Tools and Templates

The Power of Moments was John's 2017 book-of-the-year.

"How do you refresh a meeting that's grown rote?"

One approach: **"Break the script."**[2]

Refresh Your Governance Experiences!

5 Ideas for Making Board Meetings Memorable!

Introduce one new template per meeting and inspire one or two board members to customize the template so it meets your board's unique needs.

❑ 1. **Refresh Your Agenda.** Use Tool #12, "Quarterly Board Meeting Agenda & Recommendations," and build a more intentional agenda. Ensure that the agenda also includes a significant time segment for your one "heavy lifting" topic for each meeting. This will engage board members—if facilitated with all four social styles represented on your board (Driving, Analytical, Amiable, Expressive).

❑ 2. **Refresh Your Training.** Use Tool #19, "Ten Minutes for Governance," and inspire one person to be your "Leaders Are Readers Champion"—a board member who has passion for ten-minute engagement exercises to enrich your board's governance competencies.

❑ 3. **Refresh Your Policy.** Refer frequently to Tool #17, "Board Policies Manual," to ensure that your policies are changing with your changing growth/decline and/or other situations. If board discussion—on any one agenda item—seems to go nowhere, it may be time to edit or add a policy.

❑ 4. **Refresh Your Accountability.** Invest time in Tool #11, "Monthly Dashboard Report," to keep your CEO's Top-5 S.M.A.R.T. Goals on the front burner—every month—with the monthly dashboard report template.

❑ 5. **Refresh Your First 30 Minutes.** Start board meetings on time and redeem the first 30 minutes.[3] Inspire your board chair and your CEO to read *The Power of Moments* to see a new, fresh perspective on how to engage board members.

Attn: Church Boards

Read "Clinic 2: How Do You Refresh a Meeting That's Grown Rote?" on pages 89–92 in *The Power of Moments*. Learn how one leader breathed new life into a stale monthly church board meeting.

[2] Chip Heath and Dan Heath, *The Power of Moments: Why Certain Experiences Have Extraordinary Impact* (New York: Simon & Schuster, 2017), 89.

[3] Read Lesson 15, "Be Intentional About Your First 30 Minutes," in *More Lessons From the Nonprofit Boardroom: Effectiveness, Excellence, Elephants!* by Dan Busby and John Pearson (Winchester, VA: ECFAPress, 2019), 86–90.

About the Authors

Dan Busby

Dan Busby is the President of ECFA (Evangelical Council for Financial Accountability) in Winchester, VA. He has been in leadership positions with ECFA for over 20 years. Prior to coming to ECFA, Dan was the founding and managing partner of a CPA firm in the Kansas City area, and served in financial management positions with the University of Kansas Medical Center and The Wesleyan Church—International Headquarters. He has served over 110 man-years on nonprofit boards.

Dan is the author/co-author of 66 editions of 11 different titles plus numerous eBooks and booklets. Two titles published annually since 1991, the Zondervan *Minister's Tax & Financial Guide* and the Zondervan *Church and Nonprofit Tax & Financial Guide*, have set a standard as easy-to-understand resources on these topics. Now Michael Martin has joined him to author these two books.

In 2017, Dan teamed up with John Pearson to pen *Lessons From the Nonprofit Boardroom*, *Lessons From the Church Boardroom*, and *More Lessons From the Nonprofit Boardroom*. Dan's book, *TRUST: The Firm Foundation for Kingdom Fruitfulness,* is a treasure trove linked to trust, based on Busby's wit and wisdom. Joined by co-authors Michael Martin and John Van Drunen, *The Guide to Charitable Giving for Churches and Ministries* answers the important questions about the proper handling of charitable contributions for legal, tax, and accounting purposes.

An avid baseball fan and former umpire, Dan frequently consults for the National Baseball Hall of Fame concerning memorabilia acquisitions. His book about the New York Yankees, *Before and After Babe Ruth*, was published in 2018. His book about the Brooklyn Dodgers, *Before and After Jackie Robinson*, is scheduled for release in 2020.

Dan, and his wife, Claudette, have two children, Julie and Alan, and three grandchildren. His top five strengths in the CliftonStrengths assessment are: Learner, Achiever, Connectedness, Ideation, and Belief. A survivor of living in "tornado alley" in Kansas until 1987, Dan has not sought shelter from tornadoes since leaving Kansas.

John Pearson

John Pearson is a board governance and management consultant from San Clemente, CA. He served more than 30 years as a nonprofit ministry CEO, 25 of those years as the CEO of three national/international associations, including Christian Camp and Conference Association, Willow Creek Association, and Christian Management Association (now Christian Leadership Alliance).

He is the author of *Mastering the Management Buckets: 20 Critical Competencies for Leading Your Business or Nonprofit*, and the co-author with Dan Busby of *Lessons From the Nonprofit Boardroom, Lessons From the Church Boardroom*, and *More Lessons From the Nonprofit Boardroom.* He is also co-author with Dr. Robert Hisrich of *Marketing Your Ministry: 10 Critical Principles.*

Many of the boardroom lessons in this book flow from John's diverse local church and denominational background. In addition to serving on and consulting with church boards, he served five years in a denominational district office covering three Midwestern states and was on the management team at Willow Creek Community Church. He majored in Christian education and Biblical literature at Seattle Pacific University and earned a master's degree from Trinity Evangelical Divinity School.

John also writes an eNewsletter, *Your Weekly Staff Meeting*, and since 2006, he has reviewed more than 400 leadership and management books in his eNews. He writes a board blog for ECFA, "Governance of Christ-Centered Organizations," and is the creator of the *ECFA Governance Toolbox Series*. John also served five years as the lead facilitator of the M.J. Murdock Charitable Trust's Board Leadership & Development Program. He currently serves on the board of Christian Community Credit Union.

John and his wife, Joanne, have traveled and/or facilitated leadership, management, and board governance training in more than 50 countries and are blessed to live close to their son, Jason, and daughter-in-law, Melinda, and their five grandchildren (including triplet teenagers). His top five strengths in the CliftonStrengths assessment are: Focus, Responsibility, Significance, Belief, and Maximizer. A survivor of 21 winters in Chicago, John has not shoveled snow since 1994.

Visit John's website at *www.ManagementBuckets.com.*

Appreciation

In our book, *More Lessons From the Nonprofit Boardroom*, I share the poignant story of Billy Crystal's "15 Rounds" tribute to Muhammad Ali, performed for 20,000 of Ali's "closest friends." At the end, Ali whispered in Crystal's ear, "...you made my life better than it was."

This, truly, is our aspiration for every CEO, every senior pastor, every board member, and every reader—that board service will make your lives better than they were, with God's help and blessing.

So with great appreciation to all board members who serve faithfully and diligently—thank you for your Kingdom service!

Dan

In my CEO years in ministry, followed by my consulting years, I've been a zealous collector of tools, templates, and forms. You'll find more in my book, *Mastering the Management Buckets*, and even more in my *Buckets* workbook.

So when Terry Stokesbary, Senior Program Director at M.J. Murdock Charitable Trust, invited me to lead and facilitate the Trust's Board Leadership & Development Program for five years, I brought my tools and templates—and continued to tweak them for the nonprofit organizations that had passion for board development. I'm so grateful for Terry's confidence in me and for the friendship that we've developed. I'm also grateful for Dan Busby and Wes Willmer who made that connection possible. Ed McDowell had the vision for crafting this resource in book form. And so to Terry, Ed, Wes, and Dan—thank you for your inspiration!

John

About ECFA

Enhancing Trust

ECFA enhances trust in Christ-centered churches and ministries by establishing and applying Seven Standards of Responsible Stewardship™ to certified organizations.

Founded in 1979, ECFA provides accreditation to leading Christ-centered churches and other nonprofit organizations that faithfully demonstrate compliance with established standards for financial accountability, transparency, stewardship, and board governance. The Christ-centered ministries accredited by ECFA include churches, denominations, educational institutions, rescue missions, camps, and many other types of tax-exempt 501(c)(3) organizations. Collectively, these 2,400 organizations represent over $29 billion in annual revenue.

ECFA accreditation entitles a ministry to use the ECFA seal and receive other benefits. The continuing use of the seal depends on the ministry's good faith compliance with all ECFA Standards.

Worksheet #1 Resources and Worksheets

MY TOP-3 TOOLS

ASSIGNMENT:

After completing your study of these tools and templates, assess your board's strengths in each of these areas—and then identify the Top-3 tools you plan to use. What is your next step?

MY TOP-3 TOOLS:	ASSIGNMENTS	DEADLINE DATES
Tool #___ ________________	☑ ☑ ☑	
Tool #___ ________________	☑ ☑ ☑	
Tool #___ ________________	☑ ☑ ☑	

NOTES:

Worksheet #2 Resources and Worksheets

MY TOP TAKE-AWAY

ASSIGNMENT:

What is your Number One Top Take-Away from your study and discussion of these tools and templates?

My Top Take-Away Is:

To reinforce the learning, I will share my top take-away with this colleague:

Name: ______________________________

"Earlier I discussed Dr. Gail Matthew's research that individuals with written goals were 39.5 percent more likely to succeed. But there's more to the story. Individuals who wrote their goals and sent progress reports to friends were 76.7 percent more likely to achieve them"[1]

Gary Keller

[1] Gary Keller with Jay Papasan, *The ONE Thing: The Surprisingly Simple Truth Behind Extraordinary Results* (Austin, TX: Bard, 2012), 154.

Worksheet #3 Resources and Worksheets

Michael Bungay Stanier says the best coaching question in the world is the AWE question: "And What Else?"

Several years ago, John attended a seminar with dozens of other board chairs and, for an exercise, he was paired with another board chair. The assignment: ask the board chair just four questions displayed on the PowerPoint. The hardest part of the assignment? *John was prohibited from offering his advice!* "Just ask these four questions," mandated the leader.

Stanier, the seminar leader and author, says **"the first answer someone gives you is almost never the only answer, and it's rarely the best answer,"** so the AWE question is the perfect follow-up.[1] So John asked the prescribed four questions over a 4-minute period:

Q1: What's the real challenge here for you?

Q2: And what else?

Q3: And what else?

Q4: So what's the real challenge here for you?

Stanier was right! By the fourth question, the board chair began to address deeper governance issues and had an amazing moment of self-understanding about the board problem he was facing. *Even more amazing: John said nothing, other than asking just four questions!*

ASSIGNMENT:

Now, after reflecting on these tools and templates and your heart for enriching your board governance experience…is there anything else you should write down?

AND WHAT ELSE?

[1] Michael Bungay Stanier, *The Coaching Habit: Say Less, Ask More & Change the Way You Lead Forever* (Toronto: Box of Crayons Press, 2016), 58.

Worksheet #4 Resources and Worksheets

MY TOP-20 TASKS

To-Do List

ASSIGNMENT:

List up to 20 tasks and next steps for your board (or CEO or executive pastor) prompted by reviewing these tools and templates.

No.	Task	Deadline Date	Done Date
1			
2			
3			
4			
5			
6			
7			
8			
9			
10			
11			
12			
13			
14			
15			
16			
17			
18			
19			
20			

Accountability Plan:

We will give progress reports to the board on the following dates:	

Worksheet #5 Resources and Worksheets

ASSIGNMENTS:

- ❑ **Prioritize each tool: A, B, or C**
- ❑ **Assign a Point Person to each tool**

Priority A B C	Tools and Templates	Point Person	Page
	Tool #1: The Pathway to the Board		
	Tool #2: Board Nominee Suggestion Form		
	Tool #3: Board Nominee Orientation: Table of Contents		
	Tool #4: Five-Finger Feedback		
	Tool #5: Board's Annual Self-Assessment Survey		
	Tool #6: The Board's Annual Financial Management Audit		
	Tool #7: The Board's Annual Legal Audit		
	Tool #8: The Board's Annual Fundraising Audit		
	Tool #9: The Board's Annual Evaluation of the Top Leader (CEO or Executive Pastor)		
	Tool #10: The 5/15 Monthly Report to the Board		
	Tool #11: Monthly Dashboard Report		
	Tool #12: Quarterly Board Meeting Agenda & Recommendations		
	Tool #13: Board Retreat Read-and-Reflect Worksheets		
	Tool #14: The Rolling 3-Year Strategic Plan Placemat		
	Tool #15: Board Retreat Trend-Spotting Exercise		
	Tool #16: Prime Responsibility Chart		
	Tool #17: Board Policies Manual (BPM)		
	Tool #18: Job Descriptions for the Top Leader and Board Chair		
	Tool #19: Ten Minutes for Governance		
	Tool #20: Tent Cards and Tools for Leveraging Board Member Strengths		
	Tool #21: Board Member Annual Affirmation Statement		
	Tool #22: Straw Vote Cards		

Bonus Resources

ECFA Knowledge Center

ECFA.org/KnowledgeCenter

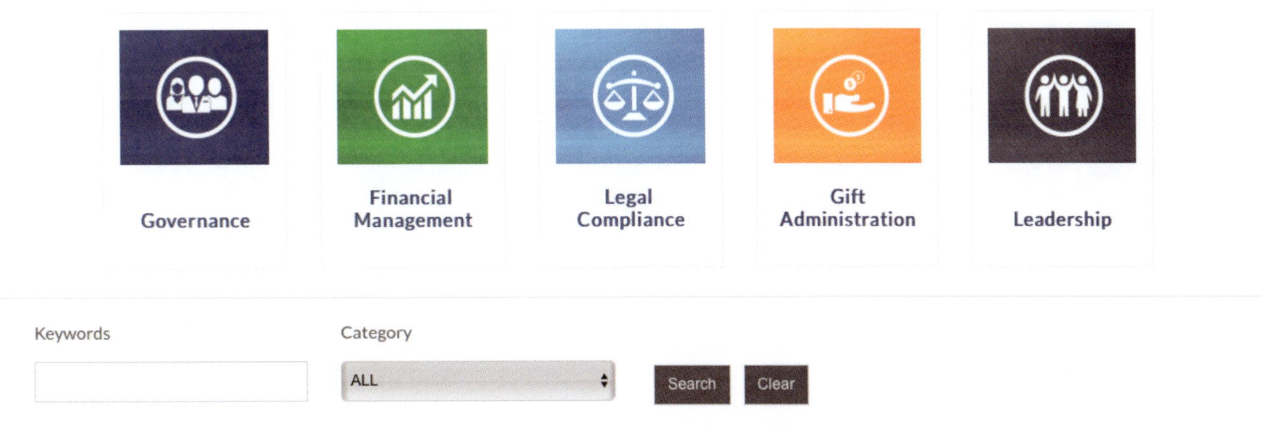

Bonus Resources

Lessons From the Nonprofit Boardroom

40 Insights for Better Board Meetings, Second Edition

by Dan Busby and John Pearson

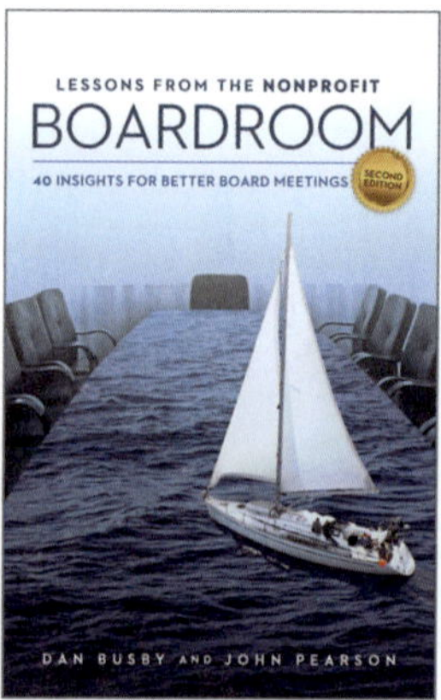

Boardroom Bloopers and More!

Boardroom Best and Worst Practices

Dan Busby and John Pearson are both passionate about good governance so they wrote 40 very short chapters in 11 irresistible categories:

Part 1: The Powerful Impact of Highly Engaged Boards

Part 2: Boardroom Tools, Templates, and Typos

Part 3: Nominees for the Board Member Hall of Fame

Part 4: Epiphanies in the Boardroom

Part 5: Boardroom Bloopers

Part 6: Boardroom Time-Wasters, Troublemakers, and Truth-Tellers

Part 7: Boardroom Best Practices

Part 8: Boardroom Worst Practices

Part 9: Holy Ground and Other Locations

Part 10: Building a 24/7 Board Culture

Part 11: Boards That Lead and Boards That Read

Sample Chapter. To read a sample chapter, visit the book's website here: *www.ECFA.org/LessonsNonprofitBoardroom/*

Listen to the Podcast. John and Dan were interviewed on October 9, 2017, by Al Lopus for "The Flourishing Culture Podcast." Listen for some learnings and laughs from the book: *http://blog.bcwinstitute.org/s3-e11-john-pearson-dan-busby/*

And by the way, Busby wrote 20 lessons and Pearson wrote 20 lessons. We will send a Chick-fil-A gift card to the first reader who correctly guesses the author of each lesson.

40 BLOGS. 40 WEDNESDAYS.

Dan and John recruited 40 guest bloggers to add their color commentary to the 40 lessons. Visit the *Lessons From the Nonprofit Boardroom* blog here:

http://nonprofitboardroom.blogspot.com/

Bonus Resources from ECFAPress

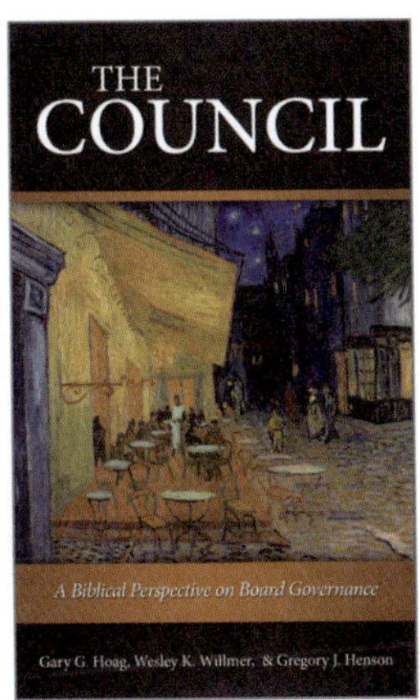

The Council

A Biblical Perspective on Board Governance

by Gary G. Hoag, Wesley K. Willmer, and Gregory J. Henson

This book seeks to answer the question, "What does the Bible say about board governance?" because followers of Jesus Christ who serve in board governance settings must start with the Scriptures. *The Council* offers an insightful, in-depth study of four governing bodies or "councils" that appear n the biblical record. By examining these historical accounts, we gain new perspective on how to think about board governance and how not to think about it. The book then goes on to present a logical, practical analysis and application of the biblical framework for governance that will impact the trajectory of your board for God's glory.

Available at ECFAPress • ECFA.org/ECFAPress

Lessons From the Church Boardroom

40 Insights for Exceptional Governance

by Dan Busby and John Pearson

You will feel like *Lessons From the Church Boardroom* is describing many of the church board meetings that you have attended.

Disarming yet authoritative, enjoyable yet challenging, the authors quickly pinpoint a challenging situation and then show you a better way to handle it. Your future service on church boards will never be the same after reading this book. You will gain many great ideas for building trust and increasing effectiveness whether as a church board leader or member.

You'll laugh and relate to painful moments, but most of all you'll walk away better equipped for your board's vital role in tackling your church's God-given mission.

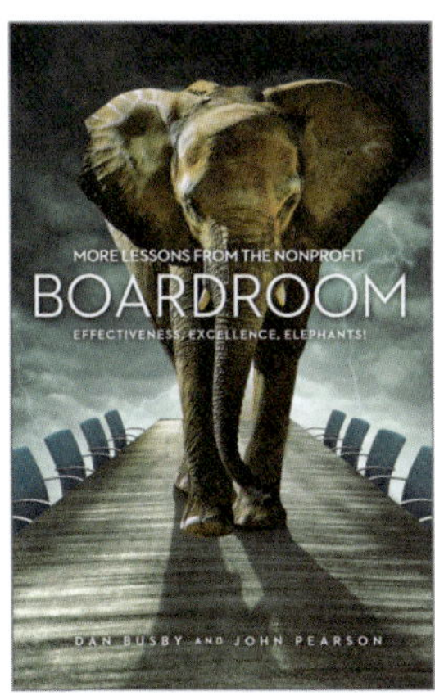

More Lessons From the Nonprofit Boardroom

Effectiveness, Excellence, Elephants!

by Dan Busby and John Pearson

Authors Busby and Pearson build on the wisdom shared in *Lessons From the Nonprofit Boardroom*. "More Lessons" is just that—40 more practical, to-the-point lessons that can be applied to your boardroom.

A special bonus lesson introduces a revolutionary resource, the NonprofitBoardScore™, an online digital resource that boards can use to evaluate their own performance. Six elements of board governance are measured: spiritual atmosphere, board-CEO synergy, intentionality, faithful administration, culture, and structure and style.

Unleashing Your Board's Potential

Comprehensive Report from ECFA's Nonprofit Governance Survey

by Warren Bird

Everything You Want to Know about Nonprofit Boards Like Yours

What would you want to ask if you could sit down with 1,662 CEOs, board chairs, and board members from Christ-centered nonprofits – all ECFA-accredited ministries? We did just that with a huge survey and have compiled everyone's responses in *Unleashing Your Board's Potential: Comprehensive Report from ECFA's Nonprofit Governance Survey* by Warren Bird, Ph.D.

More than 50 illustrated pages highlight the key findings, all with a highly practical bent designed to help your ministry's board and leadership go to new levels of excellence and effectiveness. Topics include:

- What effective boards do best (spoiler: the first one relates to clarity of roles)
- Four top challenges to governance (spoiler: "succession planning" is one)
- Where CEO and board members aren't on the same page
- How many boards have a policy and process for removing an ineffective board member

The survey is available as a free download: *ECFA.org/Surveys*

ECFA Resources

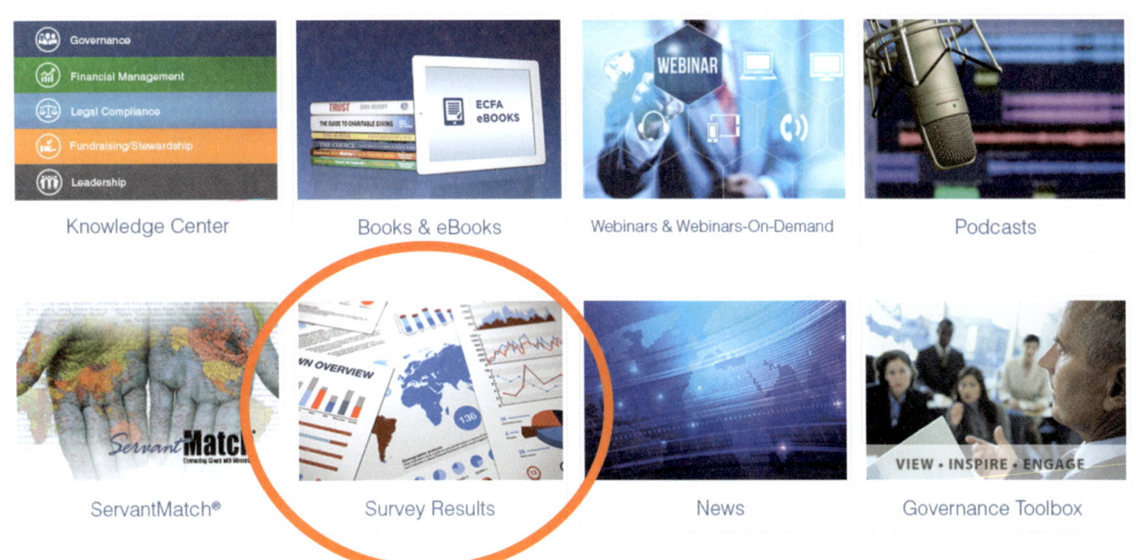

Bonus Resources from John Pearson

Mastering the Management Buckets

20 Critical Competencies for Leading Your Business or Nonprofit

by John Pearson

www.ManagementBuckets.com

Enrich your leadership and read excerpts from the 20 Buckets (core competencies) every month and every year!

Cause ✦ Community ✦ Corporation

The 20 Management Buckets are organized into three arenas—think three-legged stool. So when you read (or clip or download an article), categorize the resource into one of these 20 buckets. See the book or the website for the core competency statement/description for each bucket.

OUR CAUSE

#1: The Results Bucket
#2: The Customer Bucket
#3: The Strategy Bucket
#4: The Drucker Bucket
#5: The Book Bucket
#6: The Program Bucket

OUR COMMUNITY

#7: The People Bucket
#8: The Culture Bucket
#9: The Team Bucket
#10: The *Hoopla!* Bucket
#11: The Donor Bucket
#12: The Volunteer Bucket
#13: The Crisis Bucket

OUR CORPORATION

#14: The Board Bucket
#15: The Budget Bucket
#16: The Delegation Bucket
#17: The Operations Bucket
#18: The Systems Bucket
#19: The Printing Bucket
#20: The Meetings Bucket

Download Tools and Templates from all 20 Buckets:

www.ManagementBuckets.com/20managementbuckets

Bonus Resources From *Mastering the Management Buckets*

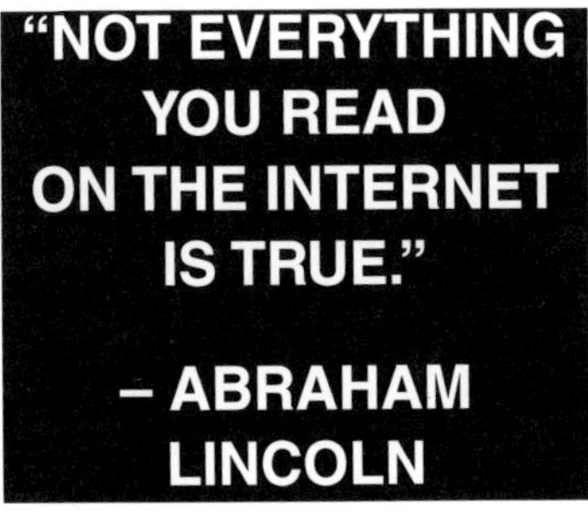

Online Tools, Templates, and Worksheets

ASSIGNMENT:

Visit: *www.managementbuckets.com/20managementbuckets*

- ❑ Click on a bucket.
- ❑ Download tools, templates, and worksheets.

#1. The Results Bucket	**WORKSHEET #1.2:** "When the Horse Is Dead, Dismount." Download this PDF and check the Top-5 answers you often hear in your organization.
#2. The Customer Bucket	**WORKSHEET #2.1:** "Local Church Simplified Segmenting Chart: Who is God calling you to reach and serve?"
#3. The Strategy Bucket	**ARTICLE:** "Entrepreneurial Wisdom: 5 Career-Saving Principles for Ministry Entrepreneurs"
#16. The Delegation Bucket	**WORKSHEET #16.1:** "Dysfunctional Delegation Diseases." Take this Delegation Gut-Check Assessment and diagnose the severity of your delegation diseases. Are you a Code Green, Code Yellow, or Code Red?
#20. The Meetings Bucket	**WORKSHEET #20.1:** "Weekly Update to My Supervisor." CEOs: download this two-page Word document and ask each of your direct reports to customize it for your weekly one-on-one staff meetings. (Read Chapter 20. If this form was good enough for a Harvard Business School case study, maybe it's good enough for you!)

Bonus Resources From John Pearson's 400+ Book Reviews

Dinosaurs Didn't Read.

Now They Are Extinct.

Since 2006, John Pearson has published more than 400 reviews of leadership, governance, and management books in his eNewsletter, *Your Weekly Staff Meeting.*

3 BONUS RESOURCES	WEBSITE
❑ Free subscription to *Your Weekly Staff Meeting eNews* (1-3 issues per month):	*www.managementbuckets.com/enews*
❑ Visit the book review archives:	*https://urgentink.typepad.com/my_weblog/*
❑ Download the master lists of book reviews (3 lists including John's Top-100 Book List):	*www.managementbuckets.com/book-bucket*

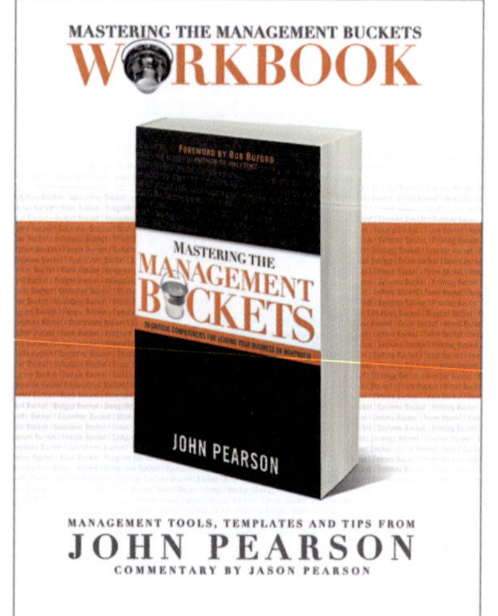

Mastering the Management Buckets Workbook:
Management Tools, Templates, and Tips from John Pearson

Jam-packed-with-practical-ideas and resources, this one-of-a-kind, 232-page workbook is the perfect complement to the book by John Pearson, *Mastering the Management Buckets: 20 Critical Competencies for Leading Your Business or Non-Profit.* Based on his two-day workshop, the workbook provides detailed templates, tips, and tools, including 99 practical takeaways that leaders, managers, and board members can implement immediately. Learn and coach others in how The Board Bucket, The Results Bucket, The Delegation Bucket, The Strategy Bucket, The People Bucket, The Donor Bucket, The *Hoopla!* Bucket, The Customer Bucket, and 12 other buckets can make or break your organization. Includes color commentaries by Jason Pearson on rebranding, understanding your primary customer, and much more.

Available at *https://amzn.to/2K6iLiy*

Bonus Resources From John Pearson: Book-of-the-Year Reviews

GARY KELLER: "One of the reasons I've amassed a large library of books over the years is because books are a great go-to resource. Short of having a conversation with someone who has accomplished what you hope to achieve, in my experience books and published works offer the most in terms of documented research and role models for success."[1]

BOOK-OF-THE-YEAR HONORS

Since 2008, John Pearson has named a "Book-of-the-Year" from more than 400 leadership, governance, and management books he's reviewed in his eNewsletter, *Your Weekly Staff Meeting.*

2018

Scaling Up: How a Few Companies Make It . . . and Why the Rest Don't – Mastering the Rockefeller Habits 2.0

by Verne Harnish

Harnish says there are three barriers to scaling up: leadership, scalable infrastructure, and marketing. To overcome these barriers, he says you must master four fundamental tools.

2017

The Power of Moments: Why Certain Experiences Have Extraordinary Impact

by Chip Heath and Dan Heath

Defy "the forgettable flatness of everyday work and life by creating a few precious moments."

2016

The ONE Thing: The Surprisingly Simple Truth Behind Extraordinary Results

by Gary Keller with Jay Papasan

"What's the ONE Thing you can do this week such that by doing it everything else would be easier or unnecessary?"

Gary Keller with Jay Papasan, *The ONE Thing: The Surprisingly Simple Truth Behind Extraordinary Results* (Austin, TX: Bard, 2012), 125.

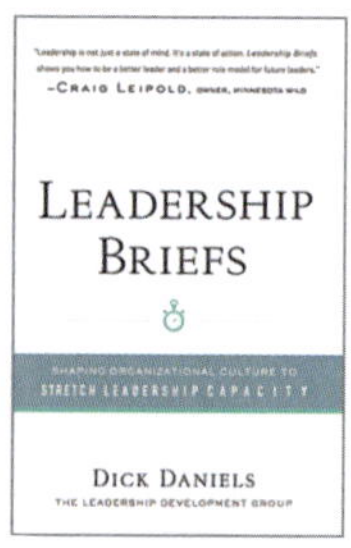

2015

Leadership Briefs: Shaping Organizational Culture to Stretch Leadership Capacity
by Dick Daniels

Daniels quotes Leroy Eimes: "A leader is one who sees more than others see, who sees farther than others see, and who sees before others see."

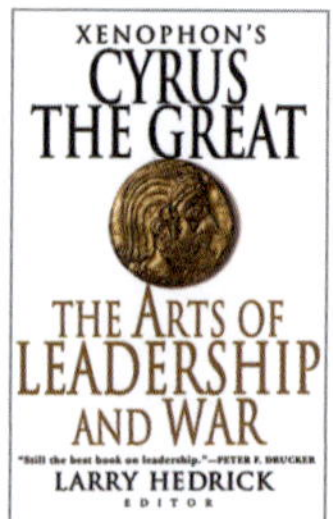

2014

Xenophon's Cyrus the Great: The Arts of Leadership and War
by Xenophon (Larry Hedrick, Editor)

What's the best leadership book ever? Peter Drucker: "…the first systematic book on leadership—the Kyropaidaia by Xenophon, himself no mean leader of men—is still the best book on the subject."

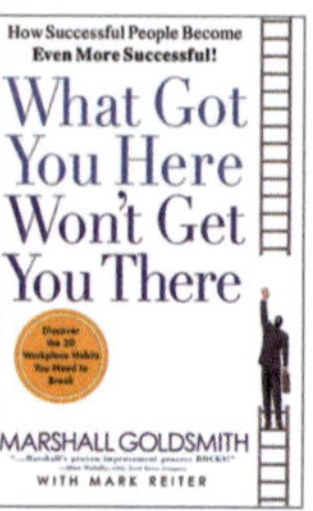

2013

What Got You Here Won't Get You There: Discover the 20 Workplace Habits You Need to Break
by Marshall Goldsmith and Mark Reiter

Chapter 12, "Special Challenges for People in Charge," encourages leaders to write a document: "Memo to Staff: How to Handle Me." If written with humility and transparency, it's a brilliant, brilliant tool.

2012

The Advantage: Why Organizational Health Trumps Everything Else in Business
by Patrick Lencioni

"If someone were to offer me one single piece of evidence to evaluate the health of an organization, I would not ask to see its financial statements, review its product line, or even talk to its employees or customers: I would want to observe the leadership team during a meeting."

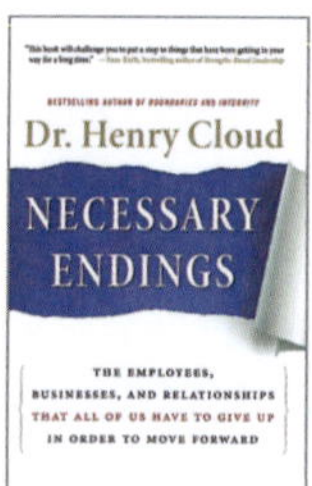

2011

Necessary Endings: The Employees, Businesses, and Relationships That All of Us Have to Give Up in Order to Move Forward
by Dr. Henry Cloud

Cloud describes those necessary endings as pruning moments: "…that clarity of enlightenment when we become responsible for making the decision to own the vision or not. If we own it, we have to prune. If we don't, we have decided to own the other vision, the one we called average. It is a moment of truth that we encounter almost every day in many, many decisions."

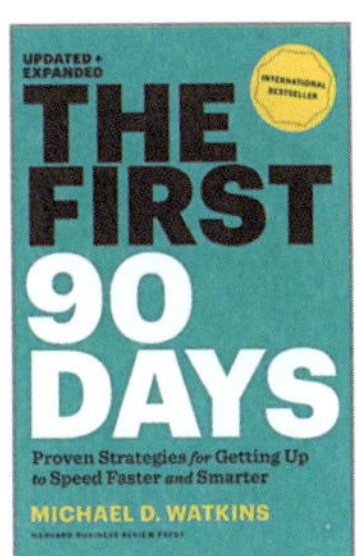

2010

The First 90 Days: Critical Success Strategies for New Leaders at All Levels
by Michael Watkins

The author's acronym, "STARS," describes four scenarios: Start-up, Turn-Around, Realignment, and Sustaining Success. Note! A successful CEO of a Turn-Around may fail at a Realignment.

2009

Strengthening the Soul of Your Leadership: Seeking God in the Crucible of Ministry
by Ruth Haley Barton

"It is also important to involve the right people. One very common leadership mistake is to think that we can take a group of undiscerning individuals and expect them to show up in a leadership setting and all of a sudden become discerning!"

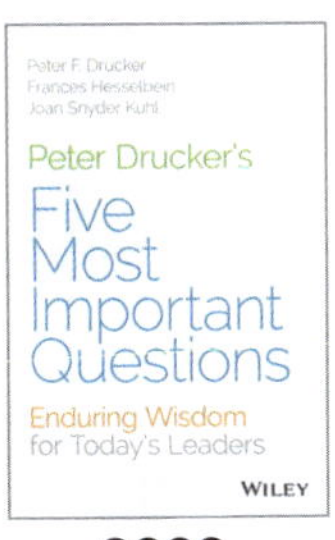

2008

This title is the 2015 update of the 2008 book.

Peter Drucker's Five Most Important Questions: Enduring Wisdom for Today's Leaders
by Peter F. Drucker, Frances Hesselbein, and Joan Snyder Kuhl

Still thin enough (90 pages, plus resources and study questions) so both staff and board members will actually read the book, this updated gem walks leaders through "The Five Most Important Questions You Will Ever Ask About Your Organization." They are:

1. What is our mission?
2. Who is our customer?
3. What does the customer value?
4. What are our results?
5. What is our plan?

READ THE FULL BOOK REVIEWS:

☑ To access a book review (and order the book), click on "Archives" at *https://urgentink.typepad.com/my_weblog/*

☑ Or Google: "[the book title], John Pearson's Buckets Blog"

***"When Larry Page, CEO of Google, was asked how he learned to run a company, he responded 'I read a lot.' For instance, he read three books on how to name things."*[2]**

Verne Harnish

[2] Verne Harnish, *Scaling Up: How a Few Companies Make It . . . and Why the Rest Don't – Mastering the Rockefeller Habits 2.0* (Ashburn, VA: Gazelles, 2014), 2.